The authors would like to thank the following people for their sterling work on this
book, whilst working in the Bdr: in particular Eirini Christofidou laboured long
and hard, particularly on image rights and researching images while Jen Langfield
and Alessandro Rigolon provided help in research and in sourcing and creating images
and drawings.

Layout and cover design
Miriam Bussmann, Berlin

Editor
Ria Stein, Berlin

Cover
Ørestad College, Ørestad, Copenhagen

Cover photographs
Adam Mørk

Library of Congress Cataloging-in-Publication data
A CIP catalog record for this book has been applied for at the Library of Congress.

Bibliographic information published by the German National Library
The German National Library lists this publication in the Deutsche Nationalbibliografie;
detailed bibliographic data are available on the Internet at http://dnb.dnb.de.

This publication is also available as an e-book (ISBN PDF 978-3-03821-547-9;
ISBN EPUB 978-3-03821-572-1) and in a German language edition
(ISBN 978-3-0346-0750-6.)

© 2015 Birkhäuser Verlag GmbH, Basel
P.O. Box 44, 4009 Basel, Switzerland
Part of Walter de Gruyter GmbH, Berlin/Boston

Printed on acid-free paper produced from chlorine-free pulp. TCF ∞
Printed in Germany

ISBN 978-3-0346-0751-3

9 8 7 6 5 4 3 2 1

www.birkhauser.com

Building Schools

KEY ISSUES FOR CONTEMPORARY DESIGN

PRUE CHILES (ED.)
LEO CARE / HOWARD EVANS / ANNA HOLDER /
CLAIRE KEMP

BIRKHÄUSER
BASEL

The Authors

Prue Chiles combines research with practice and teaching, using the skills of the design process to work with people and communities creatively. Prue Chiles is Professor of Architectural Design Research at the University of Newcastle. She set up and directed the Bureau – design + research (Bdr), set up in 2002 within the School of Architecture at the University of Sheffield to pursue 'research by design' and to raise the profile of design within the building process. Bdr has carried out over 60 commissioned research and consultancy projects with local, national and international bodies and has built up a reputation for innovation, expertise and publications in the area of school design, community visioning and regeneration and sustainable futures. This work has been supported by a small award-winning private practice with colleagues Howard Evans and Leo Care, Prue Chiles Architects (PCA). Formed in 1999, the practice has undertaken a number of innovative buildings including one of the 'Classrooms of the Future'. The practice has won several RIBA Awards such as for Prue's own house and for the Hillsborough Pavilion, a re-interpretation of the English Sport pavilion funded by Sport England.

Leo Care is an architect and teacher at the School of Architecture, the University of Sheffield. Over the last 12 years, he has helped establish a Masters course in Learning Environments, created an open access web resource, written a range of articles and delivered a series of lectures and workshops on the design of learning environments. Leo Care was director of the Bureau – design + research and has worked directly with young people, schools, architects and construction companies. His interest in a child-centred approach to designing learning environments has also been explored through collaborative design and construction projects in practice, working closely with school communities in the UK and internationally.

Howard Evans has a background in both architecture and landscape architecture and has worked in architectural practice since his graduation in 2001. He is a director with Prue Chiles Architects (PCA) and was awarded the RIBA Yorkshire 'Emerging Architect' award 2014, and Architect of the Year award in 2015. Howard Evans is also a founding member of the Bureau – design + research and has led a number of school projects within the practice, including the innovative alterations at Earlham Primary School in London. In 2011 Howard became director of the Dual BA Architecture and Landscape Architecture course at the University of Sheffield and in 2013 he established the Dual MArch course in Architecture and Landscape Architecture.

In April 2015, **Prue Chiles, Howard Evans** and **Leo Care** set up as partners the new practice Chiles Evans and Care Architects (CE+CA), combining the previous offices Bdr and Prue Chiles Architects.

Anna Holder is an architectural researcher and practitioner. Her work focuses on developing a critical understanding of the production of space as a transformative, transdisciplinary endeavour. She specialises in practice-based research as well as participation and collaborative design processes. Anna is a director of social enterprise architectural practice Studio Polpo, Sheffield, that investigates and develops sustainable models of collective housing and living, contributes design thinking for innovation in social businesses and future urban spaces and models for craftsmanship and making. Since 2009, she has taught in the Architecture and Urban Design Masters courses at the School of Architecture, the University of Sheffield, developing innovative teaching through application of Phonetic Planning Research and Actor Network Theory, and critical pedagogy with a focus on internationalisation. She is currently undertaking a Postdoctoral Research Fellowship at Århus School of Architecture, as part of the EU-funded Marie Curie Initial Training Network ADAPT-r (Architecture, Design and Art Practice Training research).

Claire Kemp developed an interest in designing buildings with, and for, young people whilst writing her undergraduate architectural dissertation 'Built Environment Education for Children' at Newcastle University. After graduating with a Masters in Architecture with distinction from the University of Sheffield, Claire Kemp became part of Bureau – design + research. At Bdr Claire co-developed and co-authored the 'Imagine: Inspirational School Design' website, an online case study resource for all those involved in the design and realisation of buildings for education. Claire also practices architecture and has recently been awarded a Sheffield Design Award from Sheffield Civic Trust and RIBA Yorkshire for the extension and renovation of an early 20th century terraced house.

Contents

Preface   **7**

Introduction: Perspectives on New School Building   **8**
9 About this book / **11** Selected school building programmes / **20** Lessons learned

1   From Ideas for Learning to Architectural Form   **24**
26 Transformational ideas / **28** The school as a workplace / **33** Subject-specific learning bases /
38 A school within a school / **42** Open Studio Learning

2   Nature, Ecology and Environmental Design   **48**
50 Linking learning to ecology – The Forest School movement – Schools and the natural elements /
54 Genius loci – Life cycles in schools – Native materials and indigenous technologies – Environmental
and social sustainability / **60** School design and environmental standards – The Passivhaus – Towards
carbon neutral schools

3   Flexible Space for Learning   **70**
72 Moving parts – Reconfiguring learning space – Dividing large spaces / **76** Large multi-purpose
spaces – Central atrium – The multi-functional staircase / **81** Temporary school buildings – Modular
solutions – Mobile lessons / **83** Long-term flexibility: adaptable space design – Manipulating internal
space – Learning cluster organisation / **87** Moving the whole school

4   Schools and the Community   **90**
92 Community access – An open facility – Bringing generations together – Schools
integrated into social fabric – Cultural cohesion and celebration of diversity / **100** Catalysts for
regeneration – Raising aspirations

5   Participating in the Design and Construction Process   **108**
110 The benefits of a participative approach – The difference between consultation and participation –
The role of young people within the design process / **111** Developing a design brief – Collaborative
brief-building – Empowering the users / **114** Design involvement – Participatory involvement in smaller
projects – Collaborative design – Getting active at the building site – Learning through building – Community self-build projects – Post-occupancy evaluation: monitoring use and performance

6   Learning Outside the Classroom   **130**
132 Settings for personalised learning – Entering a school – Entrances to subject areas / **143** Colour and
material / **147** Circulation spaces, corridors and service areas – Toilets

7 Learning in the Landscape **156**

158 Learning outside: using the school landscape – A community playground – Topography and existing soft landscape – Recreation and sport – Teaching in the landscape

8 Special Schools should be Special **172**

174 Mainstream or special schools? / **175** Legibility / **179** Inclusion and equality / **183** Co-location / **184** Community interaction / **188** Preparing for adult life

9 Refurbishment and Extension of Existing Schools **192**

194 Transforming school buildings / **203** Creating new or reinforcing existing identities / **207** Unifying the campus / **212** Strategic alterations and phased development / **214** Adaptation of other buildings and prefabrication

10 Furniture and Equipment in Learning Spaces **220**

222 Making and marking space – Chairs and desks – Creating a sense of entrance – Dividing space / **226** 'Where are we going to put everything?': furniture for storage – Fixed and mobile storage solutions – Integrating storage into the building / **229** Furniture components: a variety of approaches – Convertible furniture – Furniture integrated with fixtures and services – Using the building fabric

Bibliography 236
Index of Buildings, Architects and Locations 238
Illustration Credits 240

Preface / PRUE CHILES

This idea for this book came in 2008 whilst the neglected secondary schools in the UK were all preparing to tender for money from the government programme Building Schools for the Future. We were inspired by the local authorities who rose to the challenge of rethinking the schools in their area. One such metropolitan borough we worked with as architects was Barnsley in South Yorkshire, which had some of the least privileged children and some of the worst school buildings. Our participation in the government scheme to improve primary schools, Classrooms of the Future, in 2002 also made us think hard about the key issues and themes that make school buildings good.

In this book we have looked beyond the practical and vital aspects of light, acoustics, water and ICT to fundamental issues of design for learning. We were sponsored to look at good practice examples of schools worldwide by Balfour Beatty Construction and then subsequently to create a website on outstanding international school design, called 'Imagine: Inspirational School Design'. Sponsored also by the government agency Partnerships for Schools, this website lost funding in 2011 with the change of government, but is now being resurrected. It was created originally for everyone involved in the vast Building Schools for the Future project to rebuild all of England's secondary schools. This endeavour formed the basis of our research for this book combined with interviews with a wide range of school users on the one hand and reference to evidence-based research carried out on school environments on the other.

The authors are the university teachers, researchers and practicing architects that form **Bureau – design + research** at the School of Architecture, the University of Sheffield. This research consultancy started by Prue Chiles, Leo Care and Howard Evans in 2001 to promote architectural design to a wide public and to develop it through design and practice-based research. We have been supported by many people in this enterprise and I would like to thank the following who have been inspirational in the Bdr: Leo Care and Howard Evans, Claire Kemp, Anna Holder, Eirini Christofidou and Jen Langfield. Thanks also go to Jeremy Till, then head of the School of Architecture who saw an opportunity to bring school design into the university and supported us in our attempt to develop a different modus operandi as academics, architects and university teachers, enabling our exchange with the city and bringing the city into the university. For promoting our involvement in the design of schools in Yorkshire we would like to thank Andrew Beard, head of the School of Architecture in Sheffield; David Russell with whom we cooperated in Barnsley; Roy Fellows and David Sinclair at the Barnsley Design Centre and to colleagues Rosie Parnell and Mark Dudek. Now, seven years later, as the book finally comes to fruition, we would like to thank Ria Stein from Birkhäuser for her patience, precision and skill and above all support.

This book is timely as the first decades of the 21st century have seen unprecedented school building. Schools are a political tool and always under review. All agree we need schools but there are those who think that good, well-designed schools are an expensive luxury we cannot afford. In reality most of our contemporary schools are not good enough. The building of good schools is an important social responsibility for everyone involved; school is often the first 'civic' building children encounter and it becomes their first formative environment.

The situation has changed, both in the design and implementation of schools, in the UK. Now design is seen by the funding bodies as less important in the well-being of our children. The procurement of school buildings has also made it more difficult for many of the good smaller architectural practices to become involved. We optimistically hope the day will return when the value of design is generally appreciated; in our opinion it can inspire pupils to learn, teachers to teach and the community to participate. There are wonderful examples of new and refurbished schools around the world and also in countries with emerging economies. This book aims to remind us all how important good design is in schools and for the future of our children.   Sheffield, March 2015

Introduction: Perspectives on New School Building / PRUE CHILES

About this book

This book is for anyone interested in children's environments and the way that buildings enable children to learn. Throughout this book we encourage anyone engaged in children's learning also to be interested in the buildings they learn in: teachers, pupils, clients, local authorities, specialists and non-specialists. It is also for architects, as an accessible and discursive guide to what the authors consider to be the most prevalent themes in school design and the best ideas.

The book's focus is on secondary schools, which are analysed less than primary schools; however, we have introduced some primary schools to help with a discussion or approach. Also in parts of mainland Europe, particularly Scandinavia, primary education goes up to the age of 14. We have found many stories to tell, many victories over adversity to relate, much invention and thousands of good ideas. We show how good architecture improves the experience of our children and of the many teachers who have to implement the education our children are receiving.

School buildings should be full of good ideas. Our research and participation with young people show they respond to good ideas, to inspiring spaces, inventive solutions and elegant details. Thoughtful design raises spirits and is durable and lasting. What is clear is that to be successful the design of schools needs to develop a multi- or interdisciplinary approach – working with other people, engaging with aspects of others' knowledge and establishing tactics using research and experimentation. It is through the imagination and practical experimentation of teachers and children as much as through the educationalist and the architect that good architecture emerges.[1]

Whether the design of schools contributes to the way children learn has not been empirically proven yet. Recent research stated that it is difficult to establish firm links between capital investment in buildings and pupil attainment due to the multitude of other factors affecting attendance. Further investigation is necessary in order to assess the impact of new buildings on learning. However, there are other factors that are important: memory and experience, pleasure and comfort, and of course, fun. Schools and playgrounds, if designed well, encourage children and staff to think about issues concerning the environment, about healthy living and about interactive learning. It can also help children and adults to understand how the process of design and construction is fundamental to creating a good learning environment.

This book uses examples that have made the experience of being in a school a richer one; if a school cannot be an inspiration to children and adults, what can be? Rather than using a case study approach, however, the chapters discuss and illustrate key themes to emphasise how the best schools encompass more than architectural and spatial concerns. They have a vision and a desire to transform the educational experience.

CLAPHAM MANOR PRIMARY SCHOOL IN LONDON, UK [DeRijke Marsh Morgan Architects – DRMM, 2009]
In the atrium and circulation space it becomes apparent how the addition is joined to the existing school. It is everything this part of a school should be: full of light and places to linger, inspiring spaces, materials and details to look at, and most of all it is full of ideas.

The book begins with an introductory survey of selected government initiatives for school improvement. It describes contemporary school building in selected countries illustrating the current global socio-political concern to improve the physical environment that our children learn in. Also, it recognises an unprecedented level of investment in school buildings, by governments throughout the world at the beginning of the 21st century. All schools should be designed around an understanding of how children learn. Some schools have experimented with alternative teaching methods and pushed the boundaries of accepted ways of arranging space and facilities for learning. The schools discussed in this chapter, **From Ideas for Learning to Architectural Form**, all put new ideas in education combined with the teachers and the children first in order to transform the learning experience. The chapter **Nature, Ecology and Environmental Design** discusses how the environment is a vital factor in any school – linking teaching and learning to environmental design; integrating building services with the building fabric and the everyday running of the school is shown to be at the heart of a healthy school and healthy children. How can we think more in tune with nature? The idea of a sustainable school is emphasised as far broader than a 'zero carbon' approach, encompassing social, economic and environmental ideas and how this contributes to a holistic learning experience. For example, the generation of power and the use of water can be exhibited in the school building and thus made part of the learning experience.

In **Flexible Space for Learning** we discuss adaptable space; spaces that are good for different functions and school buildings that can be easily added on to. The most common understanding of flexibility is the ability of a building fabric to change and move but crucial, too, are multi-purpose spaces that can house a different activity every hour and that can be used for many functions. Also, it may be that a whole building is temporarily erected, changing the nature of the school for the better.

Schools and the Community shows some inspiring examples of schools knitted into their urban context, the neighbourhood or the landscape forming a unique community asset. Tapping into local resources, they can offer life-long learning thus helping communities build skills and knowledge of the area.

Although consultation, participation and engagement are carried out in designing schools, the involvement of young people is limited and often tokenistic. Usually consultation happens at the beginning of the whole building project and then the results of the work are not passed on to others involved in the ongoing process. **Participating in the Design and Construction Process** acknowledges there are still relatively few examples of participatory design processes for schools where stakeholders are involved in the building process and even fewer examples of where children and teachers have been involved in the process throughout. Research finds that involving children in the process clearly gives teachers a different impression of children. It raises children's confidence and it challenges preconceptions of their capabilities and elevates their status.

It is widely acknowledged that children can learn in spaces other than the classroom; so we look at how environments within a school can be inspirational and pedagogical wherever or however large they are. **Learning Outside the Classroom** recognises that learning can happen in any part of the school. Spaces that often go unnoticed or are forgotten about, under-utilised or simply not thought about can be the most successful spaces that children like and learn in. Entrances, corridors and toilets can all transform a school and set the teaching and learning agenda. **Learning in the Landscape** pursues the idea of learning outside the classroom, looking at the relationship between the outside and the inside of school and how the two can be combined, overlapped or integrated to create exciting spaces in which to learn. Playgrounds are often uninspiring and uninteresting and let the whole first impression and atmosphere of the school down. There are still very few examples of inspirational landscapes and playgrounds for learning and playing in.

Special schools are relatively new in the historic development of learning environments and simply do not exist at all in some countries. The chapter **Special Schools should be Special** participates in the discussion as to whether integrating students with special educational needs and mainstream learning enhances young people's education or not. What is clear is they should be exemplars for sensitive, well-researched and inspiring design.

There are many cases where a school has been extended or renovated, but true change is rare where the new part creates a complete transformation of the old and enables a new educational vision to be realised. In the chapter **Refurbishment and Extension of Existing Schools**, a number of examples are explored, where the existing school is transformed or where another type of building has been converted into a school, creating something extraordinary. The final chapter, **Furniture and Equipment in Learning Spaces**, discusses how furniture can be instrumental in the success of a school. As teaching methods change, the need for different types of furniture arises. Furniture is the closest contact the user has with the learning space and the main interface between the child and its environment. Furniture can be used to organise space or provide vital storage to support the whole gamut of learning and play activities. If not thought about carefully, furniture can also compromise an otherwise successful space.

The book is laid out for quick visual access, with drawings and images closely related and cross-referenced to the text showing the specific strength of that particular school. Rather than treating a school as a case study, certain design aspects that illustrate a chapter theme are emphasised in the building documentation. Thus, particularly seminal schools may appear several times throughout the book with footnotes pointing to the other instances where this school is being discussed. Summaries at the end of each chapter bring out the key points and there is an extensive bibliography for further reference. An index helps to find projects and locations quickly. Throughout the book the aim is to show good design in new schools clearly and concisely.

Selected school building programmes

It is useful to look at some of the school building programmes that are currently running or complete from different parts of the world. The examples of new and refurbished schools discussed in this book can all be placed within a broad framework of a worldwide socio-political concern to improve the physical environment in which our children and communities learn. The programmes included are not exhaustive by any means. We were limited to information made available by education authorities and government offices. There are undoubtedly other smaller, inventive programmes that we have not been able to include and of course individual schools not part of any programme, some of which are also discussed elsewhere in the book. The programmes highlight the unprecedented levels of investment in school building in the early 21st century. What emerged during the research were themes in common, as well as distinct differences.

There are regional differences in new schools, highlighting different climates, cultures and conditions. For example, the Northern European schools tend to use more glass owing to a desire for light, and connection with the outside from the inside, as the weather sometimes prohibits going outside. The Southern European schools tend to use more concrete and heavy mass construction. Schools everywhere are using colour more often than in the past, thus improving vibrancy, spatial definition, way finding and identity. In Scandinavia, there are many good examples of achieving a connection between design and education. However, these countries have quite small populations with a high level of wealth. Some programmes are nationwide, whilst others are local, usually run by municipalities. This implies some differences in terms of procedures and in the way the educational vision and design guidelines are developed. Local smaller programmes tend to be more specific and for this reason are often more ambitious.

Some trends, however, are global in their reach. Most prominent is the increasing civic and community role that schools, are playing, including in developing countries. In many countries this is one of the most successful aspects of the new schools, and the design of particular facilities to be used by the community is notable. Many countries have made great strides in understanding the social role of schools; the thoughtful design of social spaces both inside and outside are key to the success of schools, making them effective, enjoyable and safe places to be in. Any decline in space standards, for example the 15% reduction asked for in 2010 by the UK government, is most likely to affect these social spaces more than others. School buildings are of fundamental importance to the social mobility of children and to communities and thus to the regeneration of whole neighbourhoods.

United Kingdom

Building Schools for the Future (BSF) and Academy Schools The UK programme is prioritised here due to the wealth of information available and the authors' involvement in the Building Schools for the Future (BSF) programme. This was a UK-wide programme dating from 2004, and will be referred to at length in this book. The main focus of the programme was the construction or renovation of all secondary schools. Primary schools were not originally included in BSF, but in 2006 a parallel programme, the Primary Capital Programme (PCP), was launched. The BSF programme included about 3,500 schools, for a budget of 55 billion UK pounds, and is to end by 2023, a 20-year programme. Since the start of the programme well over 200 schools have been built or re-

newed. The original programme included 15 'waves' or stages of the programme. Inevitably the early stages were more experimental but informed the later stages, where experience of realisation and budget largely asked for more standardisation of designs and materials. The overall aim was to reach every local authority by 2011, in order to improve the situation of the schools that were more in need. The programme was managed by Partnership for Schools, a government agency supported by the then Department for Schools, Children and Families (DSCF), and private partners. The coalition government, coming into power in 2010, instigated a budget-cut plan in every branch of the public sector, including the Building Schools for the Future programme. There was a 60% budget reduction in the following four years,[2] fundamentally heralding the end of the programme.

In 2000, England's Learning and Skills Act introduced a new type of secondary school into the country known as the 'academy', being partially funded and therefore sponsored by a business, faith group or an individual. The academy model was created as a means of improving failing schools and those located in some of the most deprived areas of the country.[3] They were also part of the BSF programme but are directly funded by central government specifically and receive the additional support from personal or corporate sponsors, either financially or in kind. They are self-governing and often are constituted as charities. Most are secondary schools for pupils aged 11 to 16, but some cater for children from nursery age upwards, for children aged 4 and upwards to 18.[4] All academies have a curriculum specialty within the English Specialist school programme. In 2010 there were 203 academies in England, by the end of 2012 this number reached 1,957. It is the academies that figure most in this book, their building budget being slightly higher than that of non-academy status schools which paved the way for a number of very successful new-build projects around the country. Many of the best schools are in London and in 2014 the standard of education in London became the highest in the country.

CARLTON COMMUNITY COLLEGE IN BARNSLEY, UK [Building Design Partnership – BDP, 2011]
This college was one of the first Barnsley schools to be completed within the Building Schools for the Future programme. The school's five departments are arranged around a central spine, which cascades down a hill with different communal facilities and resources. The school has a welcoming entrance and views to the landscape beyond.

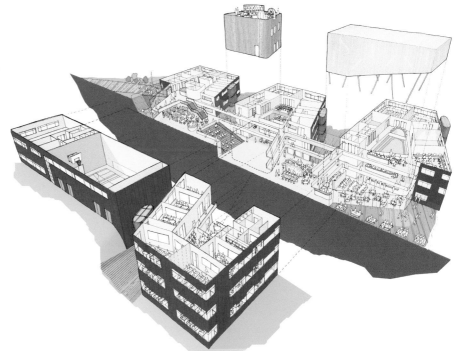

As local authorities were developing their new processes for BSF, with the help of Partnerships for Schools and CABE,[5] a number of the new schools in the UK put a strong emphasis on developing participation processes to build local ideas for secondary school education into the brief. Every local authority had to present an innovative vision for secondary education, bringing about positive change in learning and teaching. In developing that vision they needed to involve a broad array of stakeholders. This inclusive process has been criticised for being quite long and expensive, including a lot of people and different 'experts', thus resulting in an overly bureaucratic procedure. Another issue came from the fact that most major schools were funded through a Private Finance Initiative (PFI),[6] thus local education authorities could not exert financial control over the construction and management of the facilities built.

The general criticism that successful small architectural practices seldom had the chance to participate in the BSF programme, led in the Birmingham BSF program-me to inviting a number of small innovative offices to partner with bigger practices. The Birmingham 'super-team', as the architectural press described it, comprising multiple consultants, delivered a massive project for the city. The successful 'preferred bidder' for the city region of Birmingham prepared a six-stage, 15-year project to rebuild 89 schools, costing 2.4 billion UK pounds. It was considered by many as the best way to create better designed schools. The Birmingham programme gathered a huge array of design champions, 'buddy' architects and smaller 'star' architectural practices, working alongside larger commercial practices.[7] Unfortunately due to the government change in 2011 a massively reduced programme is now in place.

Barnsley Metropolitan Council in South Yorkshire, also stands out as an example of how to achieve better education through better buildings. Barnsley and its Metropolitan Council were struggling in the national education league tables and felt a new type of school was needed. The process of 'briefing' for their new schools started in

ESCOLA SECUNDÁRIA DE SANTO ANDRÉ IN BARREIRO, PORTUGAL [Pedro Matos Gameiro Arquitectos, 2010]
Part of the 'Parque Escolar' refurbishment programme, this school was remodelled with the addition of a new building and interventions to achieve interconnection between the existing buildings. The landscape was redesigned to increase permeable surface area and tree coverage, offering a space for not only students but also the wider community to congregate in.

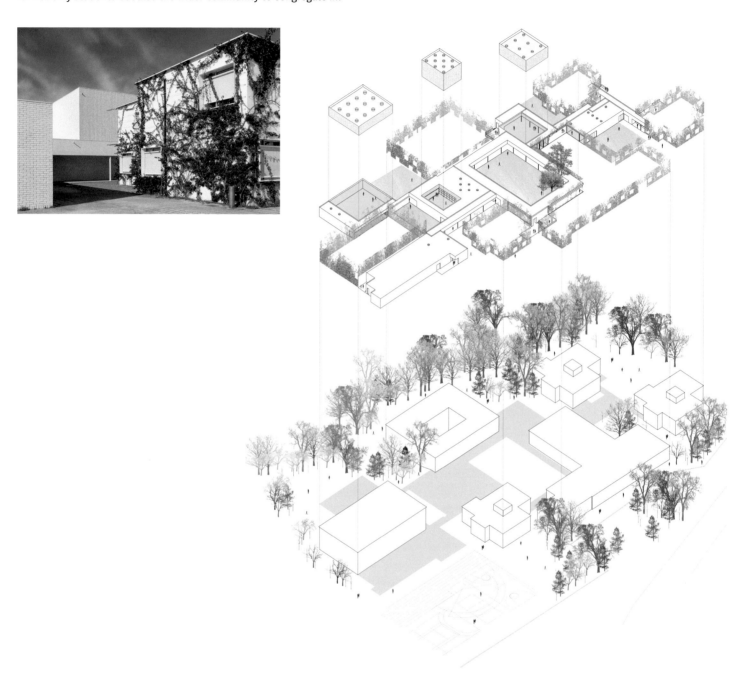

2005 with a vision for education and the concept of 'Advanced Learning Centres'. The ALCs are open 48 weeks of the year and serve as community hubs for uses in the evening and at weekends. The BSF process in Barnsley has been exemplary in many ways and lessons have emerged from interviewing some of the key participants in the process.

Prior to the actual bidding process,[8] a number of architecture-related organisations carried out consultation and engagement work[9] to inform headteachers about architecture and design issues and raise their design expectations. These projects were intended to develop the vision for their new schools and start the briefing process. They also worked with children in Barnsley to design with them specific ideas for their new schools based on their interests – particularly in sustainability. A design panel was set up to review the designs from an early stage for all teams bidding for the contract to build the schools.[10]

The process Barnsley devised delivered 11 new schools. The key players in the process, i.e. the client, the school and the consultants all wanted to achieve the best quality and, most importantly, put design and innovation high on the agenda.[11] All the successful teams were obliged to develop their proposals along a series of design principles developed by the council and the schools from their vision.[12] This enabled most of the bidders to provide school designs offering a clear and forward-looking vision for learning.

In summary, one could say that the most successful aspects of Building School for the Future were the massive scale of the programme and the real desire to improve what had been a neglected and underfunded area of public buildings for over 20 years – between the 1970s and the 1990s only a handful of schools were rebuilt. There are positive results about the educational transformation and the correspondence of the buildings to the pedagogical needs, but still little empirical evidence on how the buildings are actually performing. Also, there was quite a strong emphasis by some local authorities on creating a more environmentally sustainable school; although this rarely reinforced sustainable everyday practices and routines in schools. This was the biggest rebuilding scheme since the Second World War in the UK and it saw great triumphs but also problems: delays, overpricing by contractors, lack of good design by architects, lack of vision by headteachers are commonly quoted by observers. Restricted supply chains and contractors' budgets meant there was a limited palette of interesting materials and poor detailing. Mainly the large practices and hence only a tiny proportion of the architects in the UK were involved.

The University Technical College An interesting new paradigm for schools in the UK is the University Technical College (UTC).[13] As part of the academies programme UTCs enjoy more freedom on teachers' pay and conditions and the curriculum. University Technical Colleges are specifically designed to enrol students aged 14–19, whereas free schools and academies can choose the age range of their pupils. Students are able to pursue their specific interests and are taught in industry standard facilities by teachers with real-life practical experience. There is a guaranteed involvement with local businesses and a university. The university helps develop the curriculum and staff development and allows its specialist facilities to be used to inform and inspire the students. The most distinctive element of UTCs is that they offer technically oriented courses of study, combining National Curriculum requirements with vocational elements. A good example of this new type of school in Sheffield is described in Chapter 9, pp. 216–218 where design engineering is a specialism, building on industry research and initiatives in the two Universities in Sheffield. UTCs are supposed to offer clear routes into higher education or further learning or apprenticeships in high-technology workplaces.

Priority Schools and Baseline Designs In October 2012, the standardised design guidance for schools was released by the Department for Education (DfE) describing the suite of 'baseline' designs. These have been criticised by Royal Institute of British Architects RIBA as inflexible and likely to have a negative impact on the quality of school environments in exchange for short-term savings. The baseline designs have been developed due to the James review of capital spending on education buildings,[14] which called for standardisation as a means of targeting a 30% cost reduction compared to the now replaced Building Schools for the Future programme. The standardised designs demand a 15% reduction in space standards for secondary schools and 5% for primary schools. The new area allowance for a secondary school is 1050m² (with an additional 350m² if there is a sixth form) with 6.3m² allocated to each pupil for 11–16 year-olds, and 7m² for 16+ students. Primary schools use a similar formula to determine the total size of the school with 350m² respectively 4.1m² space per pupil. Key concerns over the baseline designs are that they may fail to create functional spaces for excellent teaching through a 'one-size-fits-all' approach. There are also concerns over accessibility and inclusion, with student discipline and well-being affected by minimal circulation spaces, as much of the space saving is achieved by reducing the corridors. Long-term sustainability and value intended may not be delivered due to lack of co-operation between design teams, educationalists and end users. The heady days of BSF are well and truly over.

Portugal

In 2007 the Portuguese government launched a major refurbishment programme for secondary schools. Through the government agency 'Parque Escolar' the aim was to refurbish 205 schools by 2011, partially through funds given by the European Union.[15] The focus was on improving the physical environments of schools: most secondary school buildings built in the last four decades have not been renovated or undergone major maintenance. The autonomous agency, Parque Escolar E.P.E., is well-structured and includes a wide variety of expertise to manage the whole process, including post-occupancy evaluations of the completed projects. Parque Escolar E.P.E. co-ordinates four regional departments in a strategy aimed at decentralising the responsibility and giving direct support to the schools at a local level. The strategy for building new schools was based on a series of pilot projects that led the way for further new schools around the whole country. This phase was completed in 2008. Testing the procedures with pilot projects is a positive approach that allows institutions to demonstrate, experiment and adjust the procedures and their strategies.

Unlike in the UK's Building Schools for the Future programme, the focus from the beginning was on refurbishment rather than new constructions, potentially a more sustainable approach. Parque Escolar E.P.E. runs the process, helps control the cost of the interventions and continuously evaluates what has been done. One key aim in Portugal is to promote a 'community culture' in the neighbourhoods where schools are renovated. Another interesting aspect of this programme is the collaboration with the building industry in aiming to develop 'smart' standardised solutions that can keep the costs of building down. It will be interesting to compare this with other countries' efforts to achieve this difficult aim.

In Portugal the philosophy is not one of the 'ideal school', but a recognition that every school has different needs. The guidelines are quite flexible and much emphasis is given to a consultative design process with the schools; the different steps of design need to be validated both by the Parque Escolar agency and by the school. For example, the conceptual 'double ring layout', an idea developed by Parque Escolar with an inner ring for school use only and an outer ring for use by the community, intersecting in the informal learning core space, proved to be easy to reinterpret in the different designs.

Denmark

Denmark has been known throughout Europe over the last 15 years for its innovation in school design, most notably for a number of schools in the Municipality of Gentofte, located north of Copenhagen. The municipality is an amalgamation of seven towns, Charlottenlund, Dyssegård, Gentofte, Jægersborg, Klampenborg, Ordrup and Vangede. This is a demographically varied area that includes the expanding Metropolitan suburb of Copenhagen, Hellerup, which is a part of Gentofte. In 1998, with a projected 50% increase in pupils over the following eight years, Gentofte embarked upon a radical transformation of its education system by remodelling eleven existing schools and building one new facility, the innovative Hellerup School. The SKUB (The School of the Future) programme, which aimed at bringing the Gentofte public schools to the top of the country ranking, ended in 2010 with a total investment of 280 million euros, considerably more than the original projected figure of 1.5 billion Danish krones (201 million euros)[16] – a large amount of money for such a small (but wealthy) municipality. The programme has been completed and a survey has been conducted to assess its effectiveness. The results are very positive: the renovated and new facilities stimulate learning, in particular reading and writing skills, and make

MUNKEGÅRDSSKOLEN IN GENTOFTE, DENMARK [Dorte Mandrup Arkitekter, 2010]
This school was one of 12 that underwent a major transformation as a part of the SKUB (The School of the Future) programme. The dramatic diamond-like internal courtyard diffuses light across the communal and teaching spaces on the lower ground floor.

children keener to go to school (96% of them express satisfaction); teachers also appreciate the new facilities. This local programme has generated a nationwide debate about the importance of the quality of space in schools, and it has increased the attention on differentiated learning. Also, the open and transparent appearance of this programme has attracted an international interest and can be replicated in other geographical contexts.

As in all the school projects in Gentofte, school principals, teachers, educationalists, students, parents, university faculty members, architects and community facilitators collaborated in the development of this project. Their teamwork and involvement have been fundamental for the programme's good outcome. In this participatory process, all the aspects of schooling were addressed. In Gentofte, space is expected to provide children with variety and choice in their learning environments. The design shift has been successful because teachers have been trained to use this new type of space in a different way, giving to every student a personalised agenda for learning.

In Gentofte, the major assumption of the programme is that the children's learning is strongly influenced by the quality of space. Space, innovation and creativity were the main objectives of the programme. The strong connection between educators and architects brought about the construction of facilities with innovative designs in a transparent and inclusive process.

Finland

Schools in Finland are a fundamentally egalitarian institution offering free and equal education to all through a strong system of public funding both for the design and construction of schools and for the education offered in them. Chiefly for this reason, Finnish education has a reputation as being outstanding, and the country is renowned for the architecture of its new schools. Although not a specific programme, the Finnish government initiated 15 architectural competitions between 2000 and 2010 for both secondary and primary schools and this has led to some exceptional schools. Finland is unique in two ways: firstly, in the recognition that both the educa-

KIRKKOJÄRVI COMPREHENSIVE SCHOOL IN ESPOO, FINLAND [Verstas Architects, 2010]
Designed with the idea of a small, full-of-life city, Kirkkojäri School is a prime example of the egalitarian education system in Finland. The dining hall along with other common spaces and the secondary school are located in a large curved volume with a glass wall allowing the afternoon sun to come through and encouraging students to spend as much time as possible outdoors.

tion offered and the design of the school is critical. Secondly, it is acknowledged that architectural competitions may be the best way to achieve excellent school design.

Important considerations for new schools include the community aspect; Eriika Johansson, a researcher at the Museum of Finnish Architecture who contributed to the exhibition 'The Best Schools in the World',[17] points out that the school is often the only visible public building in many localities and that schools have special local value as an expression of the ethos, aesthetic sensibilities and technical expertise of their era. Schools in Finland are expected to adapt to the changing needs of new generations and to have long-term flexibility. The strong connection between educators and architects in Finland brings about the construction of facilities with innovative and well-crafted designs.

Australia

In November 2006, the state of Victoria announced its Victorian Schools Plan, an ambitious programme committed to rebuilding or modernising every public school by 2017.[18]

This initiative was set to receive further funding from the Australian government's Building and Education Revolution (BER) programme that has committed 14.7 billion Au$ to school building across Australia over a decade. It is notable that there was such a large amount of money

available in 2009, in a period of general recession. Compared to other countries, Australia was tackling the economic downturn in a better way, but this programme also highlights the fact that education is a major concern in the country. An important part of the BER project is the 'National School Pride' (NSP) programme: its focus is the support of small improvements in existing schools with the aim of enhancing children's sense of belonging by providing more welcoming and child-friendly spaces. Most of such works regard the outdoors – playgrounds landscaping and exterior learning areas – and the refurbishment of dance/drama studios.

In Australia, flexibility is a central requirement as there is no focus on a single pedagogical approach but quite an open range of options. The guidelines define a series of different noise zones in order to regroup activities that need the same level of acoustic privacy: reflective, creative and interactive, with a ranging noise level. The different zones need to be acoustically separated in order to avoid noise interferences among different types of activities.

USA

In 2006, the Los Angeles school district (LAUSD) opened 32 new schools – the largest number of school openings in a single year in the United States.[19] LAUSD's vision for the future, is an all-encompassing school construction

WILLIAMSTOWN HIGH SCHOOL IN MELBOURNE, AUSTRALIA [Spowers, 2008]
Designed as a model school for environmental education in a Melbourne suburb, it utilises natural ventilation and a highly visible rainwater collection system.

programme of repair and renewal. It is the largest in the nation's history, with approximately 150 new schools, more than 70 classroom addition projects, and a modernisation, upgrade and repair programme that addresses aging buildings throughout LAUSD's more than 800 campuses.

In the mid-1990s, a persistent population growth rate and the lack of a school-building plan resulted in severe overcrowding; the immediate reaction was to supplement existing space with bungalow-type buildings, reduce the academic calendars to a 160-days-a-year cycle and bus some children out of their own neighbourhoods to less crowded schools elsewhere. The programme intends to create facilities that accommodate students and staff and enhance productivity and performance. Key to the programme are core design principles, such as creating smaller schools within larger schools, providing spaces for students and teachers to interact and encouraging collaboration between teachers. The urban planning objective was to make every school the centre of its community. The principles incorporate all the state policy requirements as well as elements that promote quality learning environments.

Community interests and involvement are also encouraged through public access and the use of playfields and gymnasia, libraries, multi-purpose rooms and auditoria – and facilities for special needs. Lastly, the district

is pursuing broadly sustainable concepts that include the use of daylighting and natural ventilation, low-maintenance finishes and furnishings, reduced-consumption water fixtures, and more usable play spaces and trees that shade and reduce heat, among other elements. Further, state-of-the-art technology in security, safety and communications is employed. The intention is to give each school an identifiable design which is compatible with its neighbourhood.

The emphasis on sustainability is particularly strong, especially considering that the first guidelines date back to the early 2000s. However, this programme focuses on the delivery of the number of school seats needed, rather than on good design, Also, some of the schools appear too grandiose and formal, like the Central Los Angeles High School #9 from 2008, designed by Coop Himmelb(l)au, which cost almost double the originally estimated amount.

Colombia

'Nuevos Colegios' in Bogotá is the biggest project of school construction ever developed in Colombia. An investment of around 998 billion Colombian pesos (386 million euros) from 1999 on to fund the construction of 50 new large schools, 54 major enlargements of existing facilities, the structural retrofitting of 172 buildings and the improvement of 326 schools. The programme is

CENTRAL HIGH SCHOOL #9 IN LOS ANGELES, USA [Coop Himmelb(l)au, 2008]
This Performing Arts School is the Los Angeles Unified School District's flagship school and as such is designed as a gateway to downtown LA, forming part of the Grand Avenue Cultural Corridor.

led by SED,[20] the 'Secreteria de Education Districtal' (the district education secretariat) of the city of Bogotá. The school building programme is part of the larger plan 'Bogotá Positiva: Para Vivir Mejor' (Positive Bogotá: Toward Better Living). The programme started after a survey, conducted in 1998 by the Secretary of Education, on the poor condition of the school estate in the Bogotá district.

The main aim of the programme is to provide a good education for every child and young person by trying to eliminate the infrastructural differences between upper class and lower class neighbourhoods. The programme addressed a series of complex issues: Firstly, most of the city schools were illegal, chiefly due to issues about land ownership; secondly, half of the schools in the city did not respect the regulations in terms of seismic safety and 80% of them did not provide an effective physical environment for learning; thirdly, there were contractual problems with the contractors; lastly, there was a lack of co-ordination with the public utilities existed. The architecture becomes the symbol of social change in neighbourhoods characterised by crime and a lack of urban planning. Similar projects were implemented in other parts of Colombia as well. There is not the same emphasis on transforming education as in some other programmes.

Lessons learned

Educational guidelines

Clearly, there are common themes in global educational reforms today that informed those programmes; personalisation of curricula, student-centred learning and curricula based on project work are among the typical aspects. Educational guidelines highlight the important roles of individualised learning, of social relationships and of interdisciplinary learning – trying to go beyond the segregated disciplines. This promotes critical thinking and the development of problem-solving skills. A number of national governments have promoted curricular developments towards much greater use of ICT and more personalised, student-centred and laboratory-based teaching methods. Usually each individual school develops an ICT strategy, specific for its needs.

The Gentofte programme in Denmark starts with the consideration that, contrary to what was taken for granted in traditional education, everyone learns differently. Also, contemporary societies require people that are able to work independently as well as in groups and school curricula take that into account. In Bogotá, Colombia, learning is seen as a social phenomenon, thus the schools

FLOR DEL CAMPO SCHOOL IN CARTAGENA, COLOMBIA [Giancarlo Mazzanti Arquitectos, 2009]
Laid out as four rings, the school's unique form encloses playgrounds and recreational spaces for the children. The punctured outer wall creates a barrier but still allows the nearby community members to have visual access to the school. Following the outline of the school, there is a wide step for people to sit on or climb to have a peek inside the school. At night the school is lit making it the centre of this community.

aim at a pedagogical model that is based on a strong participation of pupils and parents, thus encouraging the students to active involvement in a democratic society.

The UK, Portugal, Gentofte in Denmark, Australia, Los Angeles in the USA and Bogotá in Colombia all have produced design guidelines: in every programme some form of guidance that regulates design has been elaborated. This sounds quite natural when dealing with the construction of a large number of facilities. However, most of those guidelines aim at providing a minimum quality in the new facilities, not at encouraging an exemplary quality. In the state of Victoria and in the city of Gentofte the design standards have been developed as a 'translation' of the new educational guidelines introduced. In Australia the design guidelines for schools include a series of examples of what is considered 'good design'. In the Los Angeles programme, the guidelines include requirements about size, trying to reduce the traditional large-scale facilities through the use of small learning communities. Also, spaces for student-teacher interactions and teachers' collaboration are demanded, as well as areas for developing extra-curricular and informal activities. In Bogotá, a new building regulation about school design has been introduced in order to bring about change in this

field. The new schools procurement process has been based on open architectural competitions managed by the Colombian Society of Architects.

Flexible learning spaces

All programmes discussed in this chapter address this important theme of flexible space albeit in different ways. In Portugal the emphasis on spatial flexibility is expressed mainly through a central multi-purpose space, overlapping with the library, that can become the social hub of the school. In most schools in Gentofte, classrooms have been removed from the layout to make room for open flexible spaces for learning where pupils and teachers can work in teams. The educational activities take place in a variety of spaces with different spatial characteristics. Great attention has been placed on acoustic design in order to provide a quiet atmosphere even if spaces are closely connected. In Los Angeles the school layout is required to be flexible – including movable walls – so that it can accommodate pedagogical changes.

Environmental design

Sustainability and the promotion of environmental education are major aspects of several of the presented programmes with some of them making it a primary concern. With regard to energy efficiency in the UK all newly built schools completed in the BSF and Academies programme by 2014 have cut the carbon emission by 60% compared to the average situation prior to the new School building programme. The Zero Carbon Task Force for schools,[21] established in 2008 to provide strategies that would reduce carbon emissions, has the ambitious aim to create zero carbon schools by 2016. Portugal too has implemented new standards of energy efficiency, and the emphasis on refurbishment in Portugal rather than new construction plays a positive role for environmental sustainability. In Gentofte in Denmark the emphasis has also been on renovating existing facilities rather than building new schools. This is interesting because it is more environmentally sustainable and provides continuity for children, teachers and the community.

In Australia, school buildings aim to minimise their energy consumption and minimise their impact on the site. In Los Angeles, the buildings are monitored in order to evaluate the actual consumption and the way staff use them. One of the key elements of the programme is the integration of well-being and environmental sustainability within the newly built schools. Those qualities are framed within the guidelines included in 'Collaborative for High Performance schools' (CHPS) standards.[22] There are requirements about orientation, energy efficiency, water use, waste management and material resource efficiency. In the USA, California has been one of the pioneers in integrating the idea of sustainability and green building in schools.

Participation and the building process

Involving the different stakeholders in the design process is becoming a common practice in some countries but definitely not in all. It is obviously advantageous to tailor the design to the specific school, teachers and community, to make the building more effective and last longer without substantial changes. More specifically, the programmes require visions for change (at the local or school level) in the education. Participation, by definition a multi-disciplinary work, is seen as a prerequisite for real innovation in school design – going beyond the taken-for-granted ideas from the single disciplines.

This decision in favour of participation comes from the understanding that effective schools cannot be built without consulting all the stakeholders – including members of the building industry. Transparency is a major quality of a fair participatory process: in order to achieve that, architects should provide means to make the design easily understandable by the other stakeholders.

Schools and the community

In the examples from both Los Angeles and Bogotá, schools sought to bring about tangible change in their neighbourhood. Newly built schools in Los Angeles are designed to become the centre of their community. In some new schools, housing units and community centres have been included in the same block in order to reach a functional mix. In the Nuevos Colegios programme in Bogotá, there is a strong commitment to the relationship with the neighbourhood that is expressed through the creation of spaces available for out of school activities. The new facilities have been strategically located in order to bring a new image and constitute symbols of change for neighbourhoods characterised by social issues. Within the buildings there is usually an emphasis on communal spaces aimed at creating a good social atmosphere and a sense of community.

In Portugal, too, schools have been opened to the community and part of the facilities can be used out of the school hours for adult education and cultural, sport or leisure events. Also, such new school buildings need to be strongly integrated into the surrounding physical environment. New school building may also trigger the creation of jobs in the communities where the schools are built, making a real contribution to community development.

REFERENCES

1 Catherine Burke, 'About Looking: Vision, Transformation and the Education of the Eye in Discourses of School Renewal Past and Present', *British Education Research Journal*, vol. 36, no. 1, February 2010, pp. 65–82.

2 Sarah Richardson, 'Interview: Mairi Johnson', 5 September 2014. http://www.building.co.uk/interview-mairi-johnson/5070606.article, accessed 9 December 2014. Mairi Johnson was the Strategic Director of Design at Partnerships for Schools, 2008–2012.

3 Later on, the academies initiative was expanded to accommodate free schools. The Academies Act 2010 authorised the creation of free schools and allowed all existing state schools to become academy schools. The first 24 free schools opened in autumn 2011.

4 Jessica Shepherd, 'Academies to Become a Majority among State Secondary Schools', *The Guardian*, 5 April 2012. http://www.theguardian.com/education/2012/apr/05/academies-majority-state-secondary-schools.

5 CABE (Commission for Architecture and the Built Environment) was the UK government's advisor on architecture, urban design and public space. After reviewing the BSF programme for a year, CABE called for a 'design threshold' to prevent poor designs from being built. Cf. *RIBA Practice Bulletin*, no. 456, 20 July 2008. http://www.architecture.com/Files/RIBAProfessionalServices/Practice/General/2008/RIBAPracticebulletin456.pdf. Accessed 9 December 2014.

6 Driven by an increased need for accountability and efficiency for public spending, Private Finance Initiative (PFI) had the objective to create public–private partnerships (PPPs) by funding public projects with private capital.

7 Rory Olcayto, 'A Catalyst for Birmingham – Round Table', *Architects Journal*, 12 March 2009.

8 Five contractor/design teams were shortlisted from a long list of applicants for the BSF programme in Barnsley.

9 Creative Partnerships, a research programme originally funded by the UK government, sponsored a two year project conducted by the Design Centre North, Bureau – Design + Research at the School of Architecture at the University of Sheffield and BEAM in Wakefield to work with children designing specific parts of schools.

10 The bid teams again comprised of the contractors, architects, landscape architects and all consultants.

11 As an overall building programme, Barnsley BSF was attractive to bidders because all Advanced Learning Centres were newly built, whereas many other projects around the country had significant amounts of refurbishment, a more complex undertaking for contractors. During the design process the schemes were rationalised and refined and in some instances 'value engineered' in terms of a standardised materials palette and prefabrication.

12 These design principles were the following ones:
- Each school should provide an architectural statement on the design to be discussed with the stakeholders.
- A central social space acting as the hub of formal and informal learning activities should be created.
- All schools were to have an inherent openness and transparency to surrounding communities.
- The school designs should be responsive to the primarily suburban and rural contexts where each site has a very specific microclimate and social constituency.
- Each school design should offer different opportunities for short- and long-term adaptation of the teaching spaces.
- 25% of the heating was to be provided by renewable energy sources.

13 'Q&A: University Technical Colleges', 7 October 2011. http://www.bbc.co.uk/news/education-15220425. Accessed 9 December 2014.

14 The Independent Review of Educational Capital, known as James Review, was commissioned by the Secretary of Education, Michael Grove, in 2010 to examine how schools have spent money on facilities under the BSF programme. Author of the review Sebastian James outlined 16 recommendations that would radically reform the way schools were designed, built and procured in an effort to standardise design, reduce delays and save up to £6m per school in costs (http://www.theguardian.com/teacher-network/2013/mar/26/school-buildings-design-architecture-success). The James Review is a publically available document that can be viewed here: http://www.education.gov.uk/consultations/downloadableDocs/James%20Reviewpdf.pdf

15 For further information on the Parque Escolar Secondary School Modernisation Programme cf. the programme's website: http://www.parque-escolar.pt/en/. Accessed 12 September 2014.

16 SKUB stands for 'skoleudviklings- og udbygningsprojektet' (school development and expansion project) and was implemented in Gentofte in 1998–2007. http://www.create2009.europa.eu/fileadmin/Content/Downloads/PDF/Projects/National_projects/DK_SKUB_The_school_of_the_future.pdf.
http://www.autens.dk/english/skub-skoleudvikling-og-skoleudbygning/. Accessed 16 September 2014.

17 Cf. exhibition catalogue published by the Museum of Finnish Architecture: Maija Kasvio (ed.), *The Best School in the World: Seven Finnish Examples from the 21st Century*, Helsinki: Museum of Finnish Architecture, 2011. The exhibition was on display at the MFA 8 June to 25 September 2011.

18 More on the Building and Education Revolution (BER) programme in Victoria, Australia: http://www.is.vic.edu.au/independent/facts/ber.htm. Accessed 10 December 2014.

19 http://home.lausd.net, accessed 16 September 2014. Cf. also *School Construction News*, vol. 5, summer 2006. http://www.laschools.org/fs-general/download/newsletters/newsletter_5th_ed_version_Final_Web_VERSION.pdf?version_id=3638564.

20 http://www.educacionbogota.edu.co/index.php?option=com_content&view=category&id=24. Accessed 16 September 2014.

21 http://www.cibse-sdg.org/news/zero-carbon-school-buildings-consultation. Accessed 4 November 2014.

22 http://www.chps.net/dev/Drupal/node. Accessed 4 November 2014.

1 From Ideas for Learning to Architectural Form / PRUE CHILES

It is generally acknowledged that the design of new schools should be based on an understanding of current research on how children learn. Few schools have experimented with alternative pedagogical methods or explored the boundaries of accepted ways of arranging space and facilities for learning. In some recently built schools ideas from higher education or the workplace have driven the use and form of space. However, do children need to be in an office before they are adults and is this what we want for our children? Some new schools in Denmark, Finland and Norway stand out as particularly innovative at experimenting with new spatial arrangements for new learning paradigms.

The UK's Building Schools for the Future programme, from 2004 to 2012,[1] aimed to transform education through the renewal of all the UK's secondary schools. As an important part of this programme every school was required to articulate its educational vision as part of the briefing process. Running with this programme, the new public private partnership of Academies has produced some of the most successful schools over the past decade. They display some interesting ideas for new forms of learning and architectural solutions to those ideas. Perhaps due to the sponsorship and briefing from industry partners they are often quite corporate in appearance but generally better at opening their facilities to the wider community. How much real innovation and how many new ideas were developed throughout the wider Building Schools for the Future programme is questionable. Was there, in fact, a return to old ideas?

This chapter looks at some of the imaginative and creative use of space in recent schools that is driven by new understandings of how children might learn more effectively, and the architectural vision that is built around these.

ØRESTAD COLLEGE IN ØRESTAD, COPENHAGEN, DENMARK [3XN Architects, 2007]
The circular 'pods' allow students to learn in a more social and informal space.

HELLERUP SCHOOL IN GENTOFTE, DENMARK [Arkitema, 2002]
This open-plan school has many informal learning areas, with sofas and pods branching out from the central staircase. The central staircase is the main feature of this school and it has been replicated many times in other educational buildings around the world since. It is the heart of the building, the main meeting place and the first space one encounters upon entering the school.

Transformational ideas

In England the last school building programme on a similar scale as Building Schools for the Future was half a century ago the in 1960s. In England in 1975 an international survey was published exploring schools built in the late 1960s and early 1970s, whose buildings were thought to be representative of advanced pedagogical thinking. It described 'Operational flexibility, shared community, access to facilities and the exploitation of new technologies and materials' as being the discourse of the time and 'emphasised a break with the past and projected the vision of a new dynamic relationship between school community and wider society.'[2] Rethinking pedagogical ideas and the spaces needed for new forms of teaching through new technologies and materials is very much a 'mantra' for today as is putting the school back at the heart of the community.

Transformational ideas in primary schools were perhaps, more radical in the past. In post-war England for example the experimentation by the architect and educationalist partnership of David and Mary Medd[3] in the 1950s resulted in the 'expanding classroom' and 'design from inside out'. This led to a child-centred and gentler approach to the use of space. Some primary schools were also exploring new approaches to teaching the curriculum in line with the now famous Italian educational experiment in Reggio Emilia where the actual fabric of the school is thought of conceptually as the third teacher. In secondary schools where teaching is subject-specific with students moving to a classroom or discipline-specific space, a different approach is needed and perhaps it is more challenging to break from the norm, but there is surely still room to make the spaces specific to their subject in some way.

The biggest change in the spatial configuration of schools has been exemplified in the past decade in **Hellerup School** in Gentofte, Denmark [Arkitema, 2002] in a largely post-industrial suburb of Copenhagen in Denmark. Designed for 640 6–16 year olds, Hellerup School is particularly famous for its centrally placed wide staircase in an atrium space that forms the main meeting place for the school.[4] The new configuration of space encouraged new ways of teaching and learning, treating the students as more mature and independent learners. Open-plan teaching areas with spaces with sofas and

HELLERUP SCHOOL / **Ground floor plan**

First floor plan

There are a number of unexpected places for students to discover; small informal learning spaces where they can sit and study or socialise in small groups.

pods for small groups and other areas for independent learning encourage informality and foster collaboration. It should be noted that the headteacher, who briefed the architects and was there for the opening of the new school, is sure that the new ways of teaching and new spaces created were more likely to succeed because the school was completely new. All the staff were new and were recruited for this experimental approach to teaching in more open environments and so were prepared to teach in a different way. Also families were moving into the increasingly wealthy and fashionable residential area of Copenhagen.

At **Bexley Business Academy** in London, UK [Foster + Partners, 2003] one of the first and most praised academies with its interesting open-plan spaces such as the Stock Exchange, the teachers found the open-plan, more exposed spaces somewhat difficult to use due to the background noise. Both Bexley and Hellerup, a few years after opening, had problems with excessive noise even though this was expected and addressed with acoustic walls. The acoustic problems have led to the closing in of a number of these spaces onto the central atria with partitions. This does not negate the good idea of allowing children more freedom to learn in different spaces – none

BEXLEY BUSINESS ACADEMY IN LONDON, UK [Foster + Partners, 2003]
The central atrium is known as the Stock Exchange, where a 'staged trading floor' has been constructed. In this space, every student's photograph is exhibited on the wall.

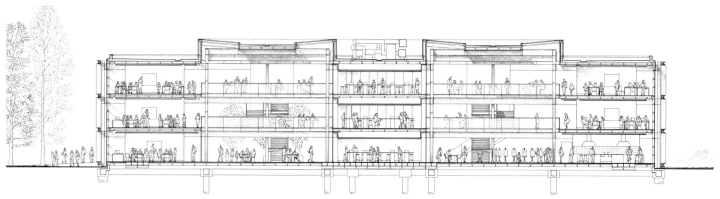

Section through central atrium

of which are a traditional classroom, but the design of these spaces and their materiality are crucial and they need to be conceived very carefully.

Today, the agenda is broadly the same as in the 1960s: to enhance the learning experience with the use of new technologies and to allow children to roam further from the traditional classroom. The biggest change is our need to think broadly sustainably; the reduction of the use of fossil fuels now being a necessity and staff, students and designers all playing a part in both understanding and implementing ecological ideas as part of other main-

stream agendas. The schools analysed in this chapter show how new ideas in pedagogy are introduced into the design and implementation of school spaces in order to transform the learning experience.

The school as a workplace

In order to prepare school children to experience what working – for instance in an office environment – is like, the school may include spaces for small group teaching, hot-desking, informal working and meeting. More formal

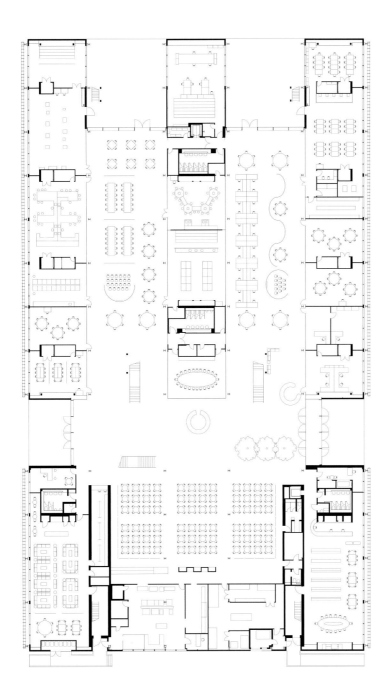

BEXLEY BUSINESS ACADEMY / Ground floor plan. Teaching areas were centred around the open-plan spaces. Because of some trouble with noise levels, parts of these open atria were closed and partitions were put up to create an acustic buffer, altering the intention of the 'trading floor'.

meeting spaces, 'boardrooms', are sometimes included giving an air of importance and sophistication. Likewise workshops are designed with an industry and workplace feel.

Situated within a new southern suburb, **Jåttå School for Vocational Learning** in Stavanger, Norway [Henning Larsen Architects, 2007] was designed for approximately 1000 pupils from age 13 to 19. It forms a gateway, with a new stadium, to the Stavanger urban quarter, adjacent to the fjord. The exterior is a large punctuated timber-clad rectangle with double-height windows allow-

ing the daylight deep into the building. A dominant formal band encases the front of the building, which is otherwise all glazed. The heart of the school – the main street with an auditorium, canteen and resource centre – melts into a fluid course with green views of atria and a roof garden as well as of workshops and spheres of educational activity. Most ingenious is the way in which this central main street becomes a sinuous piece of landscape, flowing from the entrance up into the main hall. Planted courtyards and atria provide sensory relief and views of greenery throughout the school. These afford a variety of

JÅTTÅ SCHOOL FOR VOCATIONAL LEARNING IN STAVANGER, NORWAY [Henning Larsen Architects, 2007]
Externally the school is clad in timber, frequently punctured by double-height windows. The main street, which is the heart of the school, extends out of the building into the landscape.

Longitudinal section

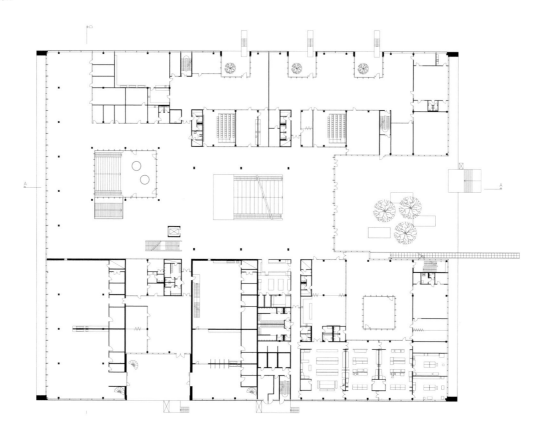

Ground floor plan. The plan displays more variety of spaces than a classroom-based school, with the central stair and atrium offering a place for learning away from the classroom.

JÅTTÅ SCHOOL FOR VOCATIONAL LEARNING / Large dramatic workshop spaces provide flexible and inspiring places for vocational learning.

The multi-use auditorium is a popular place to congregate.

The central stair and atrium offers a place for learning away from the classroom.

Working in smaller student groups in an office-based environment.

spatial experiences that support the adaption of teaching methods to suit varied learning and teaching needs. The large atrium slices right into the building, allowing even the spaces deep into the plan to be flooded with natural daylight. The generous circulation spaces create extensive internal recreation areas. Both factors are important in a country where the winters are long and cold.

Jåttå School for Vocational Learning is one of the most innovative school buildings in Norway, providing the framework for new and specific teaching methods. The open and varying spatial sequences permit teaching methods to adapt to various work scenarios, small group work space, larger meeting space and quieter, more private situations.

The school in fact functions like a modern workplace with large open teaching environments and workshops

for special subjects. However, Jåttå Vocational School is particularly striking in the way in which the architecture supports the new teaching pedagogies. Designed by the architects as a 'town within a town', the main street leads to a variety of separate learning spaces. The central atrium and open-class spaces have much in common with Hellerup School in Denmark. Both function along the principles of a modern generalised workplace, with large open teaching spaces and more closed specialised subject teaching zones; both are landmark projects within new residential areas and aim to be at the heart of their community.

The voluminous central hall at Jåttå holds the big open stepped auditorium area, the canteen, the library and the resource centre. The adjacent individual departments have zones for teaching as well as work demand-

ROC AVENTUS IN APELDOORN, THE NETHERLANDS [Jurgen Bey, Tjep., Tejo Remy and René Veenhuizen with Kunst en Bedrijf and AGS Architekten & Planners, 2004] The school takes the form of an interior 'high street' with various businesses. The floor design integrates symbols from the various vocational subjects and each department has a unique entrance to reflect the subject taught.

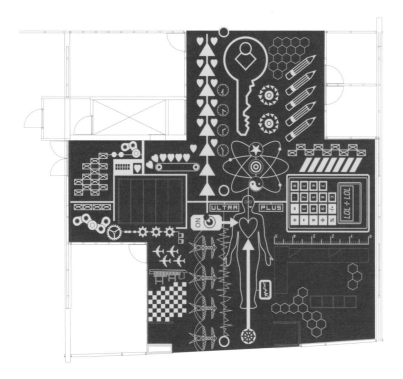

ing more concentration, thus complying with the individually adapted teaching methods. The mixture of dedicated workshop bases and more informal teaching spaces is very flexible, enabling teachers to adapt lessons to individual situations and various learning needs. This is enhanced by the variety in scale of adaptable space. Many of the classes are taught in smaller student groups, which obviously calls for an improved student-to-staff ratio. The desired choices of available teaching space and flexibility of learning environment were key drivers of the design brief given to the architects. The vocational nature of the subjects taught at the school also favours those students with a lower academic disposition who prefer more 'hands-on' learning. Subjects at Jåttå cover a broad vocational range including transport, building technology, health and sports sciences.

The vocational school **ROC Aventus** in Apeldoorn, the Netherlands [Jurgen Bey, Tjep., Tejo Remy and René Veenhuizen with Kunst en Bedrijf and AGS Architekten & Planners, 2004] is the flagship of a national programme in the Netherlands to integrate vocational and technical learning into mainstream education.[5] Its school takes the form of an interior 'high street' with functioning businesses including a travel agent and hairdresser and heavier engineering and mechanical subjects. Students can learn on the job on the high street, while in the upper floors of the building lecture theatres, classrooms and open-plan office spaces provide a setting for the more theoretical subjects. The school celebrates the craft of vocational subjects with adult reception spaces that are manned by the students. Meeting spaces are provided that are subject-specific and specially designed by imaginative designers to represent the subjects. Each subject reception is unique and fun. Walking into one of these spaces you feel welcomed, and your vocational subject is embued with significance.

In a similar way, **Lycée Marcel Sembat** in Sotteville-lès-Rouen, France [Archi5 with B. Huidobro, 2011] is a dramatic and celebratory solution to large workshop spaces. Much praised and awarded, this refurbishment and extension answers many questions of how to bring a school up to date and to value all its subjects. It is clearly a highly successful architectural landmark. The urban landscape form beautifully bridges the edge of the city and the large park – regenerating a run-down suburb of Rouen.

Educationally Lycée Marcel Sembat is innovative; it aims to raise expectations of pupils attending and offers a new type of technical school where the architecture celebrates the subjects. The vast halls with their technology aesthetic, accommodates cars and machinery and are like cathedrals to mechanics. It also celebrates the edge of the city-park environment raising the status of the college through the dramatic urban landscape profile of the buildings. It is an enhanced typology for the technical college where there is a strong relationship between the largely open-plan workshops and the classrooms for more academic work; they share a direct visual relationship, connecting intellectual and manual subjects. The brief called for a very good lighting and the curving roof allows natural light to flood into the workshops creating exceptional spaces to learn in.

Subject-specific learning bases

The educational model of subject-specific learning bases, also known as faculty-based learning spaces, refers to a university model of particular subjects being in their own building. In a secondary school this will probably mean a variety of learning spaces, from typical classrooms to larger workshop-like spaces. The learning bases may be broadly subject-based, i.e. humanities or science. Staff have a fixed base and the students move through the building with particular emphasis usually placed on providing a generous central circulation space that physically and visually connects the learning bases. Perhaps the key here is to make the spaces created for learning look and feel appropriate to their subject, to have a specific identity so often lacking in secondary schools.

Similar to the Jåttå School of Vocational Learning and ROC Aventus is the **Piter Jelles Nijlân School** in Leeuwarden, the Netherlands [RAU – One Planet Architecture, 2008]. It is part of the Dutch national secondary educational programme, offering both traditional academic subjects alongside vocational training. This new building, known as 'YnSicht', meaning 'insight' or 'in view', looks exciting and welcoming. A cantilevered prow-like entrance with a dramatic red staircase draws the students in. The external façades are partially screened by wood boarding, giving a distinct boat-like feel to the architecture. The four-storey transparent centre looks sophisticated and adult, but in this case fun. The building is top lit as well as having a large area of façade glazing, so the building is filled with light. Sustainability was one of the key drivers in the building's design; the oval form

LYCÉE MARCEL SEMBAT IN SOTTEVILLE-LÈS-ROUEN, FRANCE [Archi5 with B. Huidobro, 2011]
The school building is a powerful landmark at the edge of the city, where the city fabric ends and the landscape begins.
While the older buildings are embedded in the city, the newer workshops are part of the park landscape. The dramatic form
of the workshops creates a feeling of space and organisation.

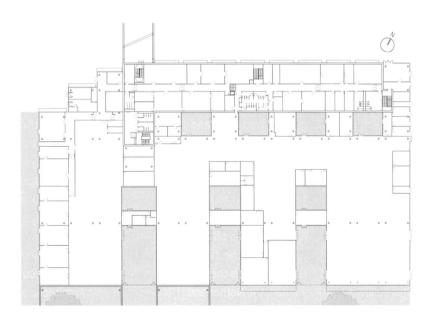

Ground floor plan of the extension

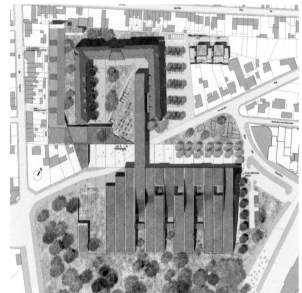

The massing diagram shows the two parts of the school
with the bridge crossing and the connection between the
landscape strips of the workshops and the city fabric.

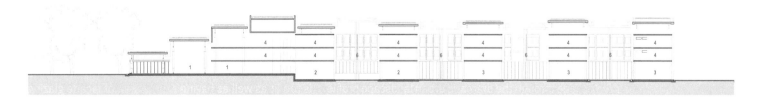

Cross section

PITER JELLES NIJLÂN SCHOOL IN LEEUWARDEN, THE NETHERLANDS [RAU – One Planet Architecture, 2008]
The wood boarding of the exterior and the cantilevered prow-like entrance are reminiscent of a ship.

with central circulation core is efficient in terms of minimising the area of external walls whilst allowing natural daylight deep into all spaces. This instills a collegiate appearance.

On a day-to-day basis flexibility of space for learning is provided through a variety of learning spaces from typical classrooms to larger workshop areas. This school is described by the architects as autonomous; the compact oval form allows the extensive use of glass while keeping heat and energy consumption to a minimum. The design goes beyond the Dutch standards for energy consumption in a new building, achieving 35% below the required level. The architects aimed to make the building as transparent as possible both from the outside and from within and to allow for changing educational needs in the future; the building's structure has been designed as a concrete frame with flexible internal partitions that can be rearranged.

The vocational training offered seeks to bridge the gap between education and 'real life'. The shops within the new building are a physical manifestation of this principle and their location at ground floor level provides a literal connection between the school building and the outside world. The fully glazed façades at ground floor level allow for the newly found skills of the students to be show-

cased to the local community. The large areas of vertical glazing and narrower horizontal glazing strips in the upper floors allow glimpses of the other activities taking place in the building. Within the building, services have been left exposed to demonstrate the functioning of the building to its users. The resulting industrial aesthetic also bears relation to the practical subjects that are taking place in the building and invites the fabric of the building to be used as a learning tool in itself.

Another strong faculty-based school, **Thomas Deacon Academy** in Peterborough, UK [Foster + Partners, 2007], is one of England's flagship academy schools. At the time it was also the most expensive new state-funded school in the country. One of the educational concepts behind Academies involves a key specialism that distinguishes the school, in this case mathematics and science (while a focus on business and enterprise would be a more usual emphasis for academies.)

However, Thomas Deacon is given further status by departing from a conventional model of education in secondary schools in favour of a university-type environment with lectures, seminars and tutorials. This school feels more like the headquarters of a large company rather than an academy school. It is an organically shaped steel and glass building surrounded by mature trees and

THOMAS DEACON ACADEMY IN PETERBOROUGH, UK [Foster + Partners, 2007]
Externally the school looks like a hi-tech research lab. Linking all the teaching spaces is a central atrium with the resource centre, social amenities and study areas at its core.

Longitudinal section showing central atrium

landscaping. Two entrances are linked by a central concourse, which directs circulation toward the central resource centre and social amenities, and creates a natural focus for meeting and informal learning. The undulating glass and steel roof over the central concourse unifies the architectural design, while providing natural daylight, acoustic control and ventilation to the main space. The triangular geometry of the roof and its innovative structure will hopefully 'inspire students to reflect on the Academy's specialised subjects of mathematics and science.'[6] This is clearly the most striking design feature of

the building, reminiscent of a similar roof soffit treatment in Foster and Partner's famous tree-like trusses of Stansted Airport.

Thomas Deacon Academy has 2200 students aged between 11–19 years[7] and joins three previous schools together in one super school. John Hinch, head of the art department when the school opened was quoted as saying: 'The different cultures that the three predecessor schools represented have come together more harmoniously than we could have imagined.' The scale is vast, at 19,000m² and some teachers struggled with the sheer

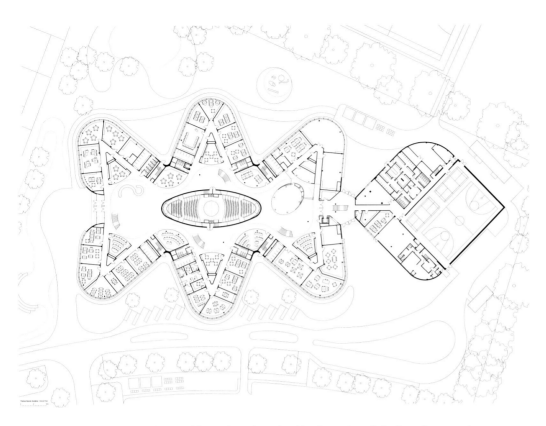

THOMAS DEACON ACADEMY / Ground floor plan. The school is planned as six 'colleges' arranged around a central atrium.

size of the school; no one had brought three schools together before. 'It was a shock to begin with,' says Rachel Baker, 18, the school's headgirl. She says it feels so much bigger, with 2200 pupils, than the three schools it subsumed. "The facilities are 10 times better though. There's a computer for nearly everyone."[8]

The school is clearly designed to resemble an adult workplace and the teaching methods, involving small group teaching and project-based team working were controversial when first introduced. However, it matches the more corporate feel of the school. To break down the scale of the building, the architects divided the academy into six smaller units, one for each of the 'colleges' that form the basis of the school's educational structure. Each college consists of a V-shaped ribbon of classrooms, formed around a three-storey central sheltered space that is the heart of each college and key to the educational and design concept.

The classrooms have either fully glazed fronts or open-plan spaces, so that you can see what's happening around the school from inside those spaces. An art gallery sits at the top of the cloud-shaped building; a dance studio at the bottom. Pupils describe it as 'lighter and brighter'.

Each of the six subject area colleges, for example arts and communications, has about 300 pupils, aged 11–19, its own reception, a showcase area for work, and a specific colour for the school ties the students wear. The college system is seen as one of the academy's 'founding factors for success'. Students feel like they belong to somewhere.

More radically, the headteacher is called the 'CEO' and some of the teachers are 'directors', for example the director of innovation. There is a boardroom, where pupils discuss 'school business' sitting on leather seats and learning to use the conference call telephone system. There are no bells, no formal break times, no registers and no staff room. The staff as well as the pupils seem happy with this set-up. For staff, who are often neglected in a school's spatial configuration, there are dedicated places for planning lessons, which have better resources and are more convenient than staff rooms. As a downside to this, however, staff report it is more difficult to keep a team together as communicating with other staff without a designated staffroom is problematic. Each college also has a 'network study area' for social and informal and collective study, allowing teaching staff to socialise with the students, and encouraging more mixing of different age groups and mentoring of younger students. However, despite these initiatives, pupils would rather go home early than have a break, because break time is when bullying might occur, so work is still to be done to make these informal learning spaces safe havens.

The university style teaching involves longer lessons; pupils have two 90-minute lessons in the morning, half an hour of form time, then another 90-minute lesson in the afternoon. Half an hour is taken out for lunch, but not everyone goes at the same time. Years 7 to 11 finish at 2.30pm, when sports activities start. Sixth-formers might have classes until 5.30pm. This creates a better flow of pupils and avoids chaos typically associated with everyone leaving together. Pupils wear ID cards around their necks. They swipe every time they enter or leave, go to the toilet, or attend a lesson. If a pupil is absent, a computer will alert staff and their parents will be called. Students also report that the 90-minute lessons work well – with time to conduct an experiment and then still time left to discuss it. The atmosphere resembles the one in a business rather than the one of a school, which helps prepare the students for university and the real world. 'It helps get us to focus rather than mess around', a student explains. '"We still get to have fun", she says. "It's just more structured."'[9]

There have been improvements in exam results in the academies but there is a growing chorus now saying that the extra spending on academies does not necessarily translate into higher results than at other new secondary schools.[10] The CEO of Thomas Deacon at the time of the school's opening, Alan McMurdo, thinks 'that as a model it has a real applicability, particularly in urban areas.' He also says: 'I'm more positive than when I started the job.'[11]

Despite mature planting and trees the site is very small and there is no real playground.[12] Mr. McMurdo said the main aim of not having a playground at the school was to help pupils' learning. On BBC News he was quoted: 'This is a massive investment of public money and I think what the public wants is maximum learning.'[13] Writer and expert on childhood Tim Gill, who led an official inquiry into children's play, said the idea 'borders on inhuman' He claims that children need to assume responsibility and argues that it is symptomatic of a way of thinking about children that we have to control and programme and manage every aspect of their lives, damaging in the long term because children need to have time when they take responsibility and make everyday decisions about what they are obliged to do and what they want to do.[14]

A school within a school

A school within a school offers an alternative building and pedagogical structure for learning. From the outside, the school appears to be a single unit; inside the school might be organised into colleges or houses where members of each house undertake most activities in their own college building. Within this college system vertical structures allow children from different key stages to work and socialise together, replicating an extended family support structure.

The college system, replicated in many academies and secondary schools in the UK is taken to its physical extreme in **Leigh Academy** in Dartford, Kent, UK [Building Design Partnership – BDP, 2010]. From the outside, the school appears to be a single building, belying the clearly demarked individual colleges that function inside. Leigh Academy is organised in four colleges or houses where students remain for most activities in their own building. 'Learning Resource Plazas' are shared between the paired colleges and classrooms are 'double-sized' to accommodate 60 pupils at a time. This is very clear in the well-organised plan of the building. According to the academy principal, this system offers a number of benefits: children learn best from each other and it replicates the 'lost' family support structure. It can also reduce gang or mob attitudes and replaces the 'factory model ' of education.

The vertically set up tutor groups and the curriculum are supported by a range of vocational programmes and

LEIGH ACADEMY IN DARTFORD, KENT, UK [Building Design Partnership – BDP, 2010]

Outside the building looks like a single unit, concealing the four individual colleges that function inside as a school within a school. The treatment of the façade, clad with rugged profiled steel, creates a contrast with the airy and light internal spaces which give a feeling of a high-end office block rather than a school. Each of the colleges is organised around a 'Learning Resource Plaza'; open-plan IT spaces rise up through the atrium.

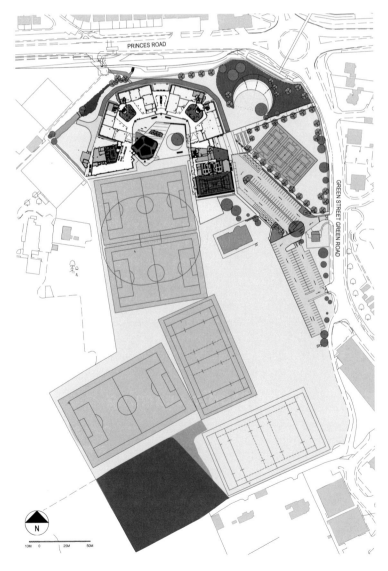

Ground floor plan

links to industry at every level. The technology specialism is also represented in the materials of the building, with a rugged profiled steel cladding. This lack of expression externally is a missed opportunity, because from the inside the building looks very different, light and airy, with verdant winter gardens separating the colleges, providing spaces to meet, socialise and undertake group working all year round. Shared sports facilities for the whole school and community use are also available.

The two 'Learning Resource Plazas' located within the central atria merge nature and technology, with computer suites at first floor level heating the space, whilst winter garden planting helps mediate the internal temperature on hot days providing a year-round space for socialising. The project architects, BDP, state that the 'exemplar' building delivers considerable reductions in carbon emissions against government benchmarks and national building regulation requirements.

Merchants' Academy in Bristol, UK [Penoyre and Prasad, 2008] is co-sponsored by the Society of Merchant Venturers, who have been supporting education in Bristol since the 16th century, and by the University of Bristol. The school provides its pupils with an inspirational environment that is both open and enclosing. The Architects worked closely with the stakeholder group to develop a brief that reflected the new academy's educational aims allowing the project to develop in a manner where the building reinforces the school's educational ethos. A successful collaboration between artist Tod Hanson and the staff, pupils and architects to develop a huge graphic to adorn the façade of the school includes the Society of Merchant Venturers' heraldic crest. This provides the school with a strong visual identity as well as representing the academy's sponsors.

The school is conceived as a series of pavilions around an open cloistered courtyard; it creates a 'learning village'. Each pavilion houses a variety of spaces that range from more traditional classrooms to labs, ICT and breakout spaces. This provides a high level of flexibility in

teaching methods. Other physical aspects of the school that contribute to the development of the school community include high degrees of transparency and openness. Large areas of glazing open out into the courtyard space, allowing views into and out of teaching spaces.

The creation of this academy sought to turn around poor attendance and low academic aspirations; the school addresses these problems in both pedagogical and physical manners. The creation of a 'house' system encourages pastoral care across the year groups. The plan form of the school with its pavilions manifests the house system. Four of the seven pavilions form bases for the 'houses', whilst one is allocated to the school's entry year. The separation of the first year is aimed at providing a transition space from primary to secondary level education. The creation of such a deliberate pastoral system strives to engender a school community based on mutual respect and maturity.

The external courtyard provides space for social interchange between the houses. In an unusual arrangement, the students' lockers are placed outside under the shelter of the cloistered walk that surrounds the courtyard. This increases the width of circulation space from an average to a generous corridor width reducing the crush experienced at class changeover and providing a place for social interaction. This also creates an incentive for pupils to stay outside a little longer.

Open Studio Learning

A new generation of schools uses the Open Studio Learning concept where each floor contains a mixture of different sizes and types of learning spaces, fully or semi-enclosed, and opening from the open-plan circulation spaces. This arrangement can provide visual stimulation and excitement with long views as well as varied teaching and learning spaces. The mixture of closed and open spaces allows maximum flexibility for different forms of teaching.

MERCHANTS' ACADEMY IN BRISTOL, UK [Penoyre and Prasad, 2008]
The school is organised as four 'houses' which are arranged around a central pavilion with shared facilities. Several types of teaching space allow for more flexible learning.

Section

A bold mural on the front entrance wall of the school creates a strong identity.

The loggia around the perimeter of the courtyard gives students a protected outdoor space to socialise and exchange ideas.

Ground floor plan
1   Entrance foyer
2   Learning resource centre
3   Assembly hall
4   Drama
5   Dining
6   Administration
7   ICT area
8   Staff area
9   General teaching
10 Year 7
11 Science
12 Sports hall
13 Changing
14 Technology
15 Bike storage
16 Technology workshop
17 Youth club

MERCHANTS' ACADEMY / The school is organised as four 'houses' which are arranged around a central pavilion with shared facilities.

The **Australian Science and Mathematics School – ASMS** in Bedford Park near Adelaide, Australia [Woods Bagot Architects, 2003] is small by European standards with approximately 260 pupils in 3455m² of space. The school is a specialist public school that caters for the three final years of schooling before entry into higher education and is designed to promote and support highly collaborative, interactive student-directed learning within an innovative curriculum.

This school specialises in mathematics and science education and uses the innovative spatial organisation to achieve high levels of engagement from all its students. The school's location, adjacent to Flinders University, enables cross-fertilisation of ideas and learning experiences. The building accommodates spaces of varying size and configuration, which allow flexibility of group teaching sizes. Traditional classrooms and laboratories have been replaced with 'Learning Commons' and 'Learning Studios'. 'Learning Commons' are the primary learning spaces and consist of zones corresponding to each year level. Each zone is a semi-enclosed space with workstations. Pupils have a 'home desk' and these are grouped in order to stimulate project work. The 'Learning Studios' are for practical research work and provide both individual and group workstations to support academic areas such as: physical sciences, applied technology, environmental sciences, life sciences, multimedia, performance, mathematics and ICT. Practical work and hands-on facilities are also found in the 'Learning Studios'. The building fabric and services are designed to be visible and legible, providing an additional learning tool. For example, some of the mechanical, hydraulic and electrical systems are exposed and used as a case study for building services in the curriculum. The environmentally friendly and sustainable design is intended to show the school's leadership in science and technology education.

The school is equipped with state of the art ICT and audio-visual facilities, remote controls and wireless technology supporting the high degree of mobility of the pupils around the school. At the heart of the school there is the 'Central Common' that promotes a sense of community. This two-storey core also provides access to the outside.

Finally, **Ørestad College** in Ørestad, Copenhagen, Denmark [3XN Architects, 2007] is an exceptional example of Open Studio Learning. The school is an established and early part of the windswept new town Orestad, a world away from central Copenhagen. It is urban, flat,

AUSTRALIAN SCIENCE AND MATHEMATICS SCHOOL – ASMS IN BEDFORD PARK, ADELAIDE, AUSTRALIA [Woods Bagot Architects, 2003]
The main entrance draws visitors into the 'Central Common'. The 'Learning Studios' and 'Learning Commons' open up off a generous double-height circulation space that is visible from the outside.

linear and organised around an artificial channel of water. The school, which now has the new town library next to it, is lined up with other large residential and office buildings along the main canal and high-level local train track. The back of the school and the view from the large outdoor raised terrace is of suburban Orestad one and two-storey 'parcel-huset' – homes on their own plots, a very Danish scene. As part of the 'new town' development, the school is important as a landmark, and hosts social and cultural activities for the local communities.

The spatial and pedagogical innovation of the school is not evident in its external form; it presents itself as a somewhat standard block, clad in a decorated skin. Semi-transparent and etched glass louvres create a responsive façade, which can be adjusted to control daylighting and views. Inside the school is visually arresting, providing a range of inviting, light, flexible and truly inspiring learning environments; these are achieved through intelligent use of structure, spatial organisation and furniture. Most dramatic is the wide spiralling timber staircase, creating an open and uplifting spatial feel to the whole volume of the school. It is conceived of as a physical manifestation of the interdisciplinary approach espoused by the school.

The structure of the building uses three huge columns as the primary load-bearing mechanism. This allows for great flexibility in the use of the floor space with wedge-shaped voids in the three upper floor plates positioned at slight rotations to one another, encouraging visual links and greater connection between the different floors and creating double- and triple-height spaces. The atrium is created by these voids. The whole school appears to be one enormous, interesting, cuboid volume.

Smaller areas are demarcated or screened with non-load-bearing structures, the intention being to allow changes in the way the space is used over time. Special-

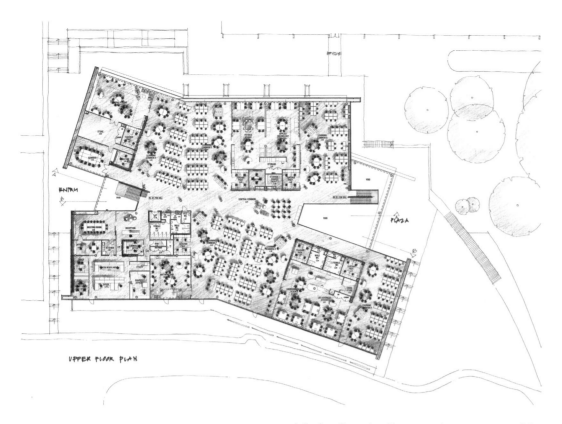

UPPER FLOOR PLAN

AUSTRALIAN SCIENCE AND MATHEMATICS SCHOOL – ASMS / **The first floor plan illustrates the open nature of the teaching.**

ly designed furniture is used to create a range of different spaces, and is designed to move and change to accommodate different group sizes. The spatial organisation of the building is designed around four floors that house the four study zones, with each floor containing a mixture of different sizes and types of learning spaces, fully or semi-enclosed from the open-plan circulation spaces. In the maths area, special pens are used to write on the glazed external walls contributing to the lived-in and educational feel of the place. Furniture ranges from desks and chairs or stools to sofas and large beanbags, allowing flexibility of use and giving students the ability to tailor their own working space to their needs. The circular 'break-out pods' are the most popular with children inhabiting these spaces long after school has finished in the afternoon, some doing their homework.

The school operates without traditional classrooms, instead encouraging students to work both individually and in groups in the various informal study areas. This approach is enabled through the provision of wireless networking throughout the building and laptops for all students. Creative use of media and communications technology is part of the school's pedagogy, and its focus on local and global connectedness through technology has led to the local nickname of the 'virtual school'. Far from virtual are the specific drama and music spaces, which again are used after school and are full of groups practising music and drama. The school here really seems to balance areas that need to be closed off with the open areas to make an exceptionally comfortable place to be.

ØRESTAD COLLEGE IN ØRESTAD, COPENHAGEN, DENMARK [3XN Architects, 2007]

The circular forms are echoed in the lighting. The clever arrangement of overlapping floor planes allows for vertical views throughout the building. The circular 'pods' provide break-out spaces for teaching and for the students to socialise.

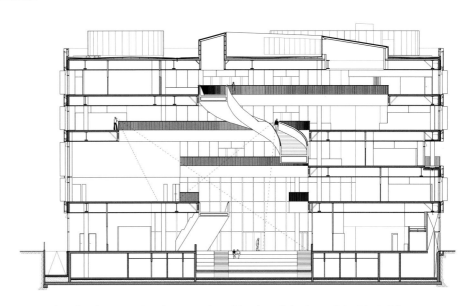

Section showing central staircase and combination of single- and double-height spaces

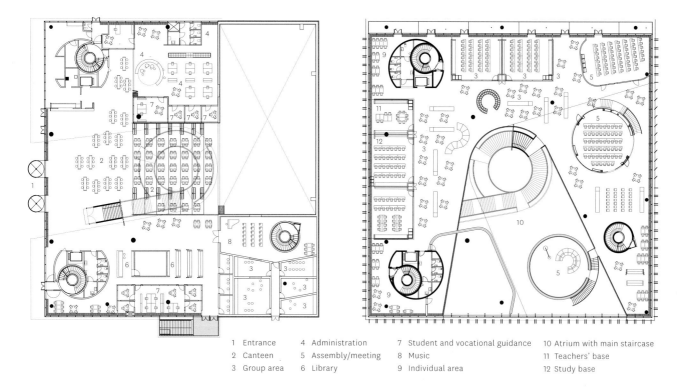

1	Entrance	4	Administration	7	Student and vocational guidance	10	Atrium with main staircase
2	Canteen	5	Assembly/meeting	8	Music	11	Teachers' base
3	Group area	6	Library	9	Individual area	12	Study base

ØRESTAD COLLEGE / Ground and first floor plan. The square external envelope provides no clue to the sinuous forms and open-plan spaces within.

A top view of the large curving staircase

REFERENCES

1 The programme is explained in the introduction, pp. 12–13.

2 Cathy Burke, '"Inside Out" A Collaborative Approach to Designing Schools in England, 1945–1972', *Paedagogica Historica: International Journal of the History of Education,* vol. 45, no. 3, June 2009, pp. 421–433.

3 Ibid.

4 The school and its staircase are also discussed in chapter 3, Flexible Space for Learning, pp. 78–79.

5 This college is looked at in detail in chapter 6, Learning Outside the Classroom, pp. 142–143, and in chapter 10, Furniture and Equipment in Learning Spaces, pp. 222–223.

6 Raw Architecture Workshop's website. http:// www.rawarchitectureworkshop.com/project6. Accessed 14 August 2014.

7 Anushka Asthana, 'No Break, no Bells in School of the Future', *The Observer*, August 26, 2007. http://www.theguardian.com/uk/2007/aug/26/newschools.schools. Accessed 14 August 2014.

8 Jessica Shepherd, 'How's Business at Thomas Deacon plc?', *The Guardian*, 4 March 2008, http://www.theguardian.com/education/2008/mar/04/newschools.schools. Accessed 14 August 2014.

9 Ibid.

10 'Certainly, there is no evidence to justify the government rush towards 400 academies,' he says. 'According to the government's own statistics, the academies showed only a 10.3% im-provement in five A*-C or equivalent including English and Maths in 2007, compared with the schools they replaced in 2002. All schools nationally went up 6.4% in this time. This means the academies added value of only 4% over that time.' Jessica Shepherd, 'How's Business at Thomas Deacon plc?', 2008, op. cit.

11 Ibid.

12 Patrick Barkham, 'Do Schools Need Playgrounds?', *The Guardian*, 8 May 2007. http://www.theguardian.com/education/2007/may/08/schools.uk3. Accessed 13 March 2013.

13 BBC News, 6 May 2007. http://news.bbc.co.uk/2/hi/uk_news/england/cambridgeshire/6629655.stm. Accessed 14 August 2014.

14 Ibid.

Summary

1 FROM IDEAS FOR LEARNING TO ARCHITECTURAL FORM

1. The most innovative thinking over the last century has traditionally been concerned with primary education seeking a more **child-centred approach** and giving more freedom of how and where to learn. Some new secondary schools are catching up now with student-centred, inviting spaces, eliciting a more mature approach to attending school.

2. It is more difficult for secondary schools **to make the learning spaces visually specific to the subject** – but some new schools have used imaginative ways to do this.

3. One popular initiative is for the **school to mimic an office environment**, including spaces for small group teaching, hot-desking, informal working and meeting. 'Boardrooms' for more formal meetings are sometimes included giving an air of importance and sophistication.

4. **Fixed learning bases**, another popular model emphasising faculty-based learning, develops a variety of learning spaces from typical classroom spaces to larger workshop-like spaces. Staff have a fixed base and the students move around the building providing a generous central circulation space that physically and visually connects the learning bases.

5. **A school within a school** offers an alternative physical and pedagogical structure for learning. From the outside, the school appears to be a single unit, inside the school might be organised into colleges or houses where members of each house undertake most activities in their own college building. Within this college system vertical structures allow children from different key stages to work and socialise together, replicating an extended family support structure.

6. In schools focused on **Open Studio Learning**, each floor contains a mixture of different sizes and types of learning spaces, fully or semi-enclosed, and arranged around the open-plan circulation spaces. Visual stimulation is provided by long views. The mixture of closed and open spaces allows maximum flexibility for different forms of teaching.

2 Nature, Ecology and Environmental Design / LEO CARE

This chapter aims to explore how some contemporary schools have grasped the spirit of environmental consciousness and created spaces for learning that 'touch the earth lightly' and use their setting as design inspiration. Environmentally sensitive design can help connect children to their natural surroundings. Making a contemporary ecological school is increasingly linked to analysing the impact of a school premises through measurement and calculations. Many schools around the world are rising to the challenge of meeting Zero Carbon status, LEED accreditation or Passivhaus standards (these standards are explained later in this chapter) and embedding the ethos of sustainable design into the school community. In order to achieve environmentally sound schools it is clear that eco-thinking needs to permeate not just the design but management, everyday use and understanding of school buildings by all users. Projects covered in this chapter also exemplify how important it is to integrate the design of the building and its landscape with the design of the school curriculum in order to provide a holistic learning experience. Starting from the origins of the Forest School movement, the outside environment and nature are emphasised as critical to the well-being of us all.

SANDAL MAGNA PRIMARY SCHOOL IN WAKEFIELD, UK [Sarah Wigglesworth Architects, 2010]
By exposing and labelling pipework, electric conduits and acoustic panels in classrooms children are actively engaged with how the building works.

L'ÉCOLE BUISSONNIÈRE IN BOSUIL, OVERIJSE, BELGIUM [Aime Ntakiyica, 2005]
The art installation by Aime Ntakiyica in Belgium explores the idea of learning in a natural setting. 'Buissonnière' literally means 'among the bushes'.

Linking learning to ecology

Linking learning to nature is a concept that without doubt goes back to our *homo sapiens* origin and was essential to our primal survival. Today, human urbanisation is contributing to 'nature deficit disorder'[1] amongst young people, generating communities and individuals that do not understand or engage with their natural surroundings. In this age of heightened environmental awareness and a dawning understanding that it is too late to resurrect the natural settings that have already been lost and that it will be a struggle to save those we still have, it is schools that are at the vanguard.

The Forest School movement

The origins of schools that make the most of the natural environment spans back nearly a century. Scandinavia is usually credited as the birthplace of natural schools and specifically the Forest School movement, where 5–7 year old preschool children used the woods as their classroom and the surroundings as their toys, curriculum and inspiration. The Forest School approach asserts that anything one can do in a classroom can also be done outside in a forest. This seemingly anti-architectural approach has been explored through a playful and provocative art installation, the **L'école buissonnière** in Bosuil, Overijse, Belgium [Aime Ntakiyica, 2005]. The juxtaposition of standard school furniture in the woodland setting, with

children's bags strung from the trees, challenges our preconceptions of what a classroom could be and hints at the freedom that children could be offered by learning outdoors.

In 1914, socialist principles led Margaret and Rachel Macmillan[2] to create an 'open-air' nursery and training centre in Deptford, London. Children from 18 months to 7 years old spent the majority of their time undertaking explorative play outside, along with gardening and animal husbandry. Across the Atlantic in the USA in 1927, Wakelin McNeel, leader of forestry and conservation in the youth development organisation 4-H, established the 'school forests', planting a huge number of trees across the state of Wisconsin and educating young people about the values of living in accord with nature. In Sweden, in 1957, Goesta Frohm created story characters to inspire children to learn through nature. In the Skogsmulle books and movement,[3] different characters depicted natural elements including mountains and the seas. The power of this vision is said to have inspired the Forest School movement, and there is no doubt that this narrative is echoed in most cultures. In 1980s Denmark, the småbørnspædagogik (early years education) programme formalised the Forest School approach.

Today, the Forest School movement still exists in Denmark, making up around 10% of preschool organisations in the country.[4] In Danish Forest Schools, children spend all day, every day outside in the woodland. There is no

OUTDOOR CLASSROOM IN ECCLESALL WOODS, SHEFFIELD, UK [Sheffield School of Architecture, 2008]
This outdoor classroom was designed and constructed by architecture students from the University of Sheffield in local historic woodland, within the city. The space is used by forest school groups throughout the year.

written curriculum to follow and activities are based on the changing seasons. Rather than sitting down and learning to read and write, children aged 3–7 years are learning about their natural surroundings. The deliberate lack of paper trail and bureaucracy is in stark contrast to the controlled curriculum-based education in other countries. In addition, children don't have access to hot food and flushing toilets, which may be difficult for education authorities to support in some countries. Having said this, the Scandinavian influence has rubbed off in many places; where natural schools are not for day-to-day use but offer a break or alternative to schools and are especially important to students with behavioural difficulties or special educational needs. Forest Schools hold fast to the belief that children need to be in touch with their natural surroundings to grow up as balanced human beings, to become responsible citizens and to foster our natural environment. The **Outdoor Classroom** in Ecclesall Woods, Sheffield, UK [Sheffield School of Architecture, 2008] was designed and constructed by Sheffield School of Architecture students. The project was commissioned by Archimedes Training,[5] who use the classroom as a base for exploring the surrounding woodland. Archimedes have since developed learning resources and training opportunities to help promote the values of the Forest School movement.

A range of schools around the world strike a balance between learning in the woods and traditional classrooms, linking natural surroundings with built learning environments and the curriculum. It is perhaps no surprise that many exemplars in this chapter are Scandinavian.

Schools and the natural elements

Many Danish schools adopt an ecologically integrated approach to learning environments, with a distinct openness and freedom to the learning spaces, blurring the boundaries between inside and out and extending the learning environment to the landscape beyond. **Kingoskolen** in Slangerup, Denmark [Rubow Arkitekter, 2000–2006] exemplifies this approach, with a series of learning hubs established around landscaped courtyards for 300 pupils. The shared facilities at the school are grouped around a wetland habitat, providing an inspiring setting for learning, an environmental basis for the curriculum[6] as well as contributing to the passive environmental design of the building.

Kingoskolen was one of the first schools to meet the agenda set by the Danish government's initiative at the

KINGOSKOLEN IN SLANGERUP, DENMARK [Rubow Arkitekter, 2000-2006]
The 'Eksperimentariat' sits over the wetland. Sliding doors and an open timber deck enable easy access from the laboratory to the pond. A covered circulation route runs around the wetland area creating an environmental buffer zone.

dawn of the millennium to develop school visions of the future based on ecological and environmental principles.[7] The expressed laminated timber frame structure gives warmth to the learning spaces and facilitates large areas of glazing, flooding the spaces with natural daylight and enabling views out onto the landscaped areas. Solar gain is dealt with through a series of external louvred shading devices and a circulation route that doubles as a ventilation buffer zone between the outside and classroom spaces. The timber structure uses less energy to make, compared to a steel frame or masonry construction, therefore reducing its environmental impact and helping to create a building with low embodied energy. There is also minimal energy used to heat and ventilate the building. The landscape courtyards play a central role in achieving this, by enabling natural cross ventilation in learning spaces. The pond helps cool air in the courtyard which can then be drawn in for ventilation in summer. In winter, the large glazing makes the most of winter sun, reducing heating costs.

Communal learning spaces are focused around the wetland area; the central *Eksperimentariat* (experimentarium) pavilion guards the pond and provides a space to explore the natural sciences. The large roof overhang funnels rainwater into the pond for recycling, enabling rainfall and water cycle studies. An internal walkway runs around the courtyard off which spring the *Naturhuset* (nature house) and *Vaerkstedhuset* (workshop). Together these areas combine spaces to research, experiment and create in. The *Mediehus* (Media House) accommodates the hall and library and the *Radhuset* (town hall) is the central administration point. Although the original school building was constructed in 2000, the courtyards provided a connection point for additional classrooms in 2006. This was achieved without compromising the connections to the natural environment.

The wetland remains at the heart of the ethos and activities of the school, providing an ongoing cycle of opportunities for exploration and learning. Unlike many schools that feel the need to restrict access to water on their premises, the timber decks and stepping stones are openly accessible to pupils. The management of the habitat is also conducted by students, engendering a sense of environmental responsibility.

Learning about the elegant natural simplicity of the water cycle in school is one of the moments of epiphany

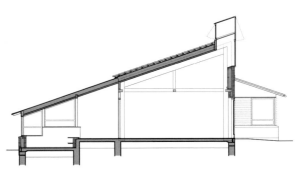

KINGOSKOLEN / The façade opens up as well, allowing for an immediate connection with the outdoors.

Section

Site plan. Buildings are clustered around courtyards with the wetland at the heart of the school.

where, as a young person, one realises the power of nature and how our daily survival relies on it. It seems incredibly sad that legislation and the fear of the danger of water has seen ponds and water courses removed from learning environments or fenced off for supervised use only. Yet, at the same time, the importance of water is being revisited in town squares, providing opportunities for play and exploration for all ages. Enlightened schools like Kingoskolen and their governing authorities have not only seen the creation of water as a place for learning but as a resource that links all the actions and culture of the school together, whilst underpinning the environmental approach to the management of the school buildings.

DARTINGTON C. OF E. PRIMARY SCHOOL IN TOTNES, DEVON, UK [White Design, 2010]
The exploded drawing shows the different elements of the classroom. The school is made of free-standing classrooms that open up to their surroundings. Children are immersed in nature with windows on all four sides. Practical instructions for reducing energy use become part of the school's fabric.

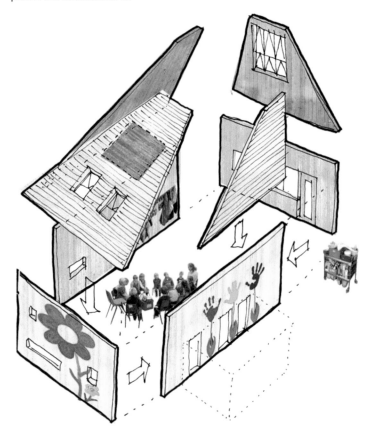

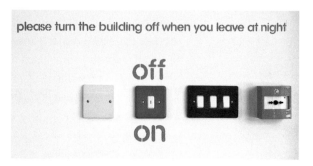

Genius loci

In the UK, the spirit of the Forest School movement is often most obvious in primary schools, whose size and scale tend to lend themselves to a more flexible approach to learning. **Dartington C. of E. Primary School** in Totnes, Devon, UK [White Design, 2010] is a publicly funded 420-place facility. The school is a recent incarnation of what the architects call eco-minimalist design. Dartington has an existing natural setting that most schools do not benefit from, but the way that this school embraces nature and the natural cycles of life could be replicated in a range of places. From the outset the school commissioning body, local community and local authorities worked in unison to create an institution that led the way in eco-design. Their approach was to immerse the children at the school in nature and connect them to their surroundings whenever possible. Like Kingoskolen the school is divided into small units, and free-standing classrooms. The rooms thus have windows on all four sides which enables pupils to experience the passage of daylight throughout the day. A large roof light renders the electric lighting unnecessary but for the gloomiest days. Solar gain is controlled through internal blinds on the roof lights and windows being set deeply within the building façade. The timber cladding also plays its part in recording the actions of the elements, with the material weathering down differently according to their orientation. Each classroom forms part of a semi-autonomous cluster, three of which are then brought together to make the school as a whole. Each cluster is located around a shared productive garden.

Life cycles in schools

Daily routines are linked to ecology through the recycling of greywater from hand basins that is purified in a reed bed, enabling children to understand the cause and effect of their actions. The building is also instructive with graphics revealing key design features; how to make best use of the building is advertised on timber panels and on electric light switches. There is also an elegant eco-logic to the design of the classroom units. A large south facing roof slope captures the energy of the sun through photo-voltaic cells, whilst the steeper north-lit window provides constant daylight for pupils to work with. The water cycle stitches the school and the landscape together, with water collection from roofs used to flush toilets and then filtered through the outside landscape, mixed with rain-water in swales and balancing ponds; this cleansing system is then used as part of the outdoor classroom. Solar water heaters are also employed for showers from which the wastewater goes into the reed bed filtration system.

Not only are these ecological features clearly expressed by the designers through the building fabric and reinforced by the school staff, but parents and the wider community are also fully tuned in to the design. Information is delivered to parents about the functionality of the school's design through presentations and a website that offers a range of information including design drawings. This level of communication has been a vital part of the successful design and the ongoing communal knowledge of how the building works.

It is perhaps not a surprise that Dartington Primary School is part of the Eco Schools Network in the UK and has an active Forest School group that forms part of the core curriculum; it is the school's mission, according to headteacher John Keats 'to take part in the existence of things'. At Dartington, the Forest School aims to replace the traditional 3Rs (in UK schools, the 3Rs humorously refer to Reading, Writing and Arithmetic) with 4Rs: Resilience, Resourcefulness, Reflection, Relationships. Trees, wood and timber are at the heart of the natural environment and forest school activities; 'children learn not just about trees and seasons but about the tools needed to craft and survive, how to "tread lightly" in a natural environment, and about themselves and their interactions with others. They have the time and space to reflect on and review their feelings, actions and learning.'[8] This approach is clearly echoed in the school building and land-scape, where timber is not just utilised, but treasured, in all its guises.

Native materials and indigenous technologies

The *spirit of place* can be captured in a school more than any other building type. Perhaps this is because the strength of optimism that pervades learning environments or the perceived need to permanently remind young people of where their roots are, reinforces a sense of belonging. Today, school buildings and their surroundings have an even greater imperative, to show children the fragility of place and the unique environmental eco-systems, traditions and heritage on which a sense of place are built. The fabric of a school can often tell a story of its location, and the environment from which it is shaped, whether in a choice of locally sourced regional materials or the use of a local vernacular.

Schools in developing countries are usually simple structures providing a basic but essential space for learning, created with minimal resources and scant budgets. In rural communities it is not uncommon for buildings to be of an exclusively domestic scale. Creating a single classroom for 30–40 pupils, some 50m^2 large, may be beyond the construction knowledge and skills of the local community and external support is often a necessity. Recently, a raft of projects has been undertaken by governments, Western NGOs and architects, to raise the standard of school buildings in developing countries. The danger is that these projects become drop-in buildings that neither relate to the place nor to the people using them. However, projects such as Gando Primary School[9] in Burkina Faso, and the **Handmade School** in Rudra-pur, Bangladesh [Anna Heringer and Eike Roswag, 2005] represent designs that reinterpret local technologies and vernacular building approaches whilst working closely with local communities. Both these projects offer innovative approaches to dealing with the challenging local climate, but also aim to create school units that can be

HANDMADE SCHOOL IN RUDRAPUR, BANGLADESH [Anna Heringer and Eike Roswag, 2005]
Brightly coloured panels animate the school building and echo the local dress. The first floor is an open classroom or meeting space, providing shelter from the sun, but enabling cross ventilation to keep the space cool.

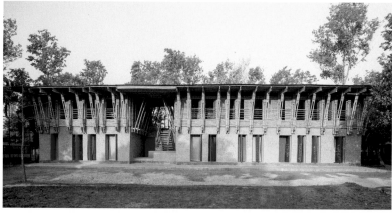

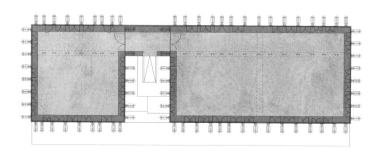

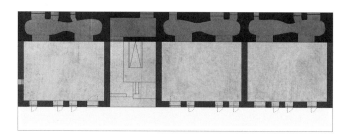

Ground and first floor plan

HANDMADE SCHOOL / A special area along one edge of the building has been created for small children to inhabit.

Cattle are employed to mix the earth and straw by trampling it.

Local residents erected the bamboo structure.

replicated and deployed elsewhere in the same country, forging a happy medium between site-specific and mass-produced.

The Handmade School, as its name suggests, is crafted by the hands of the local Rudrapur community with the German architects, Anna Heringer and Eike Roswag. Together they developed a close relationship designing and building a school grown out of local traditions and building techniques seamlessly fused with a more radical architectural and designerly approach. School children, teachers and volunteers were all involved in the construction process, making architecture that everyone has had a hand in.

Rudrapur is a small village near Dinajpur in northern Bangladesh. Its tropical climate ensures variation between a warm wet and a dry season, with the monsoon period bringing up to 400mm of rain a month. The design of the school responds to the climate by creating a thick walled ground floor structure of a mud and straw known as 'wellerbau' and a lightweight first floor structure from bamboo. The large overhanging roof disperses water away from the absorbent walls as well as providing shade and shelter to an otherwise open-sided space.

Out of necessity, the construction techniques make the most of locally sourced materials; cattle trampled the mud and straw to form the wellerbau mix and local people harvested bamboo which grows natively in abundance. The architects learnt about existing local crafts and skills and enabled the community to adapt and develop this for a larger-scale non-domestic situation. Wellerbau has commonly been used in the village, but in the handmade school a damp-proof course and brick foundation were integrated to improve the performance and longevity of the building. The earth used in the wellerbau-making process was traditionally very wet,

which makes it easily malleable, but prone to shrinkage and cracking. Experiments with a drier mix and ways of compressing the earth evenly were explored, resulting in a more stable structure. Bamboo has long been used locally in houses, but not on the larger scale that was required for the school. Techniques were developed in terms of joining, binding and overlaying the bamboo, to deal with the larger spans and cantilevered roof that the building required.

The local community and architects worked together with the regional METI (Modern Education and Training Institute) to integrate the school curriculum with the building; the more traditional classroom enclosures on the ground floor provide a setting for academic pursuits. The brightly coloured series of doors are used for access but also as chalk boards for children's work. The first floor functions as a gathering space, enabling large groups to undertake communal activities, particularly in the humid months of the monsoon season. The simplicity of the spaces supports training and more vocational pursuits. There are also more expressive and playful spaces created in the building aimed at younger children; a series of connected tunnels burrowed out of the mud walls, makes for child-sized landscapes that they can explore and inhabit, providing a framework for imaginative play.

The project has been successful on many levels, establishing partnerships, engendering a sense of community, creating new local skill specialism and providing a community facility that people can be proud of. It is integrated socially and physically into the local context, yet its design promotes a progressive educational curriculum. Architecturally, the building has a rare mixture of dignity, beauty, innovation and delight that make it of interest globally whilst evoking the spirit of its locality and people.

MAKOKO FLOATING SCHOOL IN LAGOS, NIGERIA [Kunle Adeyemi – NLÉ, 2012]
Operating in a harsh context, the Floating School has to deal with the fragile social, economic and environmental ecosystem of Makoko. On the water-level floor, the space is used both by children and local fishermen to repair their nets. Bottom right: The school under construction.

Environmental and social sustainability

Like the Handmade School, **Makoko Floating School** in Lagos, Nigeria [Kunle Adeyemi – NLÉ, 2012] tackles social and environmental issues at neighbourhood level head-on. Comparison can also be drawn in the collaborative design and construction undertaken by a western architectural practice working closely with local NGOs and craftspeople. The Floating School acts as a beacon of hope to young people and their communities in a hostile environment. Makoko is a water-borne informal settlement clinging on to the Lagos mainland. Hundreds of houses are perched on or tethered to timber posts that have been forced into the mud below the sea.

Sewage and waste goes straight into the lagoon from Makoko's 100,000 plus inhabitants. No infrastructure or services are available to residents and tensions have risen recently with reports of authorities seeking to remove Makoko to make way for prime waterside developments.[10] The Floating School is therefore a controversial development. The three-storey timber structure sits above the shanty town and literally gives children a new perspective on their surroundings. It is aspirational, yet practical, with two simple timber decks providing space for assembling and learning. The classroom spaces accommodate 100 children and can be separated by moving partitions. The space is shaded by simple timber

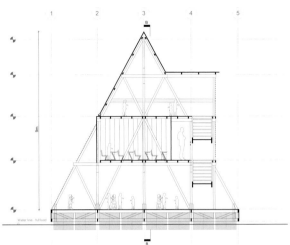

MAKOKO FLOATING SCHOOL / Location plan. Makoko is a water-borne informal settlement of over 100,000 inhabitants, attached to the Lagos Mainland.

Section. A timber A-frame forms the structure and simple timber louvres provide shade. Barrels are used for a floating platform.

Classrooms were created on the first and second floor. They can accommodate up to 100 children and can be subdivided using moving partitions.

louvres fixed to the A-frame supports. The lowest playground, at water level, doubles as a place for local fishermen to repair nets. The Floating School, a satellite of an existing facility within Makoko, can potentially move around in order to provide access to a wider range of children, facilitated by its construction of reclaimed timber lashed to some 256 plastic barrels. Power is provided by roof-mounted photovoltaic cells that provide a glimpse of technology that is otherwise beyond residents' means. The Floating School offers a clever prototype for a facility that provides basic and fundamental support to children and their families. It also delivers an intelligent response to a growing problem. With the pop-

ulation of Lagos expected to top 25 million by 2015,[11] the sustainability of Lagos' coastlines, lagoons and their ecological habitats are threatened. The pollution caused by sewage from informal settlements such as Makoko is threatening the fish stocks[12] that residents have relied upon for 120 years. By providing education for communities that depend on these areas for their livelihoods, there is an opportunity to inform people about the wider environmental concerns, helping to bring about positive change. The floating school model is one that could be replicated, creating a network of schools for a population so badly in need of support in creating a sustainable future.

School design and environmental standards

Across the world, governments, research authorities and independent organisations are forging evermore complex and holistic approaches to appraise the environmental impact of architectural designs in their early stages and when constructed. There are nearly as many different environmental assessment methods as there are countries, which means making meaningful comparisons between schools internationally is difficult. However, this is beginning to change. Successful or established systems are beginning to take hold. The USA LEED (Leadership in Energy and Environmental Design) system has now been adopted by India and other Asian countries, whilst the UK-based BREEAM (Building Research Establishment Environmental Assessment Method) is merging with the French HQE system to establish a European benchmark. There have been moves to compare the environmental impact of school buildings internationally, but it is difficult to see how any such endeavours would be meaningful, potentially reducing the interconnected issues of environment into a simplistic formula for a 'successful' school. This is not to say that environmental benchmarking is unimportant; indeed, it plays a fundamental role in setting standards but also providing an aspirational framework that school leaders and designers can buy into and strive for, not to receive a certificate, but to make a real difference to our shared environment.

There are several reasons why schools should be setting the environmental agenda and topping the environmental analysis charts; firstly, schools have an imperative to ensure that 'future generations' understand this environmental impact from an early age. This can be achieved passively by providing a school that presents a high energy rating and is inherently energy efficient, or actively by creating a learning environment that is overtly representing sustainable issues and a building that acts as a 'third teacher', offering opportunities for children to engage with the building through a sustainable curriculum. In addition, schools as a building type are not particularly demanding in terms of heating and cooling and do not tend to place specialist demands in terms of servicing, like a hospital, for instance.

The Passivhaus

In certain instances, technical environmental standards form part of a movement or contribute to a wider environmental philosophy. The Passivhaus (Passive House) movement, established in Germany in 1996, is a prime example. Initially focused on houses, as its title suggests, the approach has been adapted for public buildings. Passivhaus principles guide the design and construction of buildings that provide a comfortable interior climate that can be maintained without active heating and cooling systems.[13] This is primarily achieved through creating a building that is airtight and through controlling the ventilation by a heat exchanger, so that fresh air brought into the building is preheated with the warmth of the air that is being extracted. The concept also relies on heavily insulating the building thus reducing the heat loss through its walls, floors and roof. The attraction of this approach is that heating costs are virtually negligible without any need for space heating, as occupants provide most of the warmth required to heat the spaces. This could enable huge savings in monetary terms and in CO_2 production over the life of a building, both very attractive to schools' governing bodies. Passivhaus buildings are also considered to be healthier as damp, stale air is exchanged for prewarmed fresh air, reducing CO_2 levels and airborne contaminants, which is particularly important for young people in schools to maintain their well-being and readiness for learning.

In Hanover in Germany, the **Postfossil Ecowood Kindergarten** [Despang Architekten, 2007] accommodates 70 children and provides living proof of how an ecological benchmark can contribute to a groundbreaking learning environment, where the building design and construction ethos form the backbone of the school's environmental agenda. The main ethos of the Postfossil

POSTFOSSIL ECOWOOD KINDERGARTEN IN HANOVER, GERMANY [Despang Architekten, 2007]
Circulation spaces are generous and filled with natural light, making them great places to play in. Bottom: View from the adjoining park

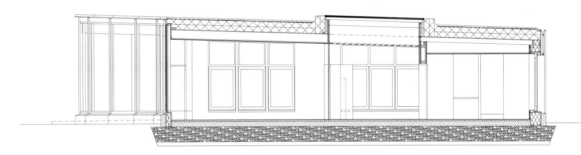

Cross section showing roof lights and full-height windows

Ecowood project is that children growing up in the catchment area of the kindergarten will become some of the first members of a postfossil generation, and that the kindergarten building will be an inspiration to this postfossil community.

The new kindergarten replaced an existing building of the same use from the 1950s. The new structure provided an opportunity to rethink the notion of early-years learning as well as creating a community hub with a focus on ecological sustainability. By creating a learning environ-

ment with such a high environmental standard, the hope is that the children will not settle for less in the future!

The vision for an environmentally integrated kindergarten is borne out through the creation of a building that is at one with its surroundings; curved classroom elements link the building and park, reflecting the curvilinear tree canopies. Within the curved spaces nestles a small group room, echoing the spaces created by tree routes and creating an inspirational space for classes to gather that is inside, yet connected to the outside landscape.

POSTFOSSIL ECOWOOD KINDERGARTEN /
Entrance with external timber cladding

From inside the classroom the surrounding mature trees provide a natural backdrop to the kindergarten.

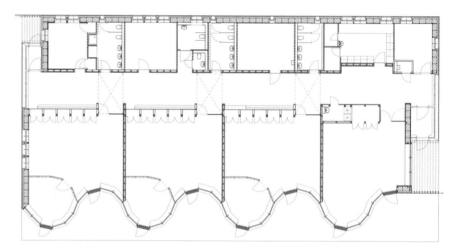

The ground floor plan illustrates the undulating façade of the building that creates bays inside the classes that are perfect for activities such as reading.

As with many Passivhaus projects, the predominant construction material used is timber, both in the laminated timber frame and the external cladding. The building utilises a relatively new type of sustainable heat-treated softwood timber which improves life and increases durability of European softwood to approximately 30 years, without chemical preservative or painting. The northside of the building is a virtually solid wall, dissolving into glazing on the southside. Triple-glazed units make the most of thermal gain in combination with a highly insulated (400mm thick) timber frame structure. Although ventilation is mechanical, there are still openable windows above external doors to provide additional ventilation if required. The cost of constructing the kindergarten

was 1800 € per m^2 in 2007. Although this initial build cost may be more expensive than a typical kindergarten construction, it is offset by the lower running costs over time. In addition the building offers added value to the school community through its environmental standards.

In 2000, U.S. Green Building Council (USGBC) established the Leadership in Energy and Environmental Design (LEED) assessment tool, to enable the 'verification of Green Buildings'. In 2007 the USGBC launched its 'Green Schools Campaign' to emphasise the importance of creating sustainable schools. Two specialist assessment tools were created, depending on whether the school was yet to be built or was an existing school looking to improve its green credentials by refurbishment. The US-

SIDWELL FRIENDS MIDDLE SCHOOL IN WASHINGTON, D.C., USA [Kieran Timberlake Associates, 2006]
Access to the wetland and entrance to the school is along a timber walkway alongside a concrete wall that was designed collaboratively with school pupils.

GBC explains the importance of greening schools in the USA: '20% of America goes to school every day. Too many of these students and teachers attend schools that are inefficient and miss important opportunities to reduce operational costs, foster learning and protect student health.' It also points out the benefits of green schools in terms of staff retention and, maybe even more importantly, recognises the learning potential of a green building. 'The school building is no longer a vessel filled with students, teachers and books, but itself an opportunity for experiential learning and discovery.' In March 2010 there were 13 schools that had obtained the highest LEED certification level of Platinum,[14] one of them being **Sidwell Friends Middle School**, Washington, D.C., USA [Kieran Timberlake Associates, 2006] for 340 pupils. Tellingly, the majority of school buildings reaching this target are private organisations that charge a tuition fee, which perhaps suggests that reaching this environmental target requires a larger budget than the one available to state maintained schools.

In reaching its LEED Platinum status, Sidwell Friends School has embraced the green imperative to create an interactive, environmentally sound school and grounds through the construction of a new wing for the middle school and the creation of a wetland and reed-bed system to recycle their greywater. Additional features include natural ventilation systems and photovoltaic banks on the roof. Perhaps the most impressive aspect of the project is how the school has embraced sustainable practices and made them central to the school's ethos in line with their Quaker ideals of sufficiency, stewardship and simplicity. In the past few years pupils have taken part in a range of lab projects that use the wetlands and school energy and ventilation systems as a base from which to compare and analyse other buildings in Washington, D.C. Interviews with local regulators, scientists and specialists help reinforce the lessons being learned. In addition, chemical levels in the recycled water are tested by pupils while biology classes look at the animal species within the wetland. English lessons also take up wider environmental issues and introduce books that trigger a range of discussions and, equally important, 'make connections between the building's systems and the world outside the building.'

Technology is integral to the process of building sustainability into the school, and an open-access online 'Building Dashboard' hosted by Lucid Design Group provides real-time outputs for energy consumption,

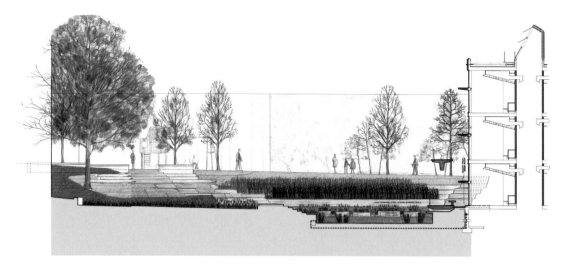

SIDWELL FRIENDS MIDDLE SCHOOL / Diagram of the wetland

View of the roof garden

Looking out onto the wetland area from behind the timber screen

production and water usage/recycling. Longer periods of usage can also be analysed and evaluated to assess the impact of the school's activities and the efficiency of the building systems over time. The dashboard is quite intuitive and provides the link between design, use and learning that many schools are striving for. A team of landscape design, environmental and engineering consultants were central to the project, exemplifying the unified working team required to realise such a holistic project.

Towards carbon neutral schools

In the UK the environmental standards are now driving schools towards carbon neutrality. In January 2010, the Zero Carbon Taskforce published its final report on how schools across England could become carbon neutral by 2016. The main issues outlined to achieve the aim of being carbon neutral were summarised as: engagement (with school users), knowledge and skills, feedback (on usage of energy and resources within schools), access to renewable energy and low carbon supplies and sufficient investment. The report also states 'behavioural change'[15] as one of four challenges to overcome in order to reach the zero carbon goal. Some of the issues and challenges identified in the report do not directly relate to the design of learning spaces, but there is an underlying imperative for designers to work with school communities as well as construction partners to fully engage people – not only in the design process, but in the creative management and use of school buildings. Such engagement will help ensure that design intention is implemented in a way that is effective at reducing carbon emissions; the design should also enable school users to be actively involved in making a positive contribution towards this goal. Achieving zero carbon emissions in schools needs to be embedded into everyday activities and routines and should be integral to learning activities. Recent research[16] has confirmed a large gap between the intended or projected carbon footprint of school buildings and the actual net carbon usage of the school in operation. This is due to the fact

MAWSON LAKES SCHOOL IN MAWSON LAKES, AUSTRALIA [GMB Architects and Russell & Yelland Architects, 2003–2008]
Pupils can access the Building Management System and adjust the ventilation to suit their needs and activities within the classroom.
The school is organised as a series of classrooms separated by gardens, thus linking the natural environment with learning
activities. Bottom: The building faces onto a town centre street rather than being set by a parking lot. Large clearstories provide south light.

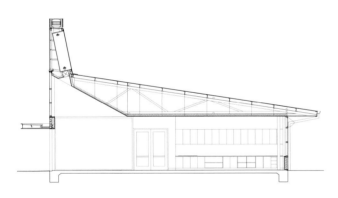

Longitudinal section showing ventilation tower

that no simulation can predict how individuals and groups will use the building; also, few building users fully understand how the school building works. Building users need training in managing the often complex heating, lighting, ventilation and energy production systems to understand the impact that they have in their everyday activities. Well-written, illustrated manuals and training courses should be offered to the occupants during the first few years of a building's life.

At **Mawson Lakes School** in Mawson Lakes, Australia [GMB Architects and Russell & Yelland Architects, 2003–2008], children not only learn from the building, but can then feed their knowledge directly back into improving the energy efficiency and quality of their learning environment. A computer interface provides student access to the Building Management System (BMS) where they can experiment with different ways of cooling by adjusting the venting through the solar and thermal chimneys

SANDAL MAGNA PRIMARY SCHOOL IN WAKEFIELD, UK [Sarah Wigglesworth Architects, 2010]
The architects tried to create an exciting building with many opportunities for its users to learn, play, socialise and engage with its environment. All spaces are naturally lit, through carefully oriented roof lights. Bottom: Located in a residential area characterised by terraced housing, the school is laid out in the parallel street pattern.

integrated into the classroom areas. This knowledge about the technical systems within the building provides the school users with a real understanding of how their building works and how building comfort may be improved, and users can also actively reduce the resources consumed. This empowerment could help overcome teething problems in some new schools, with teachers and pupils not knowing how to keep their classrooms at an appropriate temperature or light level.

Sandal Magna Primary School in Wakefield, UK [Sarah Wigglesworth Architects, 2010] sets about achieving environmental targets whilst engaging the school community in the management of the building. Described as 'one of the most carbon efficient schools in the Britain'[17], the building is heated by a ground source heat pump buried within the school grounds and powered by photovoltaic panels on the school's roof. Natural light enters the school through carefully orientated roof lights, reducing

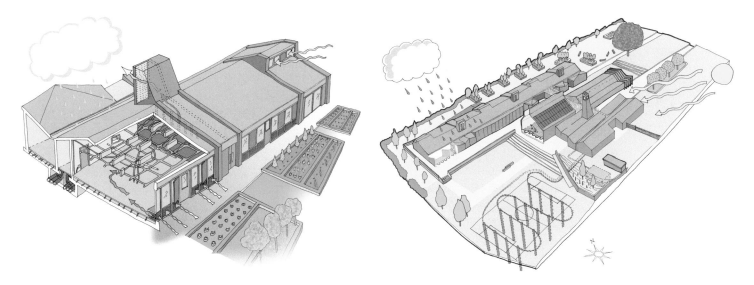

SANDAL MAGNA PRIMARY SCHOOL / Environmental diagram explaining how the school is naturally ventilated with fresh air entering at low level and being extracted through high-level brick chimneys.

The landscape in the school is productive as well as ornamental. Children have the possibility to grow their own fruit and vegetable in the allotments and the orchard on the south side.

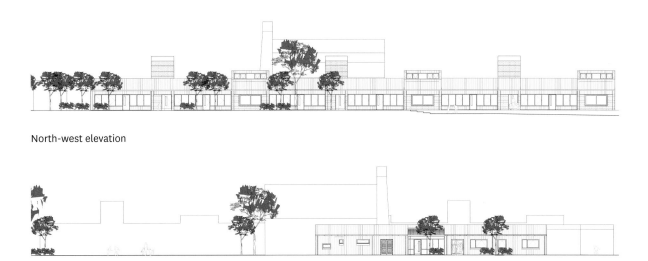

North-west elevation

South-east elevation

the need for electric lighting. Construction materials were carefully sourced and selected, including the reuse of bricks from the previous school that was demolished. Pipework and electrical conduits are exposed and labelled in teaching spaces and intertwined with acoustic panels revealing the workings of the building to children. One might expect that the effect of the building services being on show would give an unfinished appearance, but the careful design and organisation of these elements is surprisingly sculptural. Classrooms are naturally ventilated with fresh air entering at low level and being extracted through high-level brick chimneys that are a key feature of the architecture externally. Rainwater is collected from the roofs and used for toilet flushing and watering the gardens. The design of the school embodies the environmental themes of reduce, reuse and recycle.

Sandal Magna Primary School was designed hand-in-hand with the school community and local authority. The architects saw the creation of the school building as 'enriching their educational mission with activities that improve the environment and quality of life of local people.'[18] Set within a built-up area characterised by terraced housing, the school takes the parallel street pattern and creates a landscape formed out of a series of strips. A line of allotments flanks the classrooms providing a growing area for children of all ages in the school. A native hedgerow then separates the grounds from the houses beyond, creating a natural buffer. An orchard has been planted on the southside of the school delineating the entrance route from the car park. The school grounds are very much a productive landscape as well as ornamental, offering opportunities for children to learn through their surroundings. Two learning kitchens have been created, to reinforce the importance of healthy food. The spaces are used by children and families alike, to engage the wider community in healthy eating. Sandal Magna Primary School responds to its context through its use of materials and roof forms, but builds on and enhances the unremarkable existing site, creating an environmental hub in the heart of the community. The learning opportunities for children and their families offered by the school around environmental stewardship and healthy lifestyles are framed by the school buildings that reveal new opportunities to the school community on a daily basis. 'Hardly a day goes by without a new revelation from this exciting building: it could be a previously unseen view of part of the building or the way that the building is being used by the staff or children.'[19]

REFERENCES

1   Richard Louv, Last Child in the Woods. *Saving our Children from Nature-Deficit Disorder*, London: Atlantic Books, 2005.

2   Margaret McMillan, *The Nursery School*, London: 1919 (reprint BiblioLife, 2009) and Rachel McMillan, Nursery Schools: *A Practical Handbook*, 1920. (Rachel was Margaret's sister)

3   Skogsmulle is translated as Forestmulle, a 'mulle' being a fictional being.

4   Rosemary Bennett, 'Lessons in Life at the Forest School', London: *Times Education Supplement*, September 6, 2009.

5   Archimedes Training is a Sheffield-based organisation that works globally to offer training and facilities based on the core values of the Forest School movement. https://www.archimedes-training.co.uk/. Accessed 15 July 2014.

6   Further information on Kingoskolen design and curriculum can be found at the school's website: http://www.kingoskolen.skoleintra.dk/Infoweb/Designskabelon7/Rammeside.asp?Action=&Side=&Klasse=&Id=&Startside=&ForumID=. Accessed 31 October 2013.

7   Translated from Rubow Architects' website. http://rubowarkitekter.dk/. Accessed 9 January 2011.

8   From Dartington Primary School's Forest School website. http://www.dartington.devon.sch.uk/. Accessed 9 January 2011.

9   The school is described in chapter 5, Participating in the Design and Construction Process, on pp. 124–126.

10 'Destroying Makoko: One of Africa's Oldest and Best-known Slums is Being Dismantled', *The Economist*, 18 August 2012. http://www.economist.com/node/21560615. Accessed 31 October 2013.

11 Nigeria: Lagos, the Mega-city of Slums, *IRIN, Humanitarian News and Analysis – a Service of the UN Office for the Coordination of Humanitarian Affairs*. http://www.irinnews.org/report/60811/nigeria-lagos-the-mega-city-of-slums. Accessed 31 April 2015.

12 The Regional Impacts of Climate Change, Intergovernmental Panel on Climate Change. http://www.ipcc.ch/ipccreports/sres/regional/index.php?idp=30. Accessed 31 October 2013.

13 Cf. Passivhaus Institut website: http://www.passiv.de/. Accessed 31 October 2013. See also Manfred Hegger, *Aktivhaus: From Passivhaus to Plus-Energy House*, Basel: Birkhäuser, 2015.

14 The base level of the LEED assessment is 'certification', followed by silver, gold and platinum for top-performing building environments.

15 Robin Nicholson et al., *Road to Zero Carbon: Final Report of the Zero Carbon Taskforce*, London: Department for Communities Schools and Families, 2010.

16 Christine Demanuele, *Energy Performance of Schools*, London: 2010. This report was the result of a Knowledge Transfer Exchange with Max Fordham Building Engineers and the Bartlett School of Architecture. It is stated in the Research Summary that 'In many of the schools we visited, (electrical) equipment was left on all the time. This can increase the carbon emissions of the building by a massive 83% and could cost the school an additional 6700 £ a year to run (assuming 8.5 p/kWh for electricity and a 2400m² school).' The report can be downloaded from Max Fordham's website: http://www.maxfordham.com/assets/media/images/publications/Energy%20Performance/Energy_Performance_of_Schools.pdf. Accessed 31 October 2013.

17 Sarah Wigglesworth Architects' website: http://www.swarch.co.uk/projects/sandal-magna-primary-school/info/. Accessed 31 October 2013.

18 Presentation by Sarah Wigglesworth on 1 April 2011 at Sandal Magna School.

19 Julia Simpson, headteacher of Sandal Magna School. http://www.swarch.co.uk/assets/Uploads/sandal-magna/swa-sandal-magna.pdf. Accessed 31 October 2013.

Summary

2 NATURE, ECOLOGY AND ENVIRONMENTAL DESIGN

1. The **Forest School movement** holds fast to the belief that children need to be in touch with their natural surroundings to grow up as balanced human beings, to become responsible citizens and to foster our natural environment.
2. **Linking ecology, architectural design and learning** enables pupils and school staff to begin to understand their place within their local environment, both built and natural. Schools with sustainability at the heart of the design provide a knowledge base from which students can look further afield.
3. Students gain a better understanding of the fact that decisions made today have a ripple effect and **an impact on the future**. They become more **aware of the influence** that they have on their surroundings and what they can do to change this.
4. Children develop a **greater knowledge of building systems and construction**, enabling a responsible use of resources.
5. Schools that consciously contribute towards a sustainable future **raise aspirations** for everyone involved.
6. Better environmental conditions inside schools make **learning and working more enjoyable** and **reduce absenteeism**.
7. Making the sustainable design of the building and its landscape **part of the school curriculum** provides a holistic learning experience.

3 Flexible Space for Learning / CLAIRE KEMP

The call for 'flexible space' is a common requirement for many new school buildings. But what does flexibility mean in this context and how can it be achieved through design?

Flexibility is inherently related to permitting change. Schools are places in constant transformation; in the short term, they accommodate transitions between different subjects, activities and learning experiences on a daily or, more often, hourly basis. In the long term, curricula, pedagogies, student numbers and demographics are certain to change. However, even with thorough consultation and engagement it is difficult to predict exactly how people will inhabit and use a building and more or less impossible to predict how that use will change over a building's life span.

In school building architects are therefore posed with a difficult challenge: designing for the unknown. Consequentially there is a risk that spaces become 'universal': generic boxes that allow any activity or that can easily be reconfigured. Without careful design these spaces can be less flexible than those developed for specific activities and can be uninspiring places for learning.

This chapter looks at ways of providing flexibility in school buildings in both the short term and the long term. It deals primarily with physical flexibility; that is the ability of the building fabric to accommodate change, be it through multi-purpose spaces that can house a different activity every hour or through a whole school that is temporarily erected for a burgeoning population and then packed up and moved on ten years later.

BRISTOL METROPOLITAN COLLEGE IN BRISTOL, UK [Wilkinson Eyre Architects, 2009]
The covered street could be extended and additional 'learning clusters' added to accommodate
rising student numbers addressing the need for flexible space in education buildings.

OTONOHA SCHOOL IN IBARAKI, JAPAN [UZU Architects, 2006]
The first floor can be used as one large open space once the screens are drawn away. The system of doors and screens create wonderful moments throughout the building and allow for flexibility and lightness.

Moving parts

Technological advances in the design of sliding walls and moving partitions, and in particular their acoustic properties, mean that they are now a common feature in many school buildings. Typically 'off-the-shelf' sliding screens are used to subdivide large multi-purpose spaces or classrooms across their width into two or three smaller rooms to meet a demand for 'flexible' space. Where space is at a premium, such dividers have a very practical purpose. To work successfully in each configuration careful consideration of a number of practical issues including lighting, acoustics, circulation and climate control is necessary. There are countless examples where moving partitions in schools have been replaced with permanent walls due to bad design or maintenance. For example, they may be too heavy and difficult to move or the mechanism stops working after a while.

Reconfiguring learning space

But what if restructuring the learning environment through the use of flexible components (walls, screens, curtains, furniture) could become more than just a means of creating larger or smaller spaces? What if students could play a part in reconfiguring their learning environment on a daily or even hourly basis, changing the physical dimensions of the space, but also its character and in the process developing an understanding of themselves in space and their ability to manipulate it?

Otonoha School in Ibaraki, Japan [UZU Architects, 2006], is a preschool situated amongst rice fields that have served the community for years. It has a curriculum that revolves around music and agriculture. The entire first floor of the two-storey building has been designed as an open-plan space that can be broken down into smaller areas with a sophisticated system of sliding screens and semi-transparent curtains. Otonoha is an example of open-plan learning spaces that are in many cases replacing classrooms in schools; where open-plan spaces are broken down with changes in level, furniture and dividing walls, to support different types of learning such as project-based work, seminars, group sessions, individual study and traditional classroom-based activities.

Otonoha School provides an inspiring case study for designing open-plan education space that can be modified by both staff and students to accommodate different

OTONOHA SCHOOL / The façade opens up, allowing for an immediate connection with the outdoors.

The side of a ground floor classroom area can be opened up as well to the adjacent circulation space or separated by sliding screens which recess into a wall.

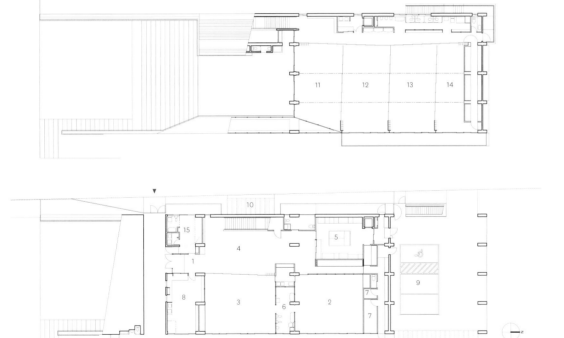

System of sliding walls

Wooden screens ———————

Lace curtains —————————

The room on the first floor can be divided by wooden screens and lace curtains into 12 spaces of varying size.

1   Entrance
2   Nursery room (age: 0)
3   Nursery room (age: 1)
4   Hall/corridor
5   Kitchen
6   Toilet
7   Locker room
8   Office
9   Parking
10 Bicycle parking
11 Nursery room (age: 2)
12 Nursery room (age: 3)
13 Nursery room (age: 4–5)
14 Nursery room (temporary)
15 Nursery room (children after illness)

Ground and first floor plan

ST. BENEDICT'S SCHOOL IN EALING, UK [HHbR (previously Buschow Henley), 2008]
Twenty-four sets of oversized doors provide a flexible space for learning at the heart of the school.

The 'hall within a hall' efficiently unites previously disparate
school buildings.

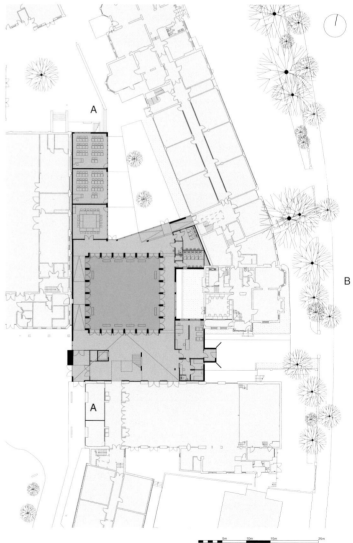

Ground floor plan

ST. BENEDICT'S SCHOOL / When the doors are open the space is transformed into the 'cloister'.

When the doors are closed the inner hall becomes an additional area for teaching and learning.

learning needs on a day-to-day basis. The grid arrangement of the nursery's deep roof structure, necessary to allow the space to be so open, doubles as the grid on which the sliding walls and curtains move. Metal tracks are integrated into the underside of the roof beams and are laid flush into the smooth timber floor finish, therefore minimising the visual clutter that can often be associated with such complex moving parts. The positioning of long strip skylights along either side of the principal roof structure allows each area to be naturally lit even when all of the sliding partitions are in place – an important consideration for any space that is to be subdivided.

Another important factor is sound penetration. In this part of the nursery complete acoustic separation is not achieved when the artist-designed semi-transparent printed curtains and low-level timber furniture partitions are slid into place due to the lightweight nature of some of the moving screens as well as gaps above the cross beams. In this part of the building this encourages the children to 'feel the rhythm' of each other in line with the school's focus on musical development. However, on the ground floor an arrangement of more typical classroom spaces, with timber-clad sliding walls along just one side, provides areas that can be completely separated both visually and acoustically.

Dividing large spaces

To accommodate occasional events such as school plays, whole school assemblies or awards ceremonies, moving elements provide the opportunity not only to reconfigure large gathering spaces, but also to change spatial qualities according to the event or time of year. For example, it became clear early on in the design process for an extension to **St. Benedict's School** in Ealing, UK [HHbR (previously Buschow Henley), 2008], that the 400m² assembly hall and the 225m² examination hall requested in the school's brief would need to be amalgamated due to space limitations. However, instead of employing the usual solution of dividing a 400m² hall across its width with a folding-sliding partition, the architects designed 'the cloister', a space that cleverly unites the existing campus whilst also embodying the school's Catholic roots and values in its design.

In what the architects describe as a 'Russian doll' solution, for the 'cloister' one hall is placed inside the other. The outer hall, square in plan, sits snugly between the existing school buildings and is linked to each with a series of ramps and hallways. Within the space 28 concrete columns form another square, the examination hall. Each of the 24 openings between the piers is furnished with a set of full-height solid double doors that, during exam times, can be closed to create a self-contained room, whilst still allowing circulation between the other school buildings in the arcade that is formed around the edges. When the doors are open the whole space becomes a grand assembly hall as well as a place to accommodate transition between lessons and chance encounters, a 21st century Benedictine monastery.

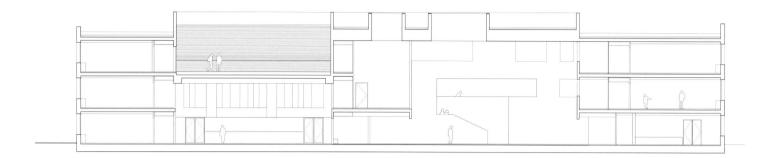

Large multi-purpose spaces

As demonstrated at St Benedict's School, accommodating large numbers of students, staff and visitors for various activities within school buildings is a difficult logistical challenge. In smaller schools it is often sufficient to provide one hall that can be used for dining, assemblies, sports and performances. In larger schools, however, the easiest solution to providing these large spaces, each with their own spatial and technical requirements, has often been to create several separate spaces: a drama studio, a dining hall, a gymnasium, an assembly hall. These days, with pressure to offer an ever-increasing plethora of facilities, schools are looking for new solutions to accommodate these space-hungry activities.

Central atrium

In some cases schools have opted for methods of providing remote space for whole school gatherings, such as broadcasting assemblies on television screens in classrooms and hiring space outside of the school for occasional events. But in many cases we have seen the emergence of a different type of space: a multi-purpose space located at the heart of the school around which the rest of the school is organised. Moving away from large disparate spaces occupied for just several hours a week, this new type of space becomes a focal point of the school: a place to arrive, to gather, to eat, to meet, to perform, to pass through and most crucially a place that is active throughout the school day.

At **Christ's College** in Guildford, UK [DSDHA, 2009], a 700-pupil newly built secondary school completed in 2009, three large spaces have been incorporated within the school building: two with dedicated uses (a sports hall and a theatre) and a third space, a multi-purpose atrium situated at the heart of the building. Every morning the school's 700 pupils arrive in this space, pause and view the day's announcements on television screens before dispersing to one of the surrounding classrooms via the circulation spaces that wrap the atrium. In the meantime staff might be wheeling out two trampolines from a nearby store into the atrium for a PE lesson that can be overlooked by accidental spectators passing along one of the corridors above.

By lunchtime the space will have seen yet another transformation; each day the kitchen servery at one end of the atrium opens up and the atrium is furnished with a series of long white mobile canteen tables. And the activity does not stop at the end of the school day; during out of school hours the atrium along with the rest of the school is available for hire for conferences, local sports practices and public events.

It is easy to see that the atrium is the most vibrant space in Christ's College, but what makes it so? Firstly, the spatial planning is very well considered. On a practical level, storage and circulation are key to making a space like this work; if it is too difficult to set up a new activity in the space staff will not use it. Acoustics and lighting are also critical especially in a location internalised within the plan. The walls and ceiling of the atrium are lined in narrow timber cladding which serves to absorb sound, but also sets this space apart from other parts of the school which are largely finished in fair-faced blockwork and concrete. Sculptural skylights draw daylight down into the space, but also into the circulation zones that surround it whilst elongated pendant lights accentuate the height and drama of the space. The

CHRIST'S COLLEGE / Timber cladding to the walls and ceiling provides acoustic absorption whilst also distinguishing the atrium from other parts of the school.

The multi-purpose atrium at Christ's College provides a grand entrance space as well as accommodating multiple functions throughout the school day, such as sporting activities.

1   Entrance foyer
2   Atrium
3   Sports hall
4   Theatre
5   Library
6   Kitchen
7   Independent
    Learning Centre

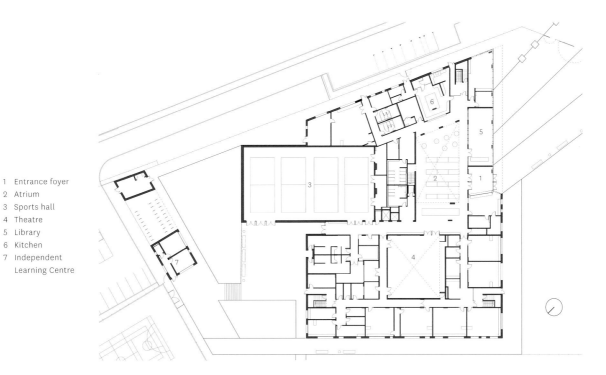

Ground floor plan

A. P. MØLLER SCHOOL IN SCHLESWIG, GERMANY [C. F. Møller, 2008]
The scale of the central atrium and grand staircase, along with a refined material palette and specially commissioned artwork, gives the building
a civic quality. The first floor landing of the grand staircase is home to the school's knowledge centre and spaces for teaching and other uses are created
in and around the stairs.

importance of this space within the school is further strengthened by its relationship to the school chapel, a double-height space sitting above one end of the atrium, an ever-present reminder of the school's Christian roots right at the centre of the school.

The multi-functional staircase

Christ's College's flexible atrium is not alone in contemporary school building, but the most influential example of this typology is almost certainly the atrium at Hellerup School[1] in Gentofte, Denmark [Arkitema, 2002], a three-storey galleried space dominated by a wide 'coliseum' stair. Countless examples of new schools in Denmark and around the world have been built around this model that combines circulation with auditorium-type seating for large group gatherings or for informal encounters.

One of the most impressive recent examples can be seen at the **A. P. Møller School** in Schleswig, Germany [C. F. Møller, 2008], serving the Danish-speaking minor-

ity in the province of the same name in Germany and designed by a Danish practice. Funded by The A. P. Møller and Chastine McKinney Møller Foundation, the school has a luxury of space and material not afforded by most school building budgets, something that is expressed by its vast central atrium. Whereas the atrium at Christ's College is only large enough to house one activity at a time, here numerous activities can occur in the space simultaneously, supporting the school's educational approach of flexible and personalised learning.

From the ground floor the grand 'Hellerup Stair' leads to an oversized first floor landing housing the school's 'knowledge centre' and then on again to the second floor. With regular steps up either side and double-sized steps in the middle the staircase not only provides the principal vertical circulation route in the building, but also forms a place where students can sit, eat lunch, read a book or gather to watch a performance occurring in the main entrance area.

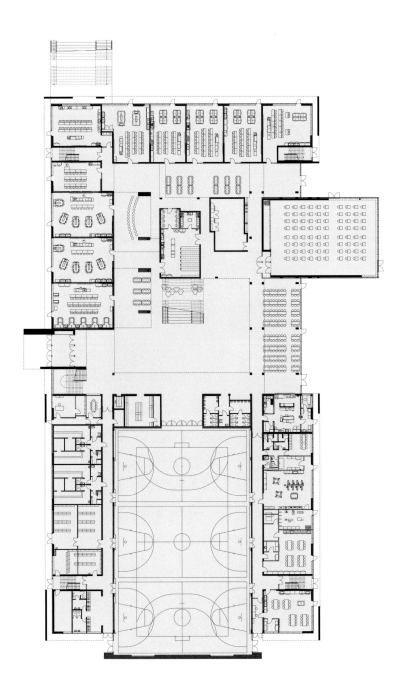

HELLERUP SCHOOL / The three-storey galleried space and 'coliseum' stair of Hellerup Primary School in Gentofte, Denmark [Arkitema, 2002] have been referenced numerous times in educational buildings around the world.

A. P. MØLLER SCHOOL / The ground floor plan shows the dominance of the large central atrium.

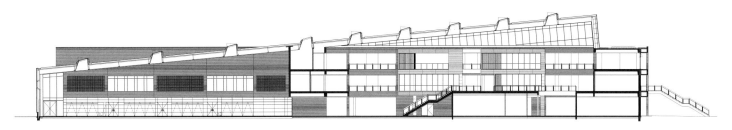

A. P. MØLLER SCHOOL / Section through the central atrium

FOURTH GYMNASIUM IN AMSTERDAM, THE NETHERLANDS [HVDN Architecten, 2008]
The modular units enclose a courtyard that provides a focus within the open landscape of Houthavens. This area of Amsterdam, undergoing regeneration, is given a vibrant landmark by this temporary school.

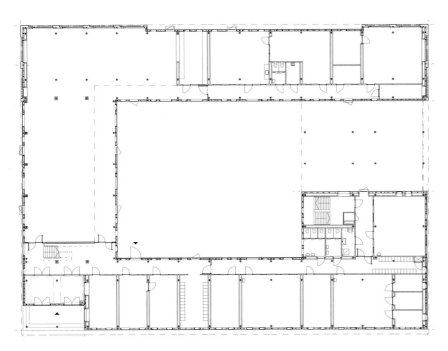

FOURTH GYMNASIUM / The ground floor plan shows the modular arrangement.

The temporary school was created using modular prefabricated components that were delivered and erected on site.

The staircases and several enclosed teaching rooms that sit within the atrium all serve to break up the vast space and create zones that, although all connected, provide places of different size and character in which to study, gather or relax.

Critical in enabling these activities to occur alongside each other is the acoustic design of the building. In fact the school's director acknowledges the 'exceptionally good acoustics in every part of the building'[2] as an important part of its success. This space is symbolic and representative of the school's core values of dialogue, community and democracy. It does indeed feel more like a civic centre than a school hall.

Temporary school buildings

Due to a number of reasons there will always be a need for temporary school accommodation. School buildings periodically need refurbishing or replacing, school populations can temporarily swell, and emergency situations such as fire or flooding can occur. In these situations, schools need access to solutions that give them the flex-

ibility to manage these changes and events in the short timescales available.

In developed countries, the most common response to the need for temporary accommodation for education is to 'drop in' one or more prefabricated modular building units. In 2006, The Modular Building Institute estimated that there were 300,000 portable classrooms in use in the United States alone.[3] If there are 30 children using each of those classrooms this number equates to 9 million children. And, whilst these structures may meet the technical standards required for educational buildings, the environments they create are not specific to learning, age group or location. Furthermore, with a life span of up to 20 years, 'portable' classrooms frequently become long-term additions to the school campus, providing uninspiring learning space for successive generations.

Modular solutions

In Amsterdam, local firm HVDN Architecten have been building a reputation for designing large temporary modular buildings that can be constructed within months, yet have a presence and architectural quality not usually as-

Volume

Programme on three floors

Completed building

The use of cut-outs creates a dynamic structure.

FOURTH GYMNASIUM / Dividing the building programme in three floors, the architects with the use of a modular structure carved out volumes to create dynamic façades and voids.

sociated with this type of construction. Their **Fourth Gymnasium** in Amsterdam, the Netherlands [HVDN Architecten, 2008], in the Houthavens area of the city, a former industrial harbour area currently occupied with a vibrant mix of temporary housing, restaurants and studios. The school is intended to attract new residents and after 5–10 years will be replaced with a permanent building whilst the temporary school will be relocated to another part of the city.

Several key innovations in modular building prevent this school appearing like a series of flimsy boxes stacked one atop the other. Firstly, a deeper than average wall build-up for modular construction allows for a sculptural façade. Secondly, the vertical joints between the modular units are made imperceptible through the application of a cladding of narrow timber slats. Similarly, at the ground floor a cladding of floor-to-ceiling glazing and coloured aluminium panels of varying widths disguise the modular joints and also provide a colourful base and some variation. The overall result is a monolithic exterior that pro-

vides a sense of permanence within this area of transition. Inside circulation occurs in generous corridors around the edge of the courtyard around which the school is constructed. In places, longer modules cantilever into the courtyard space providing 'break-out areas' from the classrooms opposite, whilst the teaching spaces themselves follow a typical classroom arrangement. The school creates a much more exciting physical presence within the urban realm and the school campus than any standard mobile classroom could.

Mobile lessons

Although the interior of the Fourth Gymnasium might not be as advanced as its exterior, it is not difficult to imagine a situation where temporary school building modules are fitted internally with state of the art learning facilities that can also be transported to different locations. Rather than selecting a classroom solely by its dimensions, schools might select a 'maths lab' or an 'art-zone' as a module for their temporary building.

MOBILE ECO LAB IN LOS ANGELES, USA [Office of Mobile Design, 2009]
Travelling to different schools in Los Angeles, ECOLAB folds out to create an informal teaching space to educate students on environmental issues.

In some cases mobile classrooms already travel to different schools in a region to deliver a specific area of learning using a 'roadshow' style approach. For example the **Mobile ECO LAB** in Los Angeles, USA [Office of Mobile Design, 2009, was constructed from a donated lorry trailer and materials from old film sets and now travels to schools in the county to teach children about environmental and ecological issues. The designers claim that when the trailer arrives at a school 'it is immediately recognisable as a place for interaction, discovery and fun'. Could this not be the case for every temporary classroom?

Long-term flexibility: adaptable space design

Societal changes will have an impact on how a school building is used over its entire life span. According to the United States National Clearinghouse for Educational Facilities (NCEF), in 1998 the average age of a public school building in the United States was 42 years. Over such a long time period population numbers have fluctuated globally and locally, pedagogies have changed and technologies have advanced beyond belief. When designing a new school building today, how can we make allowances

for these unpredictable occurrences and create buildings that can evolve over their life span rather than remain stuck in the age in which they were built?

Manipulating internal space

One of the most common ways to allow for future change in school buildings is to design the building using a concrete or steel frame and build internal partitions within that can be removed and replaced without any detrimental impact on the structure, so-called 'floating walls'. When commissioning a new building for the **Harris Academy** in London, UK [John McAslan + Partners, 2008], sponsor Lord Harris of Peckham requested a building that should be robust in terms of its short-term physical durability, but also robust enough to withstand the changes that occur over time in educational practice.

Although the brief for the academy specified classrooms of the standard 56m² recommended at the time by the UK's Department for Children, Families and Schools, it did recognise that in the future open-plan learning areas or larger classrooms with sliding partitions may be required. Therefore the building was designed using a concrete structure in which all columns were incorporated into the building envelope resulting in open floors divided with partitions that can easily be removed in the future.

HARRIS ACADEMY IN LONDON, UK [John McAslan + Partners, 2008]
The concrete structure is positioned at the outside of the building to allow alteration of internal spaces in the future. However, the structural grid does not dominate the building façade due to a carefully orchestrated window rhythm.

Learning cluster organisation

A similar construction technique was also adopted in the design for **Bristol Metropolitan College** in Bristol, UK [Wilkinson Eyre Architects, 2009]. Based on a design the architects had previously created as part of the UK government-sponsored Exemplar Designs in 2003, the secondary school also features a number of other concepts that enable future organisational change or expansion.

The school is comprised of two main elements, 'learning clusters' and central facilities, connected by a covered street or 'agora'. The architects describe that a key part of their design work for the initial concept was es-

tablishing the optimum size for each 'learning cluster', a wedge-shaped building element that contains the principal teaching facilities for 220 to 300 students that is connected to the central street. There are currently three clusters at Bristol Metropolitan College, but should pupil numbers increase additional clusters could be added with an extension to the 'agora'. In addition to classrooms each cluster contains a central resource area, its own entrance, library area, staff base, WCs, stair and lift. The architects also suggest that the model would also facilitate change to an entirely different school organisation. Currently the clusters function as 'learning zones', each

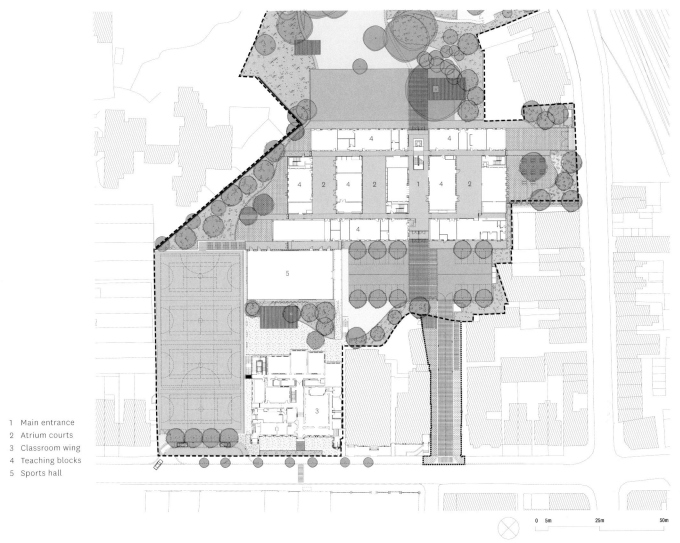

1 Main entrance
2 Atrium courts
3 Classroom wing
4 Teaching blocks
5 Sports hall

0   5m   25m   50m

HARRIS ACADEMY / Site plan. The designers had to ensure that internally the floors were open plan to allow for future changes.

Exposed services on soffits minimise disruption when reconfiguring internal spaces.

BRISTOL METROPOLITAN COLLEGE IN BRISTOL, UK [Wilkinson Eyre Architects, 2009]
Each 'learning cluster' creates a zone that can be designated by subject, age or 'school within a school'.
In the future the covered street could be extended and 'learning clusters' could be added to accommodate
rising student numbers.

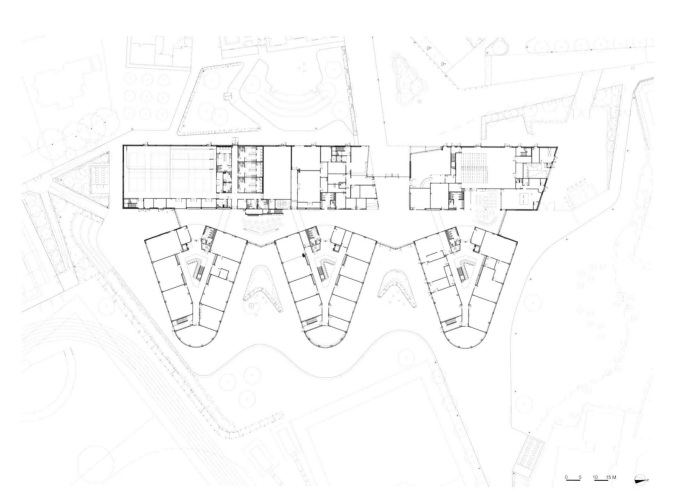

Ground floor plan illustrating the central street and 'cluster' arrangement

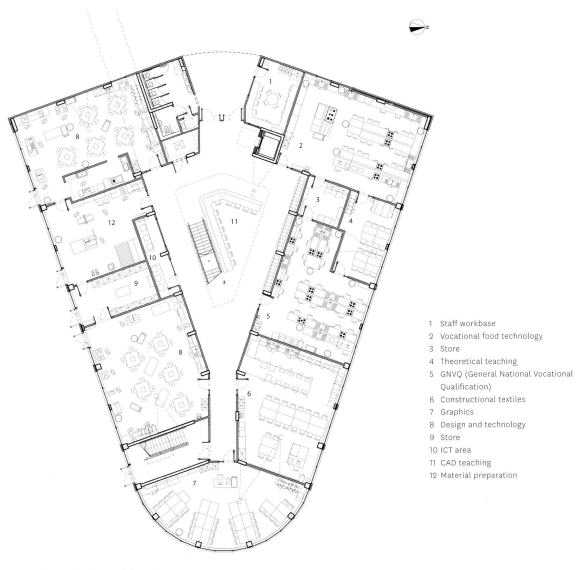

BRISTOL METROPOLITAN COLLEGE / Detail of ground floor plan

1   Staff workbase
2   Vocational food technology
3   Store
4   Theoretical teaching
5   GNVQ (General National Vocational
    Qualification)
6   Constructional textiles
7   Graphics
8   Design and technology
9   Store
10 ICT area
11 CAD teaching
12 Material preparation

serving a different area of the curriculum. However, in the future, the school could be reorganised with little physical change so that each cluster accommodates a different age group or becomes a school within a school.

Moving the whole school

An elegant and practical solution to the ultimate flexibility a school building can have – that it can move – can be see in the recent **MOVING School** in Mae Sot, Thailand, [Cole and McKillop – Building Trust International UK, 2012]. In 2011 David Cole and Louise McKillop, while near the Burmese border in Thailand, witnessed the plight of children of displaced, stateless Burmese refugees, being uprooted every few years due to the lack of land rights. They came up with an idea of a school building that could be taken down and transported with the community; that

could perhaps one day be moved back over the border into Burma, starting the regeneration of the country's small rural border towns, devastated by decades of civil war.

Following an international design competition to find the best solution they returned and built the first flexible, demountable school. This UK-based NGO has since held three more design competitions across the developing world. Building Trust International have inspired many more architects to get involved with humanitarian design projects and use their skills to help those most in need.

The first school was finished in 2012, and in spring 2013 two more were completed, leading the actual building of the schools and in the process changing the way school land contracts are organised in Thailand. The NGO encouraged young teenage migrants and local adolescent

MOVING SCHOOL IN MAE SOT, THAILAND [Cole and McKillop – Building Trust International UK, 2012]
The two schools are elevated to minimise risk of flooding and the design allows easy disassembly so that the building can be packed and moved to a new location. All spaces are naturally lit and receive cross ventilation.

apprentices to learn and subsequently share building skills such as woodwork, metalwork and bamboo construction techniques with older volunteers. All materials used for the construction of the schools are sustainable and locally sourced. The school is made of a modular steel frame with structural components of uniform size and clad with bamboo.

The schools offer comfortable, safe and inspiring places to learn for more than 500 children. Designed to enable cross ventilation and daylighting, the simple spaces give a feeling of order and calm and ultimate flexibility. They are skillfully and robustly built, although the feeling is one of lightness and delicacy.

REFERENCES

1   The school is described in chapter 1, From Ideas for Learning to Architectural Form, on pp. 26–27.

2   Quoted in David McManus, 'C. F. Møller Wins RIBA European Union Award and Worldwide Brick Award', *e-architect*, 2014, http://www.e-architect.co.uk/germany/ap-moller-school. Cf. also *Brick Bulletin*, summer 2010.

3   T. Hardiman, 'The Emerging Role of Portable Classrooms in Sustainable Design', *School Construction News*, vol. 9, no. 4, pp. 12–13, May–June 2006.

Summary

3 FLEXIBLE SPACE FOR LEARNING

1. 'Flexibility' can mean many things and it is important to **define flexibility goals** early on. Is physical, pedagogical or short-term/long-term flexibility to be achieved?
2. With **increased pressure on space** within schools, moving elements or multi-purpose spaces can be used to suit different learning scenarios at different times of the day, week or year.
3. In the long term teaching methods and the school population will change. Designing for **long-term flexibility** in schools can make it easier to accommodate that change, rather than allowing teaching and learning to be driven by old spatial requirements.
4. **Moving parts** in buildings allow children and staff to play a part in changing their environment to adapt to different learning scenarios.
5. **Temporary school buildings** can be used to quickly fulfil practical requirements for additional space, but also offer opportunities to test new pedagogies in new spaces and act as a catalyst for change.
6. Large **multi-purpose teaching spaces** can form an important communal space at the heart of a school for informal or after-school activities.
7. There is a risk when designing for flexibility of creating anonymous spaces that are not ultimately suited to any activity. It is important to **find a balance between designing for purpose and designing for complete flexibility**.
8. In all school buildings that are designed for flexibility, the design of the **structure, acoustics and lighting** are critical to their success.
9. A **movable school building** can provide much-needed spaces for learning in countries devastated by war or dispute.

4 Schools and the Community / CLAIRE KEMP

This chapter is concerned with exploring how new and improved school buildings can be designed to foster and support integration between school and community. It begins by looking at new approaches to providing shared facilities and concludes with examples of how school buildings have played a part in the regeneration of a whole town or neighbourhood.

Today, the term 'community school' is used in different ways around the world: in Australia it describes independent schools that serve a particular community group such as Aborigines, in the UK the majority of state-run schools are referred to as 'community schools' and in the U.S. it describes a small proportion of public or private schools that become centres of the community and are open to everyone – every day, evenings and weekends. The U.S. description of 'community schools' is perhaps closest to an ideal that is currently being called for in many school building programmes. New school buildings are seen as an opportunity to unite students and communities through openness, shared facilities, lifelong education and local partnerships.

At the school level benefits are cited as student improvement in academic work and personal development, encouraging stronger relationships between parents and teachers and a more positive school environment.

Within the community social and economic benefits such as increased security and pride and increased job opportunities have been attributed to successful relationships between schools and communities.

MIMERS HUS IN KUNGÄLV, SWEDEN [Wingardh Architects, 2004]
The light and airy library at the entrance to Mimers Hus provides an open-access space for both the public and the school to meet, read and study.

MIMERS HUS IN KUNGÄLV, SWEDEN [Wingårdh Architects, 2004]
This community building which includes a school has a civic presence in the centre of the town.

Community access

The idea of building facilities for both schools and communities and relationships for mutual benefit is not new. In the UK, for example, in the second half of the 19th century some schools were designed to act as both a place of worship and a community centre.[1] And in 1925, Henry Morris, who is often identified as the founder of the concept of the 'community school', wrote about his vision for 'The Village College': 'As the centre of the community it would provide for the whole of man, and abolish the duality of education and ordinary life ... There would be no "leaving school"! – the child would enter at three and leave the college only in extreme old age.'[2] Later in 1975, Italian-born architect Carlo Testa published an international survey of schools identified for being progressive in their educational approach in which community access to school facilities was found to be a shared characteristic.[3]

Management and security still determines that in most cases school facilities are only open to the public out of school hours and with the abundance of state of the art facilities (gyms, recording studios, performance spaces, IT suites) being offered by new school buildings, they are becoming increasingly popular as places for local people to visit. However, there is often little or no interaction between the students and other users and we are seeing a push for schools to build relationships with their local communities. In design terms, the question is how to support interaction between pupils and the wider community during the day, whilst also ensuring safety? And how can we move away from the school building as an institutional establishment and make it a great place for everyone to visit?

An open facility

One approach to integrating schools and communities is to co-locate open-access community facilities with the school itself. In the small Swedish town of Kungälv near Göteborg a new lower and middle school has been designed to form part of a larger community hub called **Mimers Hus** [Wingårdh Architects, 2004] which is openly accessible throughout the day. The intention is that instead of being an institutional establishment the school is combined with community and cultural facili-

MIMERS HUS / The school facilities are designed with a similar character to the shared areas giving the building a uniformity.

The theatre at Mimers Hus provides a valuable community facility which attracts people to this multi-purpose building.

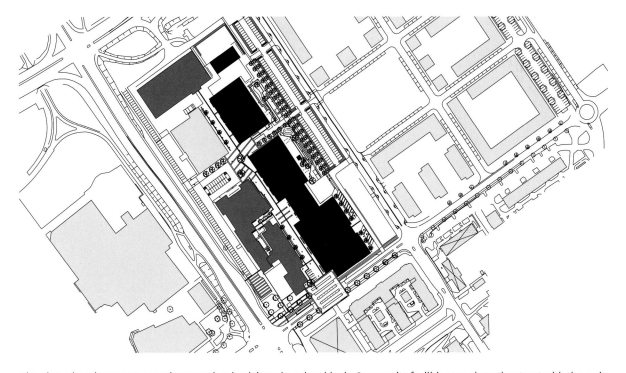

Site plan. The Mimers Hus complex stretches back into the urban block. Community facilities are along the street with the main school facilities accommodated in two blocks behind.

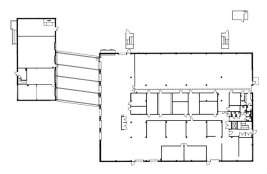

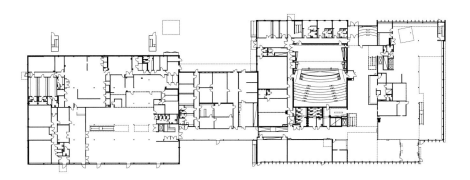

Ground floor plan

TRIANGLE CHILDREN, YOUNG PEOPLE AND COMMUNITY INTERGENERATIONAL CENTRE IN LONDON, UK

[Greenhill Jenner Architects, 2007] The Centre makes a statement on the street in this multi-cultural area of the city. A timber-lined multi-purpose hall offers a warm environment for a variety of activities while a protected courtyard provides a safe place for play and interaction between the generations.

Section A-A. The building cleverly uses the topography to create a relationship with both the main road and the park.

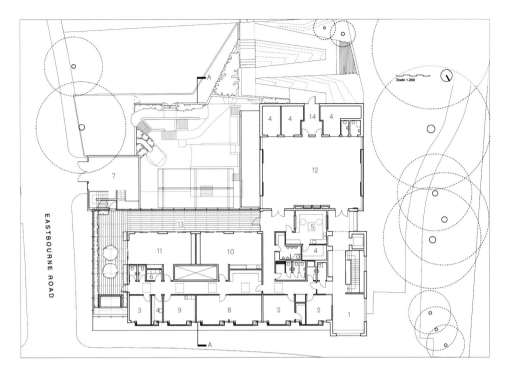

1	Foyer
2	Office
3	Plant room
4	Store
5	Kitchen
6	Laundry
7	Deliveries
8	IT/Resource
9	Staff room
10	Art room
11	Common room
12	Multi-purpose room
13	Terrace
14	Lobby

TRIANGLE CHILDREN, YOUNG PEOPLE AND COMMUNITY INTERGENERATIONAL CENTRE / **Ground floor plan.** The building accommodates a whole range of facilities for the building's numerous users.

ties that can be used by the public, but also by the staff and students. The elegant but simple building is made up of three connecting blocks: lower school, middle school and public facilities. The latter block forms the main public entrance to the building and includes a library, auditorium, restaurant and café that are used by both the local community and the school.

The Sustaining Small Expanding Towns (SusSET) project, an EU initiative, has praised Mimers Hus as an example of how small towns in particular can provide community facilities: 'The daily activities in Mimers Hus attract a lot of people. Small children come to have their first dancing or music lessons. Senior citizens come to be introduced to the mysteries of the internet. People of all ages come to listen to a concert or to go the theatre. They take part in a workshop or use the numerous public computers. They read the newspaper or they find the book they didn't know they were looking for. Or they just meet over a cup of coffee.'[4]

But what makes this project so successful? From the building plan the majority of the school accommodation seems to be quite separated from the public facilities. But perhaps that is the key; from the main entrance this building does not look or feel like a school, in fact it looks more like an art gallery. The building sits right onto the pavement, which widens out around the front of the

building into a public plaza with a tall landmark sculpture. In most cases it would be impossible to arrive at the front doors of a school without passing through imposing railings and when you get there you would enter into a small lobby, where you would be interrogated about your purpose before being allowed to penetrate any further into the building. Here, however, the highly glazed façades allow passers-by to look inside the impressive triple height library space; a space which visitors can freely enter.

But then is this not just a public building stuck onto the front of a school? Whilst a large part of the school facilities are accommodated in two connecting blocks behind the main public block, interaction between the students and other visitors occurs throughout the day. For example the chefs in the basement restaurant are pupils studying catering, the art gallery displays work of professional artists as well as school goers and the library and theatre provide resources for the school. Circulation spaces double as study areas and informal meeting places for both students and the local community. The open design of this part of the building including open staircases and galleried walkways means that passive observation makes it feel like a safe place to be; a technique now being employed in many school buildings to avoid problems of bullying in corridors and dark corners. Interestingly, the SusSET project suggests that by

USASAZO SECONDARY SCHOOL IN KHAYELITSHA, CAPE TOWN, SOUTH AFRICA [Wolff Architects (previously Noero Wolff Architects), 2004]
School buildings can play an instrumental role in creating or improving a sense of community and at times can help regenerate a whole town or neighbourhood, such as in Khayelitsha.

Section showing library

designing facilities such as Mimers Hus with young people in mind, they become more user-friendly for all. This certainly seems to be the case here.

Bringing generations together

Where typically schools were the domain of children, there is an ongoing aspiration for them to provide education, support and recreation for all members of the population. Echoing Henry Morris' hopes from the 1920s that we would never leave school, Joe Perkins, Past President of the AARP (formerly the American Association of Retired Persons) suggests that: 'Schools should be a point of unity, not division, between and among generations.'[5]

With a remit of providing a number of community facilities under one roof, **Triangle Children, Young People and Community Intergenerational Centre** in London [Greenhill Jenner Architects, 2007] gave itself the ambitious task of attracting people from 0–90 years old! The centre houses a 75-place nursery, a primary-age children's play centre and an after-school club, which

were previously operating from separate buildings. In addition, new facilities for the wider community have been provided within the building including healthcare, training and recreational activities. The design process involved 18 different local community groups from the multi-cultural area of Seven Sisters, and the resulting building is intended to express the diversity of these groups whilst also bringing them together.[6]

Given the number and diversity of organisations that use the Triangle Centre and the complexities of the sloping site which sits between a main road and a park, the building is clearly organised as an L-shape around a protected courtyard providing a safe play area for the children. Whilst separating the facilities used by different generations is still necessary for safety reasons, interaction between the age groups can be encouraged in other ways. As Amy Goyer noted in a study on intergenerational shared services, such buildings 'should be designed so that shared space and traffic-flow encourage informal interactions among participants.'[7] At the Triangle Centre

USASAZO SECONDARY SCHOOL / At street level the single-storey building has a direct relationship with the self-built dwellings opposite.

Once established planters will provide some green relief in the dense urban environment as well as providing places for students to sit.

The school comprises a library.

there is one main entrance and foyer area meaning all users come into contact with each other when entering the building. Once inside the building facilities are spread across two floors accessed by an open-plan stairwell, once again encouraging interaction between the building's users. The L-shaped form of the building around a courtyard also engenders passive interaction. Highly glazed façades from the main spaces looking onto the courtyard provide opportunity to view the other activities occurring in the building and courtyard space. An exter-nal shared terrace at first floor level and overlooking the courtyard again reinforces this.

Like Mimers Hus the Triangle Centre is accessed directly from the street; there are no physical barriers to reaching the front door. A rhythmic façade of green enamelled steel panels onto the street makes the building stand out from its neighbours, whilst also providing a relationship to the adjacent park. 'It announces itself as an important civic presence without shouting too loudly, and in this way is well pitched.'[8]

Schools integrated into social fabric

It has been widely acknowledged that 'successful schools strengthen a community's sense of identity and coherence.' [9] When designing a school building that will support successful relationships with the community, the most important thing to remember is that each community is different. A school building picked 'off-the-shelf' will have a very different relationship with the place than one designed with and for that particular community. As demonstrated by The Triangle Centre, working with future user groups can help to create a building that is equally successful for different generations. Through a deep understanding of the wider community in which it is situated school buildings also have the potential to tackle issues in the local community and reinforce the identity of a place.

An example is **Usasazo Secondary School** in the South African township of Khayelitsha in Cape Town [Wolff Architects (previously Noero Wolff Architects), 2004]. Its designers understood that the building they were creating was not only about providing a place for education but also about offering a stable place in the community: 'In an area like Khayelitsha, the schools are often the first public buildings and for a long time the only permanent, durable and expensive buildings. The schools therefore have a critical role in the formation of good quality urban environments.'[10]

The school is located within a densely populated informal settlement dominated by self-built single-storey dwellings. The plots on either side of Usasazo School are both occupied by so-called mass-produced 'cookie-cutter schools' placed with little consideration in the middle of their sites and found throughout Khayelitsha. In contrast, Usasazo School sits on the street edge directly facing the informal settlements from where the students come. Not only does this mean the school forms a physical relationship with the township, but it also allowed the architects to leave the rear portion of the site to be used for communal sports or agriculture; open land is a valuable resource in the dense community.

The brief from the Provincial Administration of the Western Cape encompassed 37 classrooms, a hall, a library, a computer suite and an administration area. As well as providing a constant place in the community, by developing an understanding of the locality, the issues facing the people of Khayelitsha and new educational legislation, the architects also saw the opportunity to develop the brief further. As well as the standard classroom spaces called for, the architects proposed including facilities for entrepreneurial teaching that would offer the opportunity to forge relationships between the school and the local community.

The single-storey street façade is lined with a series of classrooms that are designed to accommodate vocational training such as car repair and hairdressing. The solid concrete block wall is broken by a rhythm of hatches built into the wall of each classroom that allows the students to sell their products and services to local people. It provides for social interaction between the students and the community and offers services for local people.

The rhythmical street façade does not sing and shout but is given a sense of permanence and identity through the use of solid materials and bold graphics. The façade is broken by an entrance gateway leading through to what the architects describe as 'an undulating central circulation space' [11] around which the rest of the school accommodation is arranged. This external space has an informal character similar to surrounding settlements; instead of creating a formal courtyard the space weaves through the buildings, which vary in size and form, but are united by metal canopies, trees and bold graphics. The architects created a building that picks up on the essence of the place whilst also providing a sense of permanence and opportunities for integration with the local community.

Cultural cohesion and celebration of diversity

With globalisation, it is more and more difficult to retain local identity in a place, but schools – being a place where our future generations are being educated – offer

SAKARINMÄKI SCHOOL IN SIPOO, FINLAND [Arkkitehtitoimisto Sari Nieminen Oy, 2005]
The school is conceived as a series of 'barns' housing different functions including a Swedish and a Finnish language school. Timber cladding
gives a coherence to the whole. A central hall forms the main entrance to the building and also provides a place for congregating.

Site plan. The building cluster brings together the language schools with community and recreation facilities.

an ideal arena to teach about and reinforce the characteristics of a community. The Finnish municipality of Sipoo, located to the north-east of Helsinki, was once almost completely Swedish-speaking. Now only around 40% of the population speak Swedish with the remainder speaking Finnish. The right to access services, such as education, in Swedish is a contentious issue across the country, but in those municipalities with a significant percentage of people with Swedish as their first language, as is the case of Sipoo, citizens have the right to receive services in Swedish.

When commissioning the new **Sakarinmäki School** in Sipoo, Finland [Arkkitehtitoimisto Sari Nieminen Oy, 2005] the municipality chose to bring together Swedish and Finnish language schools along with other community services including a day nursery and recreation facili-

ties. The architect was appointed through an invited competition, and their winning scheme celebrates both the diversity of the different users, whilst also bringing them together. The desire for the building to contribute to community spirit was emphasised in the competition brief.

The different functions are housed in separate building forms that come together to create what appears from afar to be a group of buildings akin to groups of barns traditionally found in the area. Each of the timber-clad blocks is treated with a differently coloured stain and has its own entrance giving each part its own identity. However, the buildings are in fact joined together in the middle by a glazed foyer which forms the main entrance and a hall where the children speaking different languages come together and eat their lunch and also take part in after-school interest groups. It was the intention of the

ELMER A. HENDERSON: A JOHNS HOPKINS PARTNERSHIP SCHOOL IN BALTIMORE, USA [Rogers Partners (previously Rogers Marvel Architects), 2014] Modelled on the old row houses of Baltimore, the school campus is of high density, thus continuing the urban grid of the area. The commons building is mostly glazed and stands out.

architects to preserve culture through the use of traditional materials and building forms that were seen to be disappearing from the local area. The building seems to be a symbolic representation celebrating the differences and cohesion of the local community. Since its opening it has also become home to the Sakarinmäki Children's Library, part of Helsinki City Library housing both Finnish and Swedish texts and DVDs.

Catalysts for regeneration

Perhaps the most ambitious way to use a new school building to support a community is by using it as a catalyst for transforming an entire area. In January 2014, the **Elmer A. Henderson: A Johns Hopkins Partnership School** in Baltimore, USA [Rogers Partners (previously Rogers Marvel Architects), 2014] opened.[12] This project epitomises how a school can change a whole area. The school is run by Johns Hopkins University, a dominant institution in Baltimore, to educate teachers and give children a better education. The school, located in East Baltimore, holds 175 children in the nursery, from 0–5 with 40 staff and 540 children from grades 1–8 with 60 estimated staff.

David W. Andrews, Ph.D., Dean of Johns Hopkins University School of Education, said 'Henderson-Hopkins School will not only change the way we think about training teachers for the future, it will fundamentally change the way its students learn by providing personalised learning and a leading-edge educational experience.'[13]

Perhaps more critically this school, developed as a series of urban blocks, densifies and reconstructs a part of the city and the neighbourhood. The architects were inspired by East Baltimore's row house architecture and how this could mirror the neighbourhood's urban fabric. The buildings are designed to be flexible to accommodate experimentation and change in teaching methods and uses. Architect Robert Rogers states that 'this project represents what architecture for education can really be about: enabling students, teachers and community. Our goal was to recover and reimagine an urban fabric rich in opportunity and optimism for East Baltimore and innovate a school concept rooted in the familiar yet ever changing to fulfill a progressive pedagogy.'[14]

The school was built by a non-profit developer, East Baltimore Development, with community, government and business partners. Their mission is to regenerate greater East Baltimore and they are committed to the belief that strong neighbourhoods are built around strong community (public) schools. To promote the urban regeneration of the area further, the school's campus incorporates a family health centre, a library, an auditorium and a gym. All these resources are shared with residents and businesses in the local community.

Students are grouped by age in the small-scale 'Houses' that are set within a grid of main and side streets. Each House has a 'Commons' for lunching and flexible teaching/learning and a defined outdoor 'Learning Terrace'. This strategy of de-centralising the school is intended to promote individual learning and growth. The

ELMER A. HENDERSON: A JOHNS HOPKINS PARTNERSHIP SCHOOL / The double-height 'commons' space is also used by the local community and local business.

The two-storey commons space from above

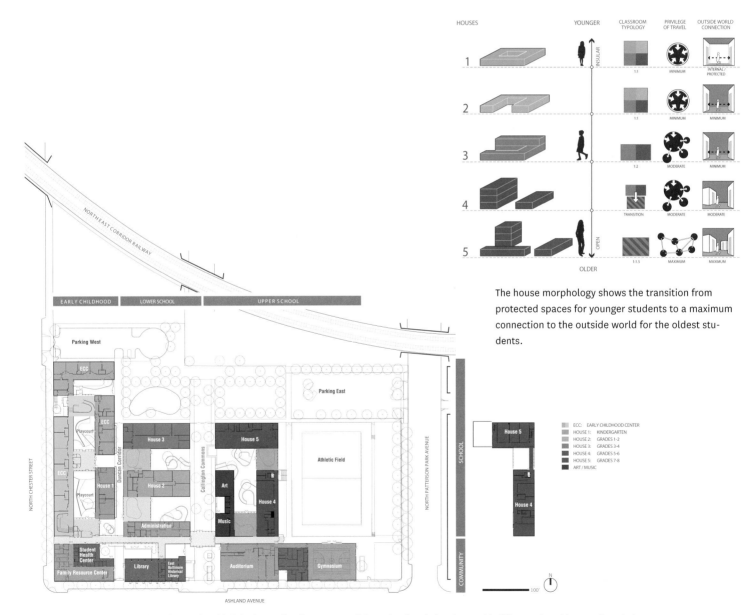

The house morphology shows the transition from protected spaces for younger students to a maximum connection to the outside world for the oldest students.

The ground floor plan and first floor plan (right) shows the three parts of the school and the clear grid of 'houses', making up the whole campus.

MOSSBOURNE COMMUNITY ACADEMY IN HACKNEY, LONDON, UK [Rogers Stirk Harbour + Partners (previously Richard Rogers Partnership), 2004]
The school is a symbol of a commitment to regeneration in the area. State of the art facilities give students a pride in their school.

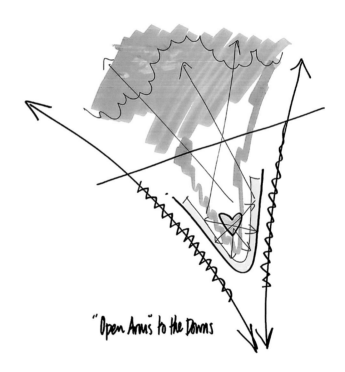

Sketch showing the courtyard as the heart of the school.

building heights are consistent with the surrounding low-rise urban form. The Commons are taller building elements that rise above the low-scale school campus, and were designed to represent education as the centre of the community: 'These vertical elements transform the school into a community landmark, following the tradition of Baltimore's church steeples, which stand as social and visual anchors for local neighbourhoods.'[15]

The UK Akademy programme In 2000, England's Learning and Skills Act introduced a new type of secondary school into the country known as the 'Academy', each being partially funded by a business, faith group or an individual. The Academy model was created as a means of improving failing schools and those located in troubled communities.

Since 2004, as part of that initiative five new academies have opened in the London Borough of Hackney alone, a borough with both wealth and poverty that can still be described as one of the most deprived areas in England.[16] The Borough's Economic Development Plan cites 'poor educational achievement and a culture unsympathetic to learning' as key contributors to high levels of unemployment in the area, one of the main determinants of social and economic deprivation.[17] In England, up until a change in policy in 2010, nearly all academies were located in new and purposely designed buildings and the government placed an emphasis on not only improving educational attainment in these areas, but also on the opportunity for these new schools to play a role in local regeneration and neighbourhood renewal.[18]

The first of the Hackney academies to open and one of the first in the country was **Mossbourne Community Academy** in Hackney, London, UK [Rogers Stirk Harbour + Partners (previously Richard Rogers Partnership), 2004]. The academy opened on the site of the former Hackney Downs School, a comprehensive secondary school which was forced to close in 1995 after being called 'the worst school in Britain' by the then Conservative government.[19] Today, Mossbourne's examination re-

sults rank among the top state schools in the country and the school's popularity is astounding; there are over eight applications for each place.[20] But what role has the new building had on achieving this success and raising aspirations in the area?

Richard Rogers saw Mossbourne Community Academy as an opportunity to put into practice many of the recommendations for urban regeneration in England made by his Urban Task Force.[21] Ivan Harbour, a Senior Director at the practice affirmed: 'This project is all about putting pride back into a community. It is about ownership, equality and heart.'[22] The provision of a new school and facilities by itself in an area such as Hackney suggests to the community that they are valued, but here it seems the architectural design has also played a large part in the success of this building. One of the largest timber frame buildings in the UK, the three-storey V-shaped building with external steel walkways and stairs sets itself apart from other institutional buildings in the area and has become a beacon in the neighbourhood. It certainly does not look like a typical school building and its unique design is clearly identifiable from both the train lines that flank two of its sides and from the open space of Hackney Downs onto which the school fronts. In the United States, the National Clearinghouse for Education Facilities recognises such an approach in its publication *Schools as Centers of Community*: 'By capturing the noble character of public architecture, they [schools] should serve as a visible symbol of community pride.'[23]

In this case the decision of the academy to appoint such a high profile architect was a sign to parents, staff and children that they are deserving of world-class facilities. It has been suggested that the new building may not have had the same impact on the community and its users, had it been designed by an unknown architect.[24]

Raising aspirations

About two kilometres away from Mossbourne Community Academy in Hackney, another new academy opened

BRIDGE ACADEMY IN LONDON, UK [Building Design Partnership – BDP, 2008]
At night the school acts as a physical beacon within the community. Views of main entrance and the roof terrace.

its doors. Whilst not part of a regeneration programme, **Bridge Academy** in London, UK [Building Design Partnership – BDP, 2008] also aspired to encourage the local community to participate in school activities, thus contributing to neighbourhood regeneration. The advantages are clear: the school benefits from facilities which it perhaps wouldn't have been able to afford and the community have access to amenities otherwise not available in their local area. In fact at Bridge Academy the sporting facilities are of such high calibre that they were used as a training base for athletes for the 2012 Olympics. What better way to raise aspirations of the students than to have world-class sports people training in their school?

At Bridge Academy the school opens their facilities not only to local residents and international athletes, but also to local businesses, organisations and community groups, thus encouraging a broad spectrum of users into the school. Its high-specification autonomous theatre space which stands separately from the main school building is flexible enough to accommodate a whole range of performance activities. But aside from the quality of the facilities, how does the building attract external users? From the outside the dynamic nature of the building form gives the impression that there is always something going on inside; this is somewhere people want to be. From the inside the clever use of the building form to

BRIDGE ACADEMY / Meeting rooms can be hired out or used for small group teaching.

The high-calibre facilities attract businesses and large organisations and their use generates extra income for the academy.

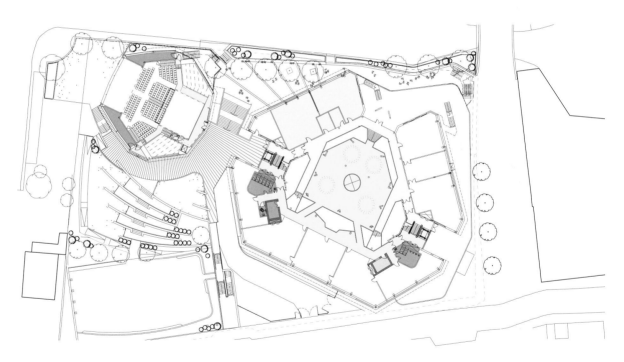

Site plan. Located on the Grand Union Canal, the new academy serves not only education, but also local residents and businesses.

provide long views out across the city also make this a place where citizens want to go. Thus, the students are being offered a much broader outlook rather than creating a focus on their immediate surroundings.

Although it is perhaps too soon to really determine if the construction of Bridge Academy can play a part in the long-term regeneration of its neighbourhood, the school itself clearly states that the building is crucial to connecting with the local community: 'The building helps create the school community and to make the school part of the wider community.'[25]

REFERENCES

1 Cf. Tony Jeffs, Mark K. Smith, 'What is a Community School? How has Theory and Practice Developed?' on the website of Informal Education, http://www.infed.org/schooling/b-comsch.htm. Accessed 16 May 2014.

2 Henry Morris, 'The Village College. Being a Memorandum on the Provision of Educational and Social Facilities for the Countryside, with Special Reference to Cambridgeshire' (1925), quoted in: 'Henry Morris, Village Colleges and Community Schools'. http://infed.org/mobi/henry-morris-village-colleges-and-community-schools/. Accessed 16 May 2014.

3 Carlo Testa, *New Educational Facilities*, Zürich: Artemis, 1975. Referenced in: Cathy Burke, "Inside Out": A Collaborative Approach to Designing Schools in England 1945–1972', *Paedagogica Historica*, vol. 45, no. 3, June 2009, pp. 421–433.

4 'Sustaining Small Expanding Towns' project (SusSET), an EU-funded programme, deals with sustainable small town development strategies. Cf. in particular 'Kungälv – Combined School and Library'. http://www.pagodagraphics.com/susset/csf_dis_more.html. Accessed 16 May 2014.

5 Kevin J. Sullivan, 'Catching the Age Wave: Building Schools With Senior Citizens in Mind', October 2002. http://www.ncef.org/pubs/agewave.pdf. Accessed 16 May 2014. The now archived NCEF (National Clearinghouse for Educational Facilities) was a U.S. programme of the National Institute of Building Sciences, a non-governmental, non-profit organisation authorised by Congress to serve as an authoritative source of innovative solutions for the built environment.

6 P. Meadowcroft and H. Braddick, 'The Triangle Squares the Circle', *Architecture Today*, no. 190, July–August 2008, pp. 38–40, 42, 44.

7 A. Goyer and R. Zuses, 'Intergenerational Shared Site Project, a Study of Co-Located Programs and Services for Children, Youth and Older Adults: Final Report', Washington, D.C.: AARP, 1998 and A. Goyer, 'Intergenerational Shared Site and Shared Resource Programs: Current Models', Washington, D.C., 2001. Quoted in: Kevin J. Sullivan, 'Catching the Age Wave: Building Schools With Senior Citizens in Mind', October 2002. http://www.ncef.org/pubs/agewave.pdf, p. 7.

8 Philip Meadowcroft, Hugo Braddick, 'Greenhill Jenner: Triangle Children's Centre, North London', *Architecture Today*, no. 190, July–August 2008, p. 38. http://www.architecturetoday.co.uk/?p=1785. Accessed 16 May 2014.

9 'Schools as Centers of Community: A Citizen's Guide for Planning and Design', Washington, D.C.: NCEF, 2003. http://www.ncef.org/pubs/scc_publication.pdf. Accessed 14 February 2014.

10 From the architects' website: http://www.wolffarchitects.co.za. Accessed 14 February 2014.

11 Ibid.

12 The Elmer A. Henderson: A Johns Hopkins Partnership School and the Harry and Jeanette Weinberg Foundation Early Childhood Center have an interesting three-headed client: East Baltimore Community School Inc., East Baltimore Development Inc., and Johns Hopkins University School of Education.

13 Press release from Hausman Communications on Hopkins-Henderson and information from the architects Rogers Partners, New York. http://www.rogersarchitects.com/category/news/. Accessed 25 April 2014.

14 Ibid.

15 Ibid.

16 London Borough of Hackney, Community Economic Development Plan, September 2000. http://www.teamhackney.org/economic-development. Accessed 25 July 2011. Based on factors such as high unemployment, high levels of social housing and low income, Hackney was ranked in 2000 as the second most deprived area in England.

17 Ibid.

18 For the first two years of the Academies programme, 2000–2002, they were known as 'City Academies'.

19 Jenny Percival, 'Ten Mossbourne Academy Students Win Cambridge University Offers', *The Guardian*, 23 January 2011. www.theguardian.com/education/2011/jan/23/mossbourne-academy-cambridge-university-offers.

20 Peter Wilby, 'Is Mossbourne Academy's Success Down to its Traditionalist Headteacher?' *The Guardian*, 5 January 2010. http://www.theguardian.com/education/2010/jan/05/mossbourne-academy-wilby-profile.

21 The Urban Task Force, chaired by Lord Rogers of Riverside, produced the independent report 'Towards a Strong Urban Renaissance', November 2005. http://www.urbantaskforce.org/UTF_final_report.pdf. Accessed 23 April 2014.

22 From the architects' website: http://rsh-p.com/rshp_home. Accessed 23 April 2014.

23 'Schools as Centers of Community: A Citizen's Guide for Planning and Design', Washington, D.C.: NCEF, 2003, p. 8.

24 'Mossbourne Community Academy by Richard Rogers Partnership is the Showpiece Experimental Replacement for the Failed Hackney Downs School', *Architecture Today*, October 2004, no. 152, pp. 20–31.

25 From the Bridge Academy's website: http://www.bridgeacademy.hackney.sch.uk. Accessed 14 February 2014.

Summary

4 SCHOOLS AND THE COMMUNITY

1. By providing facilities that feel **open and accessible** and more like public buildings than schools, more community members are encouraged to use school buildings.
2. Whilst open-access schools present challenges in terms of **security** we should plan through careful design to open some facilities to the public throughout the school day.
3. In designing a new school building that is to work with and for the community it is essential to involve as many **potential user groups** as possible in the design process.
4. School buildings can provide a sense of permanence and safety within neighbourhoods, towns and villages.
5. Through design, a school building can **support diversity in communities** whilst also bringing people together – either by encouraging physical interaction or by acting as a symbol.
6. A new school building has the potential to **act as a catalyst for regeneration** in the wider area by raising aspirations and providing facilities not only for pupils and local residents, but also for businesses and other organisations.
7. A new school can **attract families to come and to live in an area** and this in turn can start the regeneration of other buildings and new housing in the community.

5 Participating in the Design and Construction Process / LEO CARE

This chapter explores different approaches to engaging school users – young people, staff and the wider community – in the design and construction of learning environments. The value of engaging the school community in the creation of their buildings is also discussed along with the impact on the built outcome and the personal development of those involved. It is widely acknowledged that engaging building users in the design process is important to create a school that is fit for purpose and enjoyable. Early involvement of users can also install a sense of 'ownership' and discourage vandalism. School buildings in particular have many different users, different in terms of age groups, abilities and needs, which makes involving all parties challenging. The vast majority of a school's community are young people. Yet, in many school design processes the voices of children are lost or not heard. The reasons for actively involving children can be wide-ranging; the reasons for not actively involving children in the design of their schools may be the speed and complexity of procurement making engagement impossible; or that senior teaching staff believe they understand children's needs and therefore can make decisions by proxy; or a lack of understanding by teaching staff of how to involve young people in the process of designing and building a new school. Very often it is because it is thought that children do not know or understand enough about their built environment to make a valid contribution.

COWLEY ST. LAURENCE PRIMARY SCHOOL AND CHILDREN'S CENTRE IN HILLINGDON, UK [What Architecture, 2010]
As part of forming a new entrance to the school, each child was given an area in which to create a black and white lego pictogram of their own design.

The benefits of a participative approach

In her book, *Transforming Children's Spaces*, Alison Clark stresses the importance of taking on board students' perspectives. 'Listening to children about their views can challenge preconceptions about their capabilities and raise their status within the organisations they inhabit.'[1]

Headteachers often mould a new school in an image that supports their own educational ethos. This can be an effective way of realising a vision, but there are numerous cases of a design brief for a school being established by a headteacher, only for them to move on to another school during the design process. The new incumbent then has to live with, or try and rework, the original brief to his or her own ideas of what the school should be like. Whilst it is important for an individual or tight-knit team to drive the design of a school from an educational perspective, it is equally important that a broad base of building users contribute to making the school work for all, including the local community.

Although consultation, participation and engagement are often used in relation to the process of designing schools, the involvement of young people is limited at best and often tokenistic. There are still relatively few good examples of participatory design processes for schools where stakeholders are involved in the building process. It is often difficult to fully understand how different users – children, teachers and the wider school community have been involved, as it is not recorded. It is also difficult to know what impact the involvement in the design process has on the users as well as to assess the subsequent impact on the finished school.

The difference between consultation and participation

Engaging young people in the design of their school can take many forms. School management teams often understand the importance of keeping pupils and their families informed of the school realisation process through newsletters and websites. Some institutions also consult with or seek feedback from students about the design of the school, asking people what they think. Common in these situations is a lack of information about what will be done with the responses or how the responses will impact on the design. Engaging young people in a participative approach allows them to contribute to the project with a clear understanding of what impact their contribution will have on the project. For example, children may be asked to make a model of a design, or consider what the design principles should be for a new school. Children need to know how their responses will be used, whether their ideas will directly influence the design or may be put forward for consideration.

Many school projects talk about engaging students and the wider school community in the design process, but the level of involvement and influence on the design process that participants have varies considerably. Research on children's participation undertaken for UNICEF resulted in the visualisation of a ladder of involvement to explain how young people's input varies. The first three rungs of the ladder, described as 'Manipulation', 'Decoration' and 'Tokenism', are not actually participative approaches, but ways in which children are manipulated by adults, or simply informed about what is going on. The top level of participation is where 'young people and adults share decision-making.'[2] The notion of children having equal power in making important decisions is certainly nothing new in schools, with the development of 'student councils' taking an active role in day-to-day and strategic management of education institutions. However, the key to real design participation and shared decision-making is in building the knowledge and skills of young people so that they can take an educated role in the process. In the design process of a school, the specialised skills and knowledge required are usually beyond the capabilities of adults, therefore there is potential to build the capacity of adults and children alike to assume an active role. This raises the question of whether children and grown-ups should be treated differently in terms of their involvement in a school design project? It is clear from working with adults and children on school design workshops that groups have different skills and favoured ways of representing their thoughts. Children are particularly good at articulating their ideas creatively through making scale models and drawings or collages. Young people are also willing and able to explain their ideas verbally. Adults by comparison struggle to express their creative thoughts, partly through inhibitions of not being proficient enough at hands-on art-based activities but also because their thoughts are interrupted by unresolved issues, usually about functionality and pragmatic issues of how a school works and functions. Children's work can easily be disregarded as being naive, whereas a designer may instead see a clear vision from a young person's design that can be taken forward as the conceptual basis for a school.

One question often asked of participative design processes is whether they actually make for a better outcome, a better designed building. But perhaps this way of thinking misses some key points: a participatory process offers a number of benefits to those taking part, in addition to the quality of the architecture being produced. For children, the benefits of being engaged in the design of their school are numerous: their involvement is a great example of applied learning – they can understand how their knowledge can be turned into something tangible. Research has shown how beneficial it is for students to be valued within society and for young people to take an active role in the processes that shape their environment. The children become active citizens in the present and in the future by participating in a democratic process.[3] Involving children and adults in the design process creates a body of 'informed users', or people that know something about how the building came about, why decisions were made and for what reason, and most importantly know how to use the building. This knowledge is something that can be passed down to new generations of staff and pupils as the school develops.

The role of young people within the design process

Recent research undertaken at the University of Sheffield by Dr. Rosie Parnell analyses the roles that young people can play within the school design process. Parnell suggests 13 different roles including: (co)designers, creative inspirers, evaluators and trailblazers. She also refers to so-called 'Expert Consultants' and explains their role as follows: 'Users are very often positioned as experts in their own lives and by inference, experts in their experiences of places and spaces they use. Only they can really know what it is like to experience a place as they do. In this role users participate in activities that draw out their existing knowledge so that this can inform the design process.'[4] The importance of this study is in identifying the range of skills that young people have and how their skills can be harnessed to make better buildings, better places to learn and more informed communities.

Developing a design brief

Collaborative brief-building

Collaborative brief-building involves a wide range of stakeholders coming together to develop a consensus for creating a particular space or learning environment. This collaborative act can be logistically challenging, but also very rewarding. If the brief-building process is well managed it can lead to an architectural solution that goes beyond meeting the needs of clients and results in places that can be greater than the sum of their parts. The **Flexible Open Learning Space, P-12 School** in Timboon, Australia [Rowan Opat Architects, 2007] was created to act as a physical and educational 'stepping stone', linking an otherwise separate primary and secondary school. The brief-building process for the design followed the stepping-stone metaphor, connecting staff and students from both schools, along with the architects, Rubida Research and The Victoria Department of Education. Together this diverse group of people undertook a series of workshops to develop a vision for the project.

FLEXIBLE OPEN LEARNING SPACE, P-12 SCHOOL IN TIMBOON, AUSTRALIA [Rowan Opat Architects, 2007]
Externally the building is realised as a simple rectangular form, clad in corrugated steel. It was created to act as a physical and educational
'stepping stone', linking an otherwise separate primary and secondary school. Although constructed on a budget the interior of
the space has been designed to incorporate special features such as a patterned carpet.

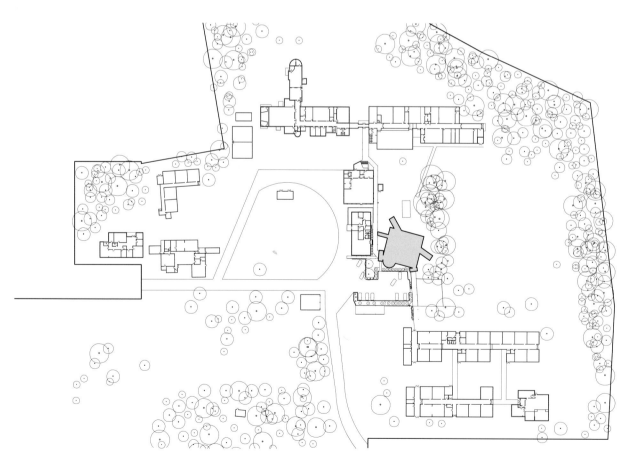

The site plan shows the linking function of the Flexible Open Learning Space (grey).

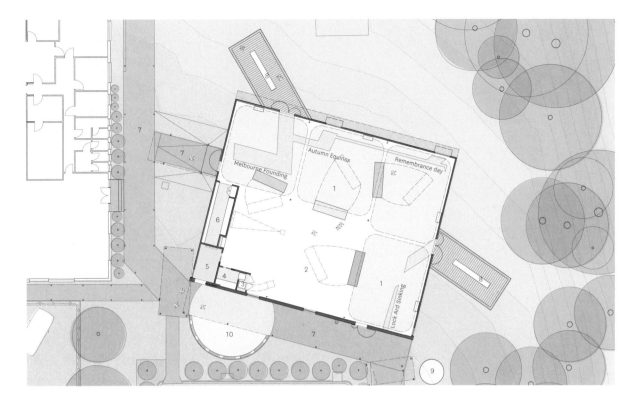

1 Home room
2 Common room
3 IT cupboard
4 IT
5 Entry
6 Storage
7 Covered way
8 Deck
9 Water tank
10 Brick bench

FLEXIBLE OPEN LEARNING SPACE, P-12 SCHOOL / **Ground floor plan**

The aim was to create a building that would aid the transition of pupils and to foster greater educational connections. The result is an unassuming building, realised on a challenging budget. From the outside it is simply clad in corrugated steel and could be mistaken for an agricultural building. Inside, an open-plan arrangement gives little away. It is only when the students inhabit the space that it comes alive, revealing itself like a 3-D puzzle that groups learn how to unlock and use to its full potential. The seemingly random patterns woven into the carpet are actually carefully calculated to match the path of sunlight through the windows on days of the year that are important to the school; bespoke moveable furniture is there for pupils to form and shape their own working spaces to suit their particular project, rather than for the teacher to control. There are also three simple outdoor spaces immediately accessible for children to use at their discretion. The so-called Flexible Open Learning Space offers the opportunity for groups from primary and secondary school to collaborate on projects, getting to know each other and coming to understand the different learning approaches that are undertaken in the senior school.

The design of the space is underpinned by a strong pedagogical belief that the school leadership teams instigated with the help of Rubida Research, a learning environment research consultancy led by Dr. Kenn Fisher.

Dr. Fisher sees learning spaces as powerful social and political tools and explains: 'Space has an impact on the performance of students and teachers and it both prohibits and establishes order.' The open learning space can be considered as a direct response to this thinking, beginning to break down the established teacher-student power relationship, enabling the students to take control of their own education rather than following the rules laid down by a teacher. In doing so, the hope was that children from different backgrounds would find it a liberating learning experience. 'Active engagement with space and place within schools can demonstrate resistant and emancipatory possibilities for those who are disadvantaged through gender, race or socio-economic position in society.'[5]

Rubida Research also worked closely with Rowan Opat Architects and the school to enable an open dialogue about the design of the building, sharing a conversation about the importance of the organisation and management of space that breaks what Fisher describes as the 'hegemony of the design professions who, by controlling the design process by excluding user input and participation, remove spatiality from the domain of teachers and students thereby increasing their sense of spatial helplessness, vulnerability and disengagement.' The outcome is a building that has architectural integrity if not beauty.

Crucially, students perceive the building as a special place where they are at liberty to work in a way that suits them, their group and the projects that they are undertaking. This has come about by an enlightened approach to developing a school building through an open and collaborative design that embraces space and education as equally important and interconnected elements.

Empowering the users

In the metropolitan borough of Barnsley, South Yorkshire, UK, an innovative programme called **'Remaking Learning'** [Bureau – design + research, 2006] funded by Creative Partnerships,[6] developed and supported Barnsley Council's approach to rebuilding all the secondary schools in Barnsley. There were initially 13 secondary schools which were consolidated to nine schools, called Advanced Learning Centres. Most new schools were rebuilt on grounds of their original sites. After construction, the old school buildings were demolished and the ground converted to playing fields and outdoor areas. The project aimed to develop teachers and headteachers into good clients in order to achieve relevant and better designed schools. The aim of the Education Department in Barnsley was to create a profound change at a cultural level; the schools were to form the centre of the community, raising expectations and levels of achievement in an area of post-industrial economic challenge. They would be designed to provide life-long learning opportunities for the whole community with centres open 48 weeks a year.

The objective was also to develop the skill and confidence of teachers to identify good practice. A set of design principles were developed for each new school led by the teachers consulting with governors, parents and pupils. These would then evolve into a final brief that architects could interpret and implement in their designs. The project took teachers on structured visits to key buildings with tours by the staff – not all of which were schools. For example, the 2002 Laban Dance Centre in London by Herzog & de Meuron was particularly popular as an inspiring teaching space while Queen Mary University Science Laboratories in London, designed by Alsop Architects in 2005 enabled teachers to see first-hand a completely different organisation of space and ways of working and learning in those spaces.

Teachers were able to link ways they wanted to teach in their new school to exemplary designs and inspiring buildings they visited. The design principles thus developed were then introduced to the pupils in workshops. One workshop for 11-year-olds, with the objective to design a school in a day, led to really imaginative ideas for forward-thinking sustainable schools with joined-up ecological processes. For example, one school was designed where the children would grow biofuel for heating and cooking, grow their own food, cook for the whole class and finally compost the waste afterwards.

The children's designs and models and the process of the whole project and the findings were then published and exhibited at the Design Centre North in Barnsley. Parents, governors and the potential building teams and consultants came to view and discuss the schemes. Many of the key issues like social space in schools, the roles of nature and technology and the inside/outside spaces all were firmly embedded in the briefs for the new Learning Centres. One of the completed schools, Carlton Community College in Barnsley, UK [Building Design Partnership – BDP, 2011] is shown in the introduction on p. 13.

Design involvement

Participatory involvement in smaller projects

Die Baupiloten is an architectural partnership between Susanne Hoffmann Architects and the TU Berlin. Together they create innovative projects through participative design approaches. Although they work with a range of clients, their schools projects are the most well known and highly acclaimed. The skill of Die Baupiloten lies in using what children understand best – stories – as a framework for their designs. The fictional, fantastical and fairy tales used by the student designers enable children

'REMAKING LEARNING' IN BARNSLEY, SOUTH YORKSHIRE, UK [Bureau – design + research, 2006]
As part of a larger programme to rebuild all the schools in Barnsley, several workshops with pupils were conducted. Students were encouraged to express their ideas in drawings. In addition, model making was a key method used to enable children to express their ideas in three-dimensional form.

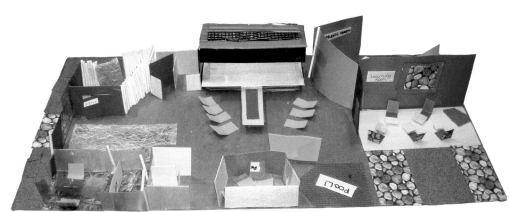

to comprehend that architecture is something that they can engage with, interpret and adapt. The influence of stories is clear in the realisation of Die Baupiloten projects, often creating magical spaces within otherwise ordinary schools. Making spatial stories within a school has a number of benefits to children's well-being and schooling; it enables the everyday realities of school to merge with the imaginative world that young children often inhabit, it brings to life the written word, enables children who are learning in their second language to engage with stories physically rather than through text.

A series of installations at **Carl Bolle Elementary School** in Berlin, Germany [Die Baupiloten, 2008], saw students of architecture working collaboratively with the school children in a series of creative workshops, devel-

oping a narrative about a spy. The children then began to flesh out the various scenes in the story through a series of drawings and collages. The architects then returned for a model-making workshop, enabling children to create their own interpretations of the story. Two pupils, Jon and Burak, developed ideas for a Summer Labyrinth, Climbing Forest, the Secret Leisure Garden and Snowworld. Die Baupiloten skilfully took the essence of these ideas and synthesised them into a series of spatial interventions. The actual architectural reality manages to deliver the dynamism and freshness of the children's ideas, bringing them to life in glorious Technicolor, using materials and lighting to dramatic effect.

The result of working closely with children is a new sequence of spaces created in the ground floor corridor

CARL BOLLE ELEMENTARY SCHOOL IN BERLIN, GERMANY [Die Baupiloten, 2008]

The concept for the architectural interventions came from a model developed by school pupils in a workshop with the architects. At different times of the day and of the year the spaces take on a different and sometimes magical character.

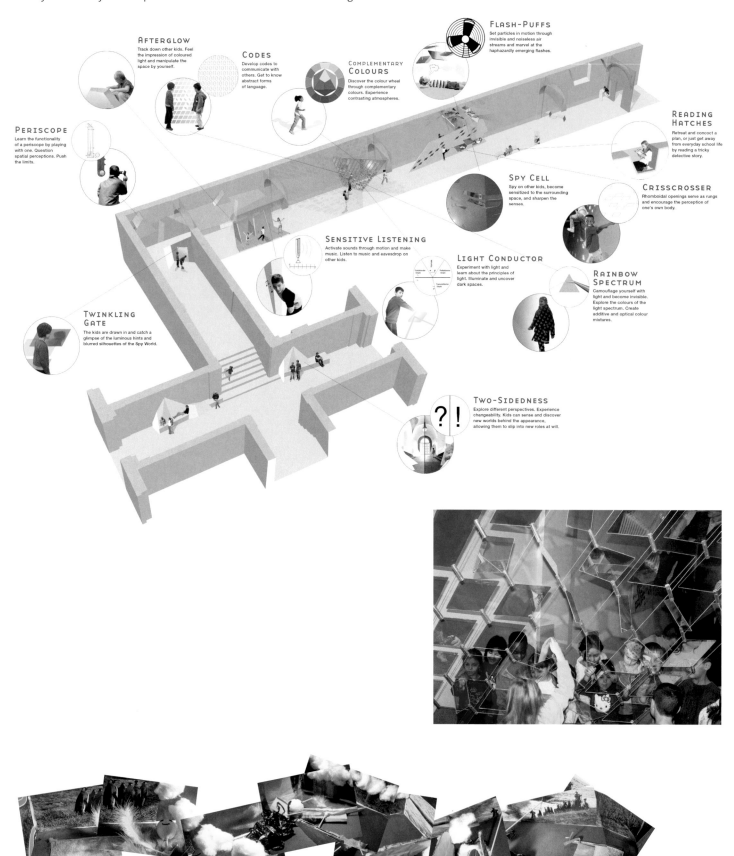

AFTERGLOW
Track down other kids. Feel the impression of coloured light and manipulate the space by yourself.

CODES
Develop codes to communicate with others. Get to know abstract forms of language.

COMPLEMENTARY COLOURS
Discover the colour wheel through complementary colours. Experience contrasting atmospheres.

FLASH-PUFFS
Set particles in motion through invisible and noiseless air streams and marvel at the haphazardly emerging flashes.

READING HATCHES
Retreat and concoct a plan, or just get away from everyday school life by reading a tricky detective story.

PERISCOPE
Learn the functionality of a periscope by playing with one. Question spatial perceptions. Push the limits.

SPY CELL
Spy on other kids, become sensitized to the surrounding space, and sharpen the senses.

CRISSCROSSER
Rhomboidal openings serve as rungs and encourage the perception of one's own body.

SENSITIVE LISTENING
Activate sounds through motion and make music. Listen to music and eavesdrop on other kids.

LIGHT CONDUCTOR
Experiment with light and learn about the principles of light. Illuminate and uncover dark spaces.

RAINBOW SPECTRUM
Camouflage yourself with light and become invisible. Explore the colours of the light spectrum. Create additive and optical colour mixtures.

TWINKLING GATE
The kids are drawn in and catch a glimpse of the luminous hints and blurred silhouettes of the Spy World.

TWO-SIDEDNESS
Explore different perspectives. Experience changeability. Kids can sense and discover new worlds behind the appearance, allowing them to slip into new roles at will.

CARL BOLLE ELEMENTARY SCHOOL / The children's ideas resulted in a series of interventions in the school corridors. The interventions transform them into a series of dynamic spaces in which the children can create new stories.

and entrance gallery. Each intervention plays out one of the scenes from the 'the spy with the shimmering coat' story, offering pupils a chance to explore the space playfully and learn creatively. Starting at the entrance gallery, you make your way through the 'twinkling gate' and past the 'wall of disguises' and end up at the 'reading benches'. Each part of the design focuses on a sensory element, encouraging looking, talking and listening, touching and feeling. The architecture also incorporates puzzles that relate to scientific investigations, such as using mirrors to reflect light and distort images at the 'wall of disguises'. The project establishes an interactive zone, at a child's scale, providing a landscape for hiding in, climbing on and sitting in. It creates a sense of place and a unique solution that is woven into the building fabric, just as the stories that it animates are part of the children's minds.

The skilfulness of Die Baupiloten's work is in converting the language of children's make-believe world into reality, with all of the wonder and vibrancy of the children. Die Baupiloten's work does not seem to be compromised by issues of building codes and everyday functional problems and is architecture with a sprinkling of fairy dust! In faithfully bringing to life children's ideas the architects are showing how much they value young people as creative designers and artists.

Collaborative design

'Mission Addition' is an innovative collaboration developed over a two-year period between **All Saints School** in Mansfield, UK and the architects from Sheffield [Bureau – design + research and Prue Chiles Architects, 2011], aimed at creating a particular space, an outdoor classroom for secondary school students. All Saints School in Mansfield has a very strong mathematics department that initiated the project, which was student-led from the outset, with young people interviewing and selecting the design team. The brief for the project was to use the subject of mathematics as a basis for the design of a structure that could be used as a physical piece of learning equipment as well as a place for student socialising.

ALL SAINTS SCHOOL IN MANSFIELD, UK [Bureau – design + research and Prue Chiles Architects, 2011]
Over a period of two years, the students in collaboration with the architects developed an outdoor classroom for secondary
school students. In a series of workshops, the design was developed using 1:10 scale models of the structure.

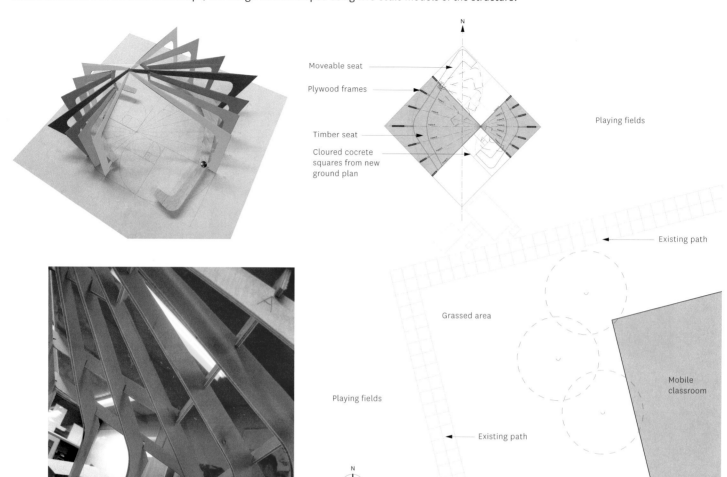

Moveable seat

Plywood frames

Timber seat

Cloured cocrete
squares from new
ground plan

Playing fields

Existing path

Grassed area

Playing fields

Existing path

Mobile
classroom

The site plan shows the new structure within its context.

A 1:1 mock-up model was tested on site.

Students bolted pieces of plywood and
sealed them with a mastic glue to form
the main structural pieces of the scale
model.

Finally the structure was assembled
as a 3-D jigsaw, using a construction
manual to guide both the staff and
the students.

An ambitious programme was devised that aimed to take students through the briefing and design process, from site surveys through to construction. A series of workshops were organised which started by looking at potential locations for the classroom with pupils, talking to staff, surveying possible locations and analysing the potential of different locations. A range of mathematical principles were explored, tracking their history through architecture, culture and civilisation and looking for examples of buildings that have been composed using such geometric principles such as the 'golden section' or Fibonacci sequence. Students explored various materials and undertook their own research based on environmental credentials, cost, availability and appropriateness for self-build.

A study visit was also undertaken to look at different types of buildings, structures and sculptures, to raise aspirations and to inspire the group, showing the potential for a classroom to be something that is beautiful, practical and inspirational! As the concept developed the group started looking at the details of the structure: how it would function, how a class could be accommodated and how the building could be utilised in different ways. The students created full-size mock-ups of seats and structural elements to explore several proposals. As part of a visit to the school of architecture, school pupils learnt about how architecture students work and learn.

The group started making a 1:10 scale model of the structure from a set of instructions and templates – structural elements were bolted together to replicate the real construction. With building contractors having cleared the site and levelled it off, a day was spent with the students, setting out the geometry of the structure, to ensure that it was orientated correctly and that it would fit on the site! The structure was developed by the architects as a kit of parts or life-size plywood 3-D jigsaw. Plywood was chosen as it was a material that could be accurately cut by a CNC machine to make the complex shapes required. The size and finish of each piece of the structure could also be controlled, to ensure that the pieces could be handled safely by the children. The main structural pieces of plywood were assembled by the students, by bolting them together and sealing with a mastic glue. This approach allowed students to be safely involved in the fabrication of the structure just like they had practised in the scale model. A construction manual was developed to enable the school site maintenance staff to assemble the structure and for pupils to be involved at specific stages.

The project process and product sought to embed the collective learning experience, for the benefit of other pupils and teachers within the school. In order to achieve this, students have documented the project at every stage and presented their work in school assemblies to inform their peers about progress. Alongside the built structure a curriculum resource was developed by the teachers and architects. The resource included lesson plans and learning activities based around the Mission Addition structure that were linked to the national curriculum. This helped to ensure that both the process and product are used to teach maths to children of different ages within the school. The result is not architecture to support the curriculum, but architecture that has been developed through the curriculum.

This project is a great example of a how a small building project can fully immerse young people in the architectural design process. It also highlights what a rich subject architecture is and how it can be influenced by other related academic subjects. Mission Addition also shows how relatively small architectural projects can be more accessible or appropriate for participation than larger projects such as building an entire school. When a close partnership is nurtured and architects take the role of facilitators, as well as designers, the results can have a big impact on pupils' learning experience, sense of achievement and improved facilities.

Getting active at the building site

Most people would agree that construction sites are potentially dangerous places and are not suitable for children: yet they are places of great energy and interest. If

COWLEY ST. LAURENCE PRIMARY SCHOOL AND CHILDREN'S CENTRE IN HILLINGDON, UK [What Architecture, 2010]
The Lego façade at the entrance gives the existing buildings a new identity. The façade construction process not only involved children, but also parents and staff.

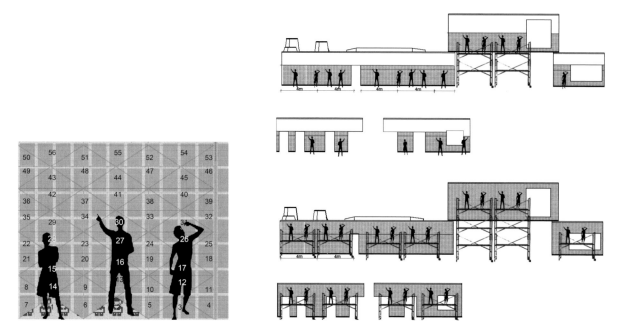

All construction drawings were based around the Lego brick modules and how they could be assembled by lay people.

only there was a way to involve children in the design and building of their school in a meaningful, playful and safe way! In the creation of the **Cowley St. Laurence Primary School and Children's Centre** in Hillingdon, UK [What Architecture, 2010] this question was answered. In forming a new entrance to the school and joining together two existing buildings, the aim was to express the creativity of the young people within the school. This was

cleverly achieved by making the outer skin of the building out of Lego! Not special Lego, but 40,000 of the same blocks that we have all played with in our formative years. What must have seemed like a crazy idea at the outset became a collaboration that has galvanised the school community and created a building that is a unique. The skill was in the organisation and synthesis of the design, enabling children to have creative input and free

COWLEY ST. LAURENCE PRIMARY SCHOOL AND CHILDREN'S CENTRE / The new entrance joins two existing buildings.

Entrance interior

reign, but carefully curated to make individual expressions part of a composition. Each child had a panel of the same size, and planned out his or her design on paper first before it was converted to fit with the Lego block modules. Like pixels on a computer screen or patches on a quilt, the pictograms form a vibrant image, but one that does not give you a headache. The initial design was going to be a multi-coloured image, but this was sensibly toned down to black and white.

The project had its technical difficulties, not least working out how to make the Lego a viable and robust building material. The architects brought in specialists to develop a spray-on fire-retardant and UV-resistant coating that would keep the surface pristine. Vandalism to the blocks was also considered with all blocks being locked in position. The only way to take away blocks is to start from the top, but the roof capping prevents anyone from trying!

Once the loadbearing and functional elements of the wall had been completed, the construction site was prepared to be inhabited by children, staff, parents and volunteers. Health and safety were key considerations in enabling unskilled workers and minors to be part of the construction process, but after careful planning and organisation the dream became reality. Children were able to turn their design input into a physical contribution by painstakingly forming their pictograms block by block. The entrance wall has become a symbol of collective community effort, combining design flair with hard work to make a better school.

In creating this opportunity to involve young people in the building of their school, the approach was to reduce the size of the material, making it lightweight, easy to handle and to connect without any fixings, mortar or glue. Rolling out this strategy to make a whole building may be impractical, but it still provides a great example of how the messy and complicated construction process can be distilled to a point where everyone can take part and contribute to something that is far greater than its individual parts.

Learning through building

The recently completed project **City in the Sky** in Wuhan, China [AA-Lab, 2013] is reacting against the status quo: a construction industry dominated by use of concrete and an education system that lacks experiential learning opportunities. The dual aims of the City in the Sky are therefore to reconnect young people with their surroundings and explore alternative Chinese building materials in a contemporary way. AA-Lab see the project as a learning experience rather than a piece of architecture and hope that through their involvement, the young participants will 'more truly understand nature, tools, construction and even life itself.'[7]

The building is not actually a formal learning institution, but rather a place of learning by making. Through a

CITY IN THE SKY IN WUHAN, CHINA [AA-Lab, 2013]
Developed in collaboration with Natur Organic Life, the project was to encourage young people to reconnect with their surroundings as well as to explore alternative Chinese building materials in a contemporary way. Over a period of three months, workshops for 36 children and their parents were organised to design, construct and maintain the treehouses.

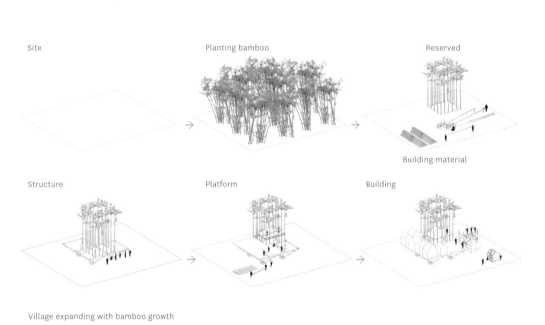

The axonometric drawing shows the construction sequence.

The City in the Sky consists of 18 cabins and two viewing platforms on a deck held up by a series of inverted pyramid structures.

CITY IN THE SKY / Elevating the City sends a message that children's work is valuable and deserves prominence in the community.

Children were learning by making the City and managing it afterwards. Small section timber form the structure and cladding of the cabins. All of them were then personalised by painting murals.

collaboration between the architects and Natur Organic Life, weekend workshops were organised for 36 children and their parents at over a three-month period. Through the workshops, children aged 5–12 years were engaged in the design process from the development of initial ideas through to fabrication, construction and crucially the management of the City afterwards. Involving parents within the process has many benefits, including passive supervision and supporting children with more difficult physical tasks. However, this relationship needed to be carefully managed to ensure that children didn't defer to the adults or let them take over!

The deck of the City in the Sky is composed of 8m high 3 x 3m square units, and sits around 1.5m up in the air. The architects see the undercroft below, made from a series of inverted pyramid structures, as key to making the city appear as if it was floating above the ground. On top of the deck perch a series of 18 cabins, made by pairs of young people using small section timber to form the structure and cladding. The children have personalised the insides of the cabins with painted murals, giving them a sense of identity and ownership. Around the cabins are a number of shared spaces to explore, including the raised bamboo houses. These enclosures provide chil-

GANDO PRIMARY SCHOOL IN GANDO, BURKINA FASO [Kéré Architecture, 2001]
A self-build approach was chosen for cost reasons, resulting in a real sense of local identity. The construction of the school offered local people the opportunity to learn new skills. Bottom right: Women lay a compressed clay floor.

dren with the opportunity to interact socially. The maintenance of the bamboo houses by the children is crucial to the ongoing health of the City: the architects recently sent a message to Natur Organic Life asking if anyone had remembered to 'water the house' – a reminder that the survival of the City requires an ongoing group commitment from the children.

As a construction material, bamboo has been used indigenously in countries throughout Asia and South America. Famed for its incredible strength to weight ratio, bamboo is well suited to participative construction projects where children are involved. To create the platform for the City in the Sky, the sizes of structural elements and their construction were carefully co-ordinated to enable

groups to handle, manoeuvre and install them. This would not have been possible with concrete or steel. Bamboo also has the potential to be used in construction as a living entity, something that the City in the Sky exploits.

The Architects see the City in the Sky as an ongoing collaboration and a living organism rather than a finished piece of architecture. They believe that the children who created the City should have the skills to carry on refining and improving their spaces in the future. City in the Sky provides an example of how architecture can be the medium for learning as much as a receptacle for learning. It also shows that by giving children the opportunity to shape their learning environment, they can generate new skills and even develop a new perspective on life.

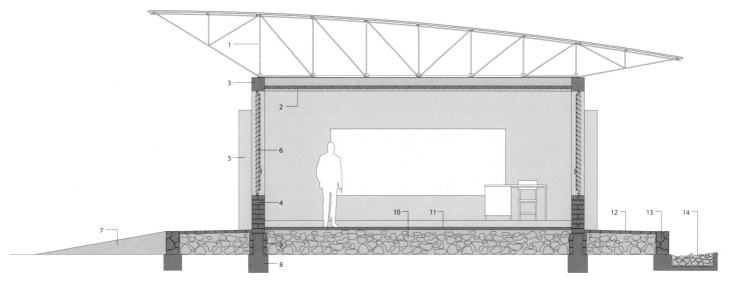

1 Roof: corrugated metal sheets, girders of welded reinforcing steel
2 Suspended ceiling: clay bricks
3 Ring beam: reinforced concrete
4 Supporting clay walls
5 Buttresses
6 Windows: steel lamella elements
7 Stair: natural stone or concrete
8 Foundation: non-reinforced concrete
9 Permanent shuttering: edgewise bricked-up adobe
10 Clay and stone filling
11 Compressed clay
12 Terrace: clay bricks
13 Terrace edge: natural stone masonry
14 Rainwater conductor filled with gravel

GANDO PRIMARY SCHOOL / Cross section. The school was designed to use materials that were easy to source and could be constructed by local people.

Community self-build projects

The creation of **Gando Primary School** in Gando, Burkina Faso [Kéré Architecture, 2001] takes participation in the design and construction process to the next level. Where Cowley St. Laurence involved children in the design and creation, it is really an experiment in how to collectively decorate a school. At Gando, the wider community were involved in making the raw fabric of the school. The architect, Francis Kéré, grew up in Gando as the eldest son of the village leader. Whilst studying in Germany he answered the call from his village to return and create a much-needed school. Kéré fulfils a multiple role, being designer, fundraiser and community member. From the outset, he understood that the creation of school should be the beginning of an ongoing initiative to develop skills and opportunities for life-long learning within the community. The collaborative design and construction was not just about one building, but about bringing new opportunities to a place and its people.

Engaging local people in the design and construction of the school was not a lofty aim but a practical imperative in this situation. The cost of building the school needed to be kept to a minimum as it was funded by charitable donations. Therefore using local and easily accessible materials was central to a workable solution. The skills needed to build the school had to be held lo-cally, partly to keep costs low, but also to ensure that any future repairs could be undertaken by local people with knowledge of the original construction. As literacy skills are low in the region – hence the need for a school – involving the community in the realisation of the school was difficult in terms of communication. The architect commented: 'The biggest challenge was how to explain the design and drawings to people who can neither read nor write. This problem accompanies the architect the whole time during his entire project time in Burkina Faso.'[8]

The materials used in the project were intended to be evolutionary rather than revolutionary. Francis Kéré introduced simple manufacturing processes for existing construction techniques, to create materials that were easy to source, work and use, but also, where possible, native to the site. With the help of a mechanical press, local people formed their own compressed earth bricks, using the plentiful clay-rich earth found in the locale. A small amount of cement was added to the earth to improve adhesion. Commonly used steel rods were welded together to form steel trusses. Coupled with a cheap and easily available tin sheet, the roof provided a wide overhang, keeping the hot sun off the children during the day, and the numerous gaps between the trusses allowing much-needed high-level ventilation. Concrete was used sparingly to make a beam on top of the walls that would

GARTHWAITE CENTER FOR SCIENCE AND ARTS IN WESTON, MASSACHUSETTS, USA [Architerra Inc., 2007]
The environmentally conscious building forms an important learning tool: In an effort to raise awareness of energy use, the school itself became part of the science education programme. For instance, energy usage is being monitored. Bottom right: View of atrium

support the roof. Through the process of making the school, Kéré worked to show the community that clay and earth were as good as concrete in terms of functionality, but that earth blocks gave the building a sense of local identity. As the architect explains, the project has had a profound impact on the Gando community and further afield: 'All the people involved in the project management were native to the village, and the skills learned here will be applied to further initiatives in the village and elsewhere. The way the community organised itself has

set an example for two neighbouring villages, which subsequently built their own schools as a co-operative effort. The local authorities have also recognised the project's worth: not only have they provided and paid for the teaching staff, but they have also endeavoured to employ the young people trained there in the town's public projects, using the same techniques.'[9]

Since its completion in 2001, the school has attracted over 300 pupils from surrounding villages, which prompted the creation of an extension, incorporating new class-

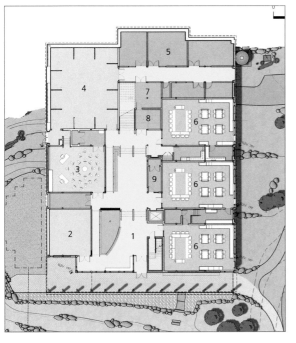

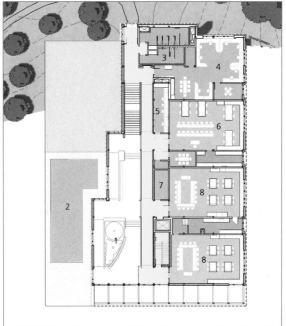

Ground floor
1 Science display atrium
2 Small gallery
3 Integrated studies
   classroom
4 Community meeting/
   large gallery
5 Mechanical gallery
6 Biology labs
7 Gallery storage
8 Installation room
9 Campus data centre

First floor
1 Open to atrium below
2 Green roof
3 Bathrooms
4 Faculty office suite
5 Independent studies
   classroom
6 Physics lab
7 Campus data centre
8 Chemistry lab

GARTHWAITE CENTER FOR SCIENCE AND ARTS / Ground and first floor plan

rooms and a library completed in 2006. Additional teachers' accommodation was also developed nearby. This addition marked a significant improvement in the outlook of the Gando community and neighbouring groups, broadening their range of civic buildings and in doing so helping themselves to learn and develop skills and knowledge. Having already seen the benefits of the original three-classroom school, students contributed to the new project in a very practical way. 'For one year every student carried a brick for the construction to the school.'[10] The practical act of carrying bricks for construction represents the fact that the young people have 'their future in their hands' and the power to make of it what they will.

Post-occupancy evaluation: monitoring use and performance

Studying how a completed building functions is important for designers and users alike. For designers there are few opportunities to learn from mistakes or to improve a building once it has been constructed. Post-occupancy studies are helpful for building users because they often highlight to what level people understand how to use the building, or how they feel about the building. Collecting computer data on fuel efficiency for heating/cooling spaces, or interviewing people about personal responses to a building can be hugely valuable and often highlight

issues that can be easily resolved. There are numerous things that put people off a building, like a shade of paint or not being able to control the temperature in a room. However, rather than this being an exercise for consultants to undertake, school children and staff can help themselves by analysing their school building and the way it is used. This area of participative design is often forgotten about, but can have a big impact on people's understanding of a building and also their enjoyment of it.

The Cambridge School in Weston, Massachusetts, USA, has an environmentally sensitive building called **Garthwaite Center for Science and Arts** [Architerra Inc., 2007]. The design of the building incorporates a heat recovery system, a wood pellet biomass boiler heating facility, stormwater management and composting toilets. The school and particularly children worked closely with the design team throughout the process, continually feeding their thoughts and ideas into the project. This collaborative approach has been carried through to the use of the building, where the school analyses how it performs as part of the science education programme and as a way to raise awareness of energy use in the wider community. 'Students have been involved in thinking about the building design from its inception. They debated the best forms of renewable energy for the building, have monitored energy usage on campus and have surveyed the community about energy

GARTHWAITE CENTER FOR SCIENCE AND ARTS / **View of classroom.**

issues. Now that we are actually in the building, we will be tracking its systems and see if it is living up to its potential regarding energy and water use. We are also monitoring atrium light levels to compare with the daylight monitoring by the architects … Our hope is to reach out into the community and bring other schools on campus to learn about sustainability via the building.'

Using the building as an experiment – taking measurements and testing its performance – offers rich potential for learning, but also ensures that the maximum value is being rung out of the building. Usually buildings are deemed so complex to run and maintain that they are out of most people's control. Undertaking studies like those in the Garthwaite Centre helps to ensure that the building is understood and therefore used fully by its occupants.

Whilst the architects should be commended for enabling this through an accessible design, the fact that it is not considered by most schools is cause for concern.

'Our new centre offers an exciting array of environmentally friendly features, but we are particularly proud of the building's value as a major teaching tool.' [11] The notion of a school building as a teaching or learning tool is one that many schools aspire to. However, in order to achieve this goal, by definition teachers and children need to know how it works and understand what factors have shaped it and made it the way that it is. This can only be realised where children, teachers and the community have been engaged in the design and construction process.

REFERENCES

1   Alison Clark, *Transforming Children's Spaces: Children's and Adults' Participation in Designing Learning Environments*, London: Routledge, 2010, p. 43.

2   Adam Fletcher, Ladder of Youth Voice. Washington: The Freechild Project, 2011. http://freechild.org/ladder.htm. Accessed on 20 December 2012. Ladder diagram developed from Roger A. Hart, *Children's Participation: The Theory And Practice Of Involving Young Citizens In Community Development And Environmental Care*, London and New York: UNICEF, 1997.

3   Alessandro Rigolon, 'A Space with Meaning: Children's Involvement in Participatory Design Processes', Research Paper, University of Bologna. 2009.

4   Rosie Parnell, *School Design Involvement*, Sheffield: University of Sheffield, 2011. http://

rosieparnell.staff.shef.ac.uk/DSIU/yourprocess/roles.html. Accessed on 20 December 2012.

5   Kenn Fisher, *Re-voicing the Classroom: A Critical Psychosocial Spatiality of Learning*, Adelaide: Rubida Research, 2002.

6   Creative Partnerships was the UK's flagship creative learning programme running throughout England from 2002 until 30 September 2011 when funding was withdrawn by Arts Council England. The Creative Partnerships programme brought creative workers such as artists, architects and scientists into schools to work with teachers to inspire young people and help them learn.

7   http://www.gooood.hk/City-in-Sky-By-AA-lab.html. Accessed on 15 November 2013.

8   http://www.designboom.com/architecture/diebedo-francis-kere-at-small-scale-big-change-new-architectures-of-social-

engagement-exhibition/. Accessed 26 April 2015. Cf. also Andres Lepik, *Small Scale Big Change: New Architectures of Social Engagement*, New York: The Museum of Modern Art and Basel: Birkhäuser, 2010, pp. 33–42.

9   http://www.kere-architecture.com/projects/primary-school-gando/. Accessed on 15 October 2013.

10   http://www.fuergando.de/index.php/de/our-work/primary-school. Accessed on 15 October 2013.

11   Marilyn DelDonno, CSW Science Chair, The Cambridge School of Weston. http://www.csw.org/podium/default.aspx?t=204&nid=521466&bl=back&rc=0. Accessed on 15 October 2013.

Summary

5 PARTICIPATING IN THE DESIGN AND CONSTRUCTION PROCESS

1. The **key principles of consulting with young people are respect, trust and an ability to listen**: it is important to treat pupils in a professional way and don't underestimate what they're able to do as children.

2. Involving young people in the design process has a number of benefits: enabling pupils to become active citizens in school and in society, being involved in decision-making, positive and creative contributions in a range of situations. It proves to young people that they have a **role in a democratic system**.

3. Pupils can **develop a range of new skills** participating in design projects, reinforcing the link between academic and vocational learning through the design and construction process.

4. It is important to **develop an engagement strategy at the earliest opportunity in the design process**. If the initial project brief can introduce the intention to involve staff and students in the design process it is much more likely to be achieved.

5. It is crucial to ensure that all participants **understand the rules of engagement** and their **roles and responsibilities** in the design process. Make it clear that people understand what the anticipated outputs of their involvement will be. When people know what their contribution is and how it will be used they are in a better position to add value to the project.

6. **Managing the expectations** of those engaged in a design process is really important to ensure that people don't get carried away. All participants need to understand how long projects can take from design to realisation.

7. **Building people's capacity to engage** with the subject is crucial. People can only make an informed contribution if they have the skills and knowledge of the design and realisation process.

8. Be creative about the nature of participation, particularly when young people are involved; provide **a range of approaches**, whether using stories as a starting point, using children's voices to help build a project brief, treating young people as co-designers or engaging them as builders.

6 Learning Outside the Classroom / PRUE CHILES

This chapter recognises that children can learn in school spaces different from the traditional classroom or other formal teaching spaces. It can be argued that they learn as much outside the classroom as within. Many of these incidental spaces go unnoticed or are forgotten about; they are under-utilised or simply not prioritised in the design and use of the school. Often, entrances are bland and disorientating, corridors are dark, long and monotonous, and toilets are unpleasant and to be avoided. It is often when extending a school that these new learning and socialising spaces can be carved out and used creatively.

Entrance spaces are the first thing the visitor and the pupils see as they enter a school and they are vital to the image of a school and the possibility of exhibiting what the school has to offer; these spaces need to be welcoming, spacious and inspiring. Corridors and other circulation spaces are an opportunity to create small intimate spaces to meet and work in small groups. Toilets are a good example of a space that may not get mentioned in a case study, but are often a good indicator of the design quality and innovation of a school building. Further, they can inspire children to learn and provoke ideas. This chapter captures thoughtful design in specific areas of the school that can make a big difference to the children's and teachers' experience of school. Perhaps most importantly it is these and other new types of education space that teach children both how to socialise and how to learn independently.

HIGH SCHOOL IN CANEÇAS, PORTUGAL [ARX Portugal, 2013]
Taking in the idea of a 'learning street', the High School has dynamic break-out and outdoor spaces, encouraging students to explore and take ownership of these spaces.

ORDRUP SCHOOL IN CHARLOTTENLUND, DENMARK [Bosch and Fjord, CEBRA Architects and Søren Robert Lund, 2006]
Revered as having one of the leading child-centred educational practices in Europe, the existing school underwent a major transformation. Following the theme of 'peace and absorption' set by the school, the designers created 'reading tubes' for younger children to allow for time off to read. Bottom right: Creating a feeling of an indoor playground, the interventions were designed to fit the needs of each age group.

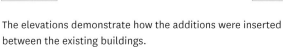
The elevations demonstrate how the additions were inserted between the existing buildings.

Settings for personalised learning

Most of us are motivated by social experiences; we enjoy talking to and watching other people. We all feel safer with others around. A school with pupils everywhere, with movement and activity and a sense of openness is more desirable.[1] Central atria, wide staircases, with places to linger and the more intimate spaces discussed in this chapter are all becoming more popular in today's learning environments. The spaces discussed in this chapter support individual and small group learning and it is in this respect that they are conducive to personalised learning, a popular new direction in education. They provide alternative spaces for working on tablet or palm top computers and for getting away from the more formal classroom environment.

In many countries in the 21st century the pedagogical shift towards 'flexible' or 'personalised' learning acknowledges that individuals learn in different ways. This approach focuses on the development of students' own skills and aspirations rather than imparting knowledge to

ORDRUP SCHOOL / Older children have 'concentration booths' and moveable 'carpet islands' to help create a more personalised learning environment in a public building.

Utilising disused spaces like corridors, the architects and designers intervened by creating learning oases that allow children to socialise or concentrate whilst learning.

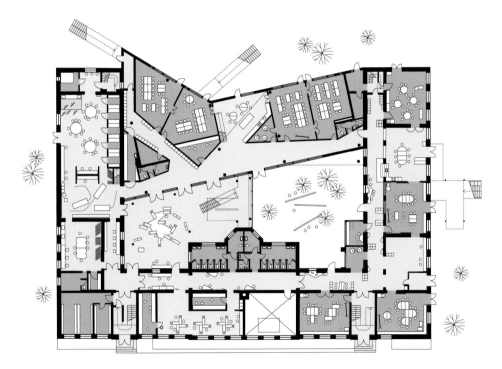

Ground floor plan. Working within three existing buildings, the architects created 15 interventions that provide an alternative learning space to the classrooms.

the whole group. Such a large change in both teaching methods and the physical environment requires research and experimentation. In the UK, the government sponsored the project 'Space for Personalised Learning'[2] to explore how new or existing schools can develop a physical environment which supports a student-led approach to learning. In other countries, where the changes in edu-

cational pedagogies are more advanced, whole schools have already been built to support this emergent educational paradigm of personalised learning space.

An example is **Ordrup School** in Charlottenlund, Denmark [Bosch and Fjord, CEBRA Architects and Søren Robert Lund, 2006] in the municipality of Gentofte in Denmark. Gentofte has one of the most progressive and

CORLAER COLLEGE 2 IN NIJKERK, THE NETHERLANDS [Broekbakema Architects, 2006]
'Instruction classrooms' serve the needs of specific teaching and learning styles, such computer research and individual studying. The architects played with the idea of transparency achieved by different types of openings and glazing.

widely published school building programmes in Europe and has physically transformed 12 schools to support new child-centred educational practices.[3] Fundamental to the programme is the belief that the innovative and considered design of school buildings can enrich learning.

Within the programme, three existing buildings at Ordrup School in Charlottenlund have been rationalised and extended by CEBRA Architects and Søren Robert Lund to create one school building. It is on the inside, however, where the architects have worked with visual artists Bosch and Fjord, that this school has really been transformed. Whilst traditional classrooms still remain, a series of 15 new settings for learning have been woven into the school building. Based on three key ideas within the school's personalised learning strategy – 'peace and absorption', 'discussion and cooperation' and 'security and presence' – the new interventions play a part in supporting learning and teaching rather than merely providing a space in which it occurs.

Whilst the interventions, such as sunken 'hot pots' for small group discussion, may look more familiar to an indoor playground than a school environment, the settings have been carefully considered to meet the needs of different age groups and individuals. For the youngest children, the desire for quiet time has been accommodated with upholstered 'reading tubes' which provide individual cocoons in which children can curl up with a book on their own or in pairs. For older children, once merely functional corridors have been given new life and purpose with the insertion of 'concentration booths' and moveable 'carpet islands'. Importantly, these insertions are not just tables and chairs that have been put in a disused corner, but are stimulating additions with bold graphics and striking lighting to give them a common language. These are places that children want to go to and learn and socialise at the right times; many are placed in corridors or other spaces which might be neglected otherwise.

In Nijkerk in the Netherlands, the need for a whole new secondary school building for **Corlaer College** in Nijkerk, the Netherlands [Broekbakema Architects, 2006] was again combined with a shift away from traditional classroom-based teaching methods towards students exploring their own learning needs and styles. In designing the new building, Corlaer College 2, the architects and the school had the opportunity to create a whole new spatial paradigm for educating their students, aiming to nurture the individual and the aspirations of every child who inhabits it. The resulting building is more like an open-plan office building than a school environment: the school is arranged into a series of 'teaching domains'

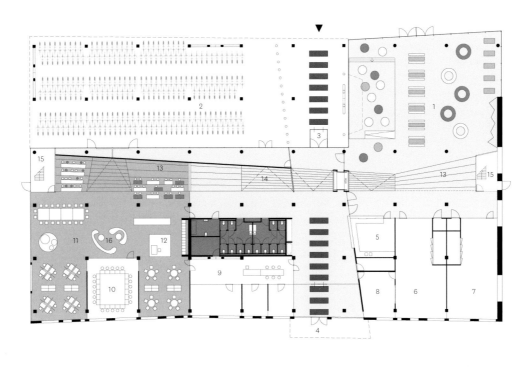

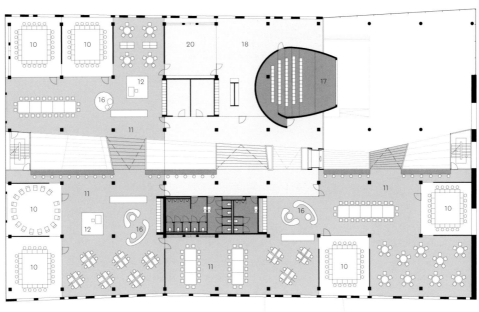

1 Auditorium
2 Bicycle shed
3 Student entrance
4 Main entrance
5 Caretaker
6 Music education
7 Drawing
8 Studio
9 Administration
10 Classroom
11 Education domain
12 Supervisor
13 Grandstand
14 Main staircase
15 Emergency staircase
16 Relaxation isles
17 Lecture room
18 Staff room
19 Biology
20 Teachers' area

CORLAER COLLEGE 2 / Ground and first floor plan. Resembling an open-plan office building, the 'teaching domains' are arranged around a central 'knowledge canyon' that is three storeys high.

either side of a central 'knowledge canyon' that rises through the three-storey building.

Although the key to this educational concept of personalised learning is freedom and flexibility, a sense of structure is also necessary. It is crucial to find the balance between offering a setting in which students have the freedom to work individually or as a team while also providing a structure in which they can learn how to do that. At Corlaer College 2 the solution has been to create

a number of common elements and designated zones within the open-plan educational domains. Firstly, each domain is broken up by the insertion of one or two 'instruction classrooms' for quiet study. The classrooms are carefully placed to break up the space and to create a series of zones in the open-plan area that are furnished to accommodate different learning styles such as computer research, individual studying, small or large group-working. 'Relaxation isles' provide a place for students to

HIGH SCHOOL IN CANEÇAS, PORTUGAL [ARX Portugal, 2013]
The main entrance to the building has a dynamic presence in the community, due to its scale and the relief lettering that wraps from the wall around under the soffit that acts as an invitation to students to enter the school. The aerial view shows the insertion of the extension between existing pavilions.

break from their study and a fixed base within each domain is designated for the supervisor, offering a constant point of reference within this fluid environment. There is an overwhelming sense of transparency within this new building for Corlaer College that is central to the educational concept.

Originally built in the 1970s, the **High School in Caneças**, Portugal [ARX Portugal, 2013] is part of the Parque Escolar programme that attempted to establish a new culture for learning in Portugal and indeed standards have risen enormously and over 200 high-quality schools have been completed through this programme.[4] Caneças is a fragmented suburb of whitewashed houses and pantile roofs on the periphery of Lisbon with a major highway into Lisbon through the middle – the schools and other public buildings need to act as a centre for the community.

This is an exceptional example of a school completely transformed by architectural design to enhance the student experience of school. New internal circulation spaces and other facilities link the four 1970s flat-roofed classroom blocks providing a completely new and exciting sculptural environment allowing students to explore and enjoy. The building actively participates in the learning by challenging children to explore and discover.

The uniformity of materials, chiefly flat white plaster walls, ceiling and hard floor, appears uncompromising but it enhances the sculptural appearance. The columns are reminiscent of a dense and dangerous forest – creating a bewildering and thus stimulating environment completely different from the children's homes! The complex concrete topography of the new forms weaves around the space between the original 1970s classroom volumes. The Parc Escolar programme's idea of the learning street

HIGH SCHOOL IN CANEÇAS / The use of plastered white concrete creates a uniform appearance.

New internal circulation created opportunities to both staff and students to inhabit these break-out spaces found between classrooms.

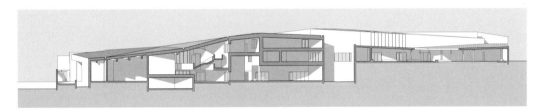

Longitudinal section

1 Classroom	6 Technical area	11 Laboratory	16 Student lounge
2 Storage	7 Archive	12 Meeting room	17 Dining hall
3 Staff room	8 Library	13 Teachers' room	18 Kitchen
4 Toilet	9 Auditorium	14 Gallery	19 Teacher office
5 Office	10 Study area	15 Reception	20 Atrium

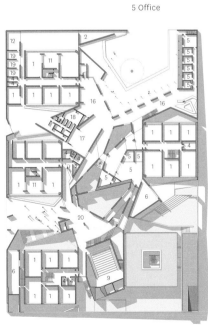

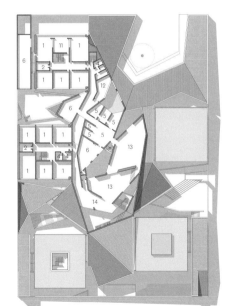

Lower level, ground and first floor plan. New sculptural elements were introduced in the courtyard that weave between the existing four 1970s pavilions, thus creating an interesting landscape for students to explore.

ST. MARY MAGDALENE ACADEMY IN ISLINGTON, LONDON, UK [Feilden Clegg Bradley Studios, 2009]
The lower glazed wall directs students, staff and visitors to the school's main entrance. The many doors to the school open up to a wide pavement. Inside, the central space enjoys natural light; its open plan offers places to sit. Bottom left: The façade provides the school with a strong visual identity and marks its presence in the community.

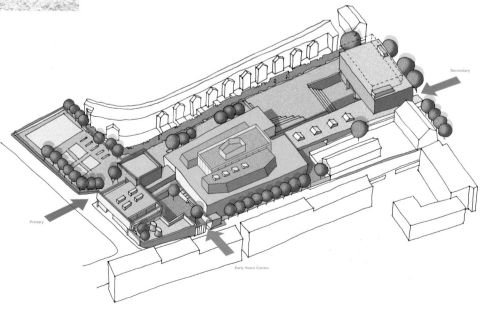

The axonometric sketch shows how memorable approaches to the school are created, with playful, partially glazed façades that allow peaks into the building.

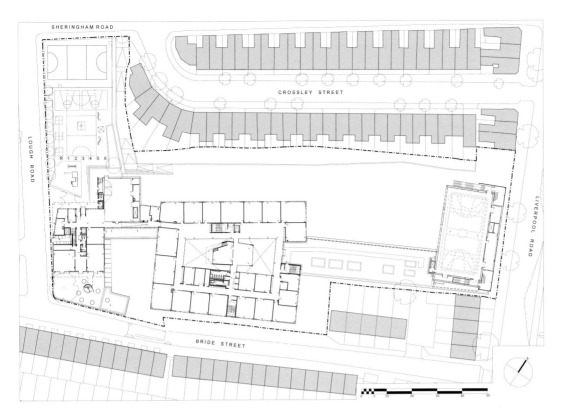

ST. MARY MAGDALENE ACADEMY / Site plan. As this multi-cultural school specialises in global citizenship, it was important to create an entrance that is inviting not only to the students but to the community the school is embedded in.

is taken to extremes here. The programme also aspired to make the school more central to the communities and used by the people they serve. There are a series of dynamic inside and outside spaces that are asking to be inhabited and used. The large entrance to the eastside of the school, for instance, has giant relief lettering wrapping around under the soffit, physically pulling the students into the school. There is a public courtyard to the south with a colonnade running around it where one of the teaching pavilions was demolished, which forms a generous entrance to the public facilities and connects to another courtyard opening onto a large sports area. This school takes architecture as a physical space which students can learn to explore and fathom to yet another level.

Entering a school

The entrance of a school is crucial to how the whole school functions. An experience shared by many visitors of school buildings from the last few decades is of walking round the outside of the building looking for the entrance only to find a set of double doors buried somewhere in a bland elevation. Entering the reception area of a school is usually uninspiring: one often encounters a badly designed reception desk with no-one behind it or an anonymous hatch to the adjoining school office, and just a pile of disorganised leaflets or paraphernalia. Entering a big secondary school or college is often an unnerving experience: uninviting and confusing at best and like penetrating Fort Knox at worst.

Some new schools, however, have reversed this trend. **St. Mary Magdalene Academy** in Islington, London, UK [Feilden Clegg Bradley Studios, 2009] has an outstanding entrance. It is light, airy and well-designed with a glazed screen and many doors open straight off a wide pavement into a generous and clear space. A long and low reception desk invites visitors in. This is particularly appropriate to the school's multi-cultural intake and its unusual specialism of humanities and global citizenship. The reception space has places to sit and linger; attractive views from the street have been created past the reception to the outdoor areas and a wide glazed corridor. There is room to exhibit and for the children to learn from each other's work and activities. To the side a huge glazed framed window looks down into a gym, full of activity and movement well after the school day has finished. The whole entrance is indicative of the unified feel of the school driven largely by the clarity of the layout and the beautifully detailed timber façades. The school is

KVERNHUSET MIDDLE SCHOOL IN FREDRIKSTAD, NORWAY [Pir II Architects with Duncan Lewis, 2005]
The school is located on the site of a disused quarry. The wooded route leading there makes for a very dramatic entrance.

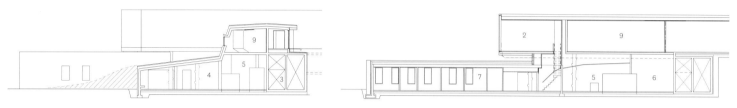

Cross sections

1 Music, drama, dance
2 Cafeteria
3 Air culvert
4 Arts and crafts
5 Hall
6 Storage
7 Administration
8 Drawing studio
9 Library

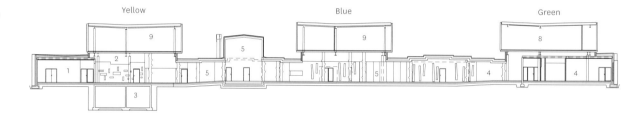

Longitudinal section

The entrance area is a multi-functional space, which is used not only as a point of arrival, but also as a space to sit, talk, play, learn from the surroundings and eat lunch.

full of glimpsed views far into the distance, all of which encourage exploration.

Completely different and even more dramatic is **Kvernhuset Middle School** in Fredrikstad, Norway [Pir II Architects with Duncan Lewis, 2005]. Originally won in a competition with Duncan Lewis in 1998 the school is built in a quarry in Fredrikstad in southern Norway. The site is now wooded and approaching the school offers a wonderfully dramatic entry sequence. Coming towards the school entrance in winter is like walking towards what can only be described as a remote arctic scientific laboratory. The visitor crosses a bridge and enters into a technical-looking glazed tower; the experience is completely different from entering school premises normally. When the snow melts the landscape becomes a rocky wetland. Inside the entrance area, the outside reappears with a pond replete with planting and fish. From here the building opens up to various spaces for mixed use: there is

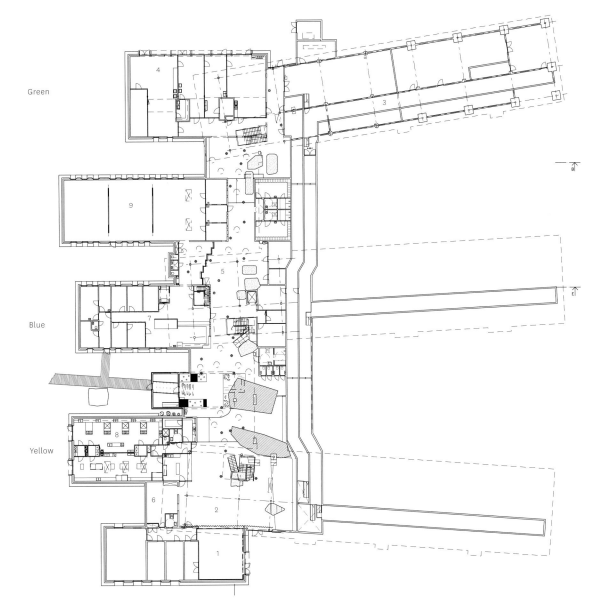

Green

Blue

Yellow

1 Music, drama, dance
2 Cafeteria
3 Air culvert
4 Arts and crafts
5 Hall
6 Storage
7 Administration
8 Home economics
9 Teachers' workrooms

KVERNHUSET MIDDLE SCHOOL / Ground floor plan. The entrance hall is the bridge between the outdoors and learning spaces.

After crossing a bridge and stepping into the building, students unexpectedly enter into a technically looking glazed tower.

At the entrance area one finds different types of rock, which connect the indoors to the outdoors but also to the original use of the site as a quarry – thus incorporating the history of the site and its unique geology and topography into the fabric of the school.

ROC AVENTUS IN APELDOORN, THE NETHERLANDS [Jurgen Bey, Tjep., Tejo Remy and René Veenhuizen with
Kunst en Bedrijf and AGS Architekten & Planners, 2004]
Each department of this vocational school has its own reception and meeting area that opens up to the indoor 'street'.

room to sit, to talk or to learn from the descriptions of types of local stone built into the floors. The entrance becomes a dining room, becomes a stage, becomes a table tennis venue, becomes small tutorial spaces. Looking up towards a teaching laboratory a stuffed badger in a glass case in the wall suggests that is where you go for 'biology' and you can look straight through the glass case into the laboratory. The three wings are colour-coded: the yellow wing is devoted to learning about the use of solar energy, the blue wing focuses on water and the green wing is dedicated to ecology, comprising a greenhouse and biology classrooms.

Entrances to subject areas

It seems obvious that schools should make the most of their entrance spaces to exhibit work and to create informal meeting areas but this is still relatively rare and these spaces often remain without an identity or specific feel. However, the vocational school **ROC Aventus** in Apeldoorn, the Netherlands [Jurgen Bey, Tjep., Tejo Remy and René Veenhuizen with Kunst en Bedrijf and AGS Architekten & Planners, 2004][5] is a brilliant example of how a school can tackle the issue of lack of identity, where both visitors and students cannot distinguish between departments and subjects.

ROC Aventus is situated on a prominent site opposite Apeldoorn's main station and positions itself geographically, politically and commercially at the heart of town

life. The main entrance is light, clear and spacious, located at one end of the main organisational atrium, an indoor 'street', where shops, salons and workshops offer intriguing glimpses of tractors being examined on the one hand and heads being shampooed on the other. This arrangement, with the atrium of the indoor street bringing in natural light and providing visual connection, gives this large building a sense of immediate clarity, transparency and openness. At first floor level, walkways bridge an indoor street, leading to clusters of teaching spaces and facilities divided by subject. The college offers a number of educational options ranging from full-time education for post-18 olds, to day-release apprenticeships and short courses. Many of the short courses are run through a commercial concern, where students learn 'on the job'. Examples of this include a travel agency, hairdressing salon, careers centre and café, all open to the public on a regular basis.

The teenagers arriving at ROC Aventus are leaving mainstream academic school for vocational educational training (VET), and the environment created by the inspirational design makes it a positive and attractive choice. The exceptional design creates the feeling of a new style of facility, bridging academic and on-the-job learning. Each of the subject clusters has its own reception, with an interior reflecting the topic studied in that area. These separate reception areas, with a contemporary, youthful atmosphere created by graphic designers Jurgen Bey,

ROC AVENTUS / In the Optical Nursing area one can see the subject matter reflected in the interiors. The reception area has a carpet with various medical illustrations of eyes printed on it.

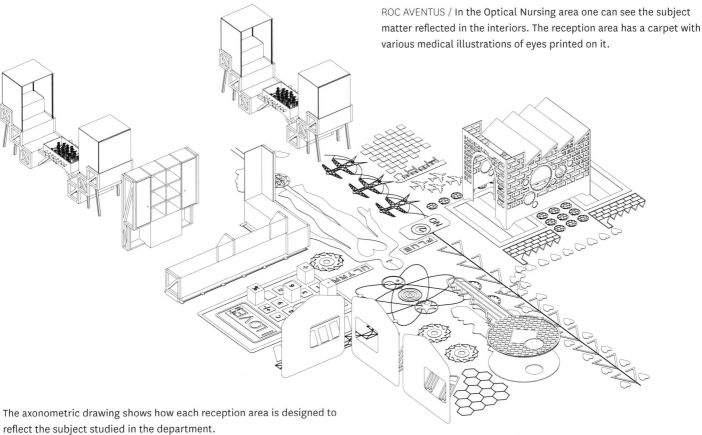

The axonometric drawing shows how each reception area is designed to reflect the subject studied in the department.

Tjep., Tejo Remy and René Veenhuizen, also provide flexible space for break out, individual meetings or discussion in small groups. The spatial arrangement and choice of materials strike a tone somewhere between a modern college and that of a contemporary office, or fashionable shop fit-out. They all encourage activity and ask to be used. More than that, they are intriguing and a talking point. The area for optical nursing has a beautifully crafted reception desk with a graphically printed carpet with the eye drawn in detailed medical perspective. The design department has a meeting area that can be private with the curtains drawn or allowed to be part of the open experience of the entrance - it invites comment on what a meeting space should be like.

Colour and material

Located on a square urban block bounded by four roads, **Joensuu Lyceum** in Joensuu, Finland [Lahdelma and Mahlamäki Architects, 2006] is a primary school for 250 pupils. A windmill-shaped plan form divides the school into four three-storey wings that are connected by a cen-

JOENSUU LYCEUM IN JOENSUU, FINLAND [Lahdelma and Mahlamäki Architects, 2006]
Approaching the building, one might mistake the school for a university building because of its uncommon choice of materials
and crisp treatment of the façades. The central foyer is the first space that greets students when entering the school. The space feels
'grown-up' due to its clean aesthetic, designer furniture and white walls juxtaposed with bright lime green and orange hard surfaces
and glazed balustrades.

tral foyer housing the dining area at ground level with the
main hall above. The crisp lines and sophisticated finishes on both the inside and outside of the building mean
the school could easily be mistaken for a university building. However, the teachers are clear that the children respect this 'grown-up' environment as it makes them feel
like the young adults they are becoming.

Entering the school, the central foyer is immediately
revealed in all its spatial glory, a dramatic and powerful

entrance. However, it is the very materiality and the colours which are outstanding. Each child is provided with
their own full-size locker to store the multiple layers of
outdoor clothing necessary in Finnish winters. The result
of this considered storage is an uncluttered environment that helps to create the mature ambience of the
whole school. The architects have not opted for 'school-
like' primary colours, but a more fashionable palette including lime green and bright orange. The spectacular

JOENSUU LYCEUM / Ground floor plan. This primary school is located on a busy urban block site. The school is arranged around a central foyer that connects the four wings housing the teaching spaces.

0 m   5 m   10 m

colours and the finesse of the detailing, such as the elegant yellow glass balustrades, make the space feel sunny and sophisticated and somewhere to linger.

As one enters the school, the interior finishes, with clean lines, designer furniture and white walls with injections of colour, all contribute to the school's 'grown-up' feel. Colour again is used selectively to identify each wing through large-scale graphics and huge light fittings. The layout of Joensuu Lyceum has been carefully chosen to allow the classrooms to be naturally lit and ventilated. The stepped plan form of each block creates a large surface ensuring that each classroom has glazing in at least two faces to admit as much light as possible in this country of dark winters. Each of the four teaching blocks is

provided with its own ancillary facilities and storage towards the inside of the school, again helping to clarify both the plan and the whole concept of the school and encourage students to respect and enjoy the spaces.

Another colourful example, **Ratoath College** in County Meath, Ireland [McGarry Ní Éanaigh Architects, 2007], was built for approximately 850 pupils from an area of new housing in the community. It is the first significant public building in an undistinguished new area of commuter expansion outside Dublin. The external articulation of the interesting non-orthogonal form clearly defines the entrances, social areas and areas for private learning. The external spaces around the building respond to the mature trees on the site, making the build-

RATOATH COLLEGE, COUNTY MEATH, IRELAND [McGarry Ní Éanaigh Architects, 2007]
A panoramic view of the south facing central entrance which overlooks the enclosed garden. All circulation routes meet at the central entrance, making it the heart of the school.

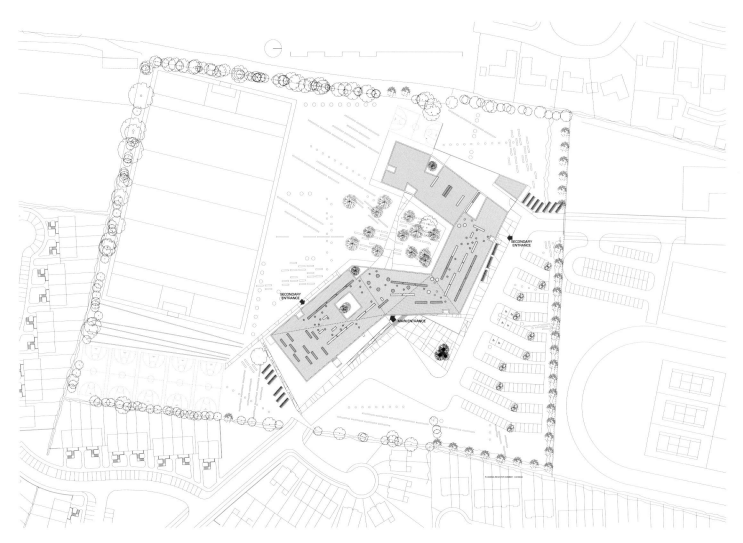

The site plan shows the interesting non-orthogonal layout embracing the mature trees on site whilst defining social areas and entrances to the building.

RATOATH COLLEGE / Cut-outs in the exposed charcoal blockwork give depth to the elevations of the school and bring light into the sports hall and staircases.

Using materials with a rich texture, the fabric of the school prompts children to take notice of their surroundings. Colours are reflected from the roof lights onto the blockwork.

ing very legible from both the outside and the inside. The articulation of both the plan and section produces a silhouette of the building that establishes an appropriate scale contrasting with the neighbouring landscape of smaller two-storey houses. Indentations or cut-outs into the brick form are in exposed charcoal block work and the windows are all timber.

The building provides the stringent Irish Department of Education and Science recommended room layouts in terms of size and adjacencies but uses the circulation and social space to resolve geometries and create an inspiring set of spaces. The main entrance leads directly into the heart of the school which is the focus of all the circulation. The central area is a south facing volume looking into the enclosed garden. The taller volumes are an important contrast with the horizontal organisation of the building and provide vertical and diagonal visual connections from space to space.

The architects were keen to encourage the young students to develop a sense of the materiality and particularly colour. They 'sought to create an environment which linked the formal teaching rooms by means of a fluid joyous social/circulation space characterised by a memorable material quality, colour, culminating in a volume – the heart of the school facing into its garden and the sun.'[6] Colour is used deliberately against a background of

stained blockwork for contrast and to help the children orientate themselves and identify parts of the school. Important locations for colours are the glazed screens between classroom and corridor and the coloured rooflights.

Materials are often under-valued in new school design; here they are used as found: exposed blockwork, reinforced concrete piers and soffits, rendered planes of colour, exposed steel balustrades and benches, precast concrete external seats, exposed pipework etc. The brickwork is recessed in some areas to give depth and to filter light into the sports hall and staircases. This school has cleverly created a better quality and volume of space by using utilitarian materials placed ingeniously and so keeping the building within the Department of Education and Science costs limits for secondary school buildings in Ireland.

Circulation spaces, corridors and service areas

Circulation spaces

At Kvernhuset School, discussed earlier in this chapter, the most popular parts of the school, according to the pupils are the linear spaces outside the tripartite class-

RÅHOLT SECONDARY SCHOOL IN EIDSVOLL, NORWAY [Kristin Jarmund Architects, 2004]
The school is made up of three main learning zones, each centred on a large brightly coloured tower that houses a small auditorium. The towers puncture the roof and filter light deep into the building, making the coloured hard surfaces more playful and vibrant.

rooms for each year group. They form, in essence, a wide circulation corridor, with their own entrance to the outside and racks for outdoor shoes and coats. They also have areas to eat snacks and make hot drinks as well as individual lockers. Each one of these year spaces has a pair of toilets. The materials, particularly the exposed brickwork make the space feel robust and a little external. Only the year group are allowed in this space – others have to be invited into this private domain. There are nearly always children in these spaces. The teachers say that the only problem with these highly successful spaces is that the pupils will not go outside – they prefer to stay inside over the lunch break in these comfortable and friendly spaces.[7]

There are no corridors at all at **Råholt Secondary School** in Eidsvoll, Norway [Kristin Jarmund Architects, 2004] – instead one encounters an open flowing series of spaces. 420 pupils aged 13–15 attend this lower secondary school, conceived as a glazed pavilion floating above the surrounding rural and agricultural landscape. Råholt is an agricultural area located 60km outside Oslo. The need for a secondary school in this area was particularly important due to perceived problems of young people having to travel further afield to go to school. The creation of such a vibrant learning environment is a strong social statement. The architect Kristin Jarmund explained: 'We have built a tiny city covered by a big roof for the youth of this rural community – a real alternative to

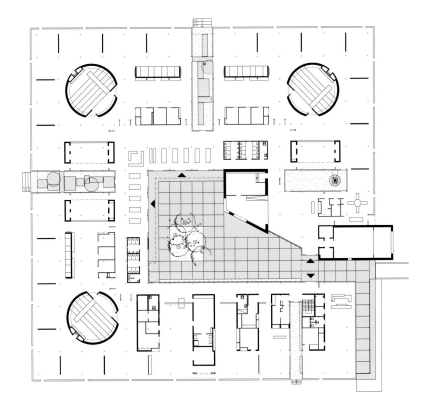

Specialist work areas accommodate the needs of a specific subject; they exist as colourful interventions in the learning zones.

RÅHOLT SECONDARY SCHOOL / Ground floor plan. A perfect square is arranged as a small city around four smaller courtyards and a larger central courtyard.

getting on a train for half an hour, going to Oslo and landing in trouble. We find to our great pleasure that the kids in Råholt take pride in their school and sense that their needs, dreams and ambitions have been taken seriously by educators, politicians and architects alike.'[8]

Råholt Secondary School forms a 75 x 75m 'perfect' square plan with a large central courtyard. Four additional long narrow external courtyards are cut into the structure from the external edge of building. These inverse spaces allow for additional daylight to penetrate deep into the building, flooding it with light. The school is made up of three main learning zones, each with a large elliptical and brightly coloured tower denoting the centrally placed small auditorium in each learning zone. They puncture the roof slab, boldly advertising the contemporary and innovative feel of the school. The building is designed as a village, with houses for teachers, specialist silent working areas and auditoria. There are no formal classrooms, but open learning zones punctuated with colourful insertions that denote specialist work areas. The balance between openness and enclosure is particularly well-organised at Råholt. Specialist areas allow focused learning activities to take place in an appropriate space specifically designed for that purpose. The three auditoria can hold up to 120 pupils and allow a year group to con-

gregate for briefing and multi-media presentations. Small, quiet and intimate workspace 'corrals' allow students to work alone or in small groups, without interruption, allowing the open learning zones to accommodate the natural liveliness of pupils in larger groups. The more open-plan school is still taking time to get used to, with teachers being supported in actively learning how to use the building, how to get the most out of it. It is clear that the teachers have had to adapt their teaching to the new spaces.

The 1175 pupils of **Westminster Academy** in London, UK [Allford Hall Monaghan Morris, 2007] are mostly – over 90% – bilingual and come from a wide ethnic background in a challenged neighbourhood. The global perspective on learning that the school offers, is a celebration of the cultural diversity of the area. The school specialises in global commerce and appears more like a fashionable office development than a learning institution, both in- and outside. The building is squeezed between high-rise tower blocks and a motorway flyover, and its bright green terracotta cladding stripes light up an otherwise harsh urban environment. The architects borrow elements from a range of building types to create a learning environment that feels both professional and playful. According to the teachers, bullying, violence and other misdemeanours

WESTMINSTER ACADEMY IN LONDON, UK [Allford Hall Monaghan Morris, 2007]
The bright green terracotta cladding stripes on the façades create a stark contrast with the urban high-rise blocks and the motorway flyover that surround the school. The main circulation routes open up to the large central atrium. All corridors are visible, reducing theft and other misdemeanors in the school.

have been common in this school. Last year, when the academy was in temporary accommodation up the road, there was nearly always a police car parked outside and even now community police officers are often on the premises. But, according to the police, behaviour has improved since pupils moved into the new building, and this is largely due to its design. The large atrium is an effective security device due to the ample visibility. In addition, pupils' lockers are in very open and visible corridors, which has virtually eradicated theft.

Over-scaled graphics and signage are used both as a learning device in the circulation spaces and as something that gives the whole school its particular character. The development of a graphic identity for the school has been clearly pursued in the building design and through to the school's website. This 'corporate' identity sets the school's agenda as a business organisation that holds its pupils as its key asset. In 2008, the Principal of Westminster Academy, was quoted as follows: 'The kids love the building. It's all been positive so far. They love being able to see who's coming and going; you don't miss anything. Behaviour has improved dramatically. There was always gang warfare going on. This year, though, no problems.'[9]

Toilets

One of the most innovative parts of Westminster Academy are the solutions to some of the more intimate areas of the school. Usually one of the least pleasant spaces in a school, the toilets at Westminster were traditionally associated with vandalism, bad smells and potentially the threat of violence. But these new toilets are well-designed and detailed, creating a 'cared-for' and adult atmosphere. They consist of a long, tiled room with individual cubicles along one side. The toilets are unisex and are individual cubicles with floor-to-ceiling partitions with the stainless steel sink/dryers inside the cubicles. There is a door at either end of the room. If bullies attempt to corner a pupil, the idea is that there is always another exit.

Even more extraordinary are the toilets at **Munkegårdsskolen** in Gentofte, Copenhagen, Denmark [Dorte Mandrup Arkitekter, 2009], Arne Jacobsen's school masterpiece extended underground in 2009 with four glazed courtyards by Dorte Mandrup.[10] According to the architects the extension was designed 'to embrace interaction and diversity and allow students to learn from each other, formally and informally, through the adaptability and flexibility of the learning spaces.'[11] The original school con-

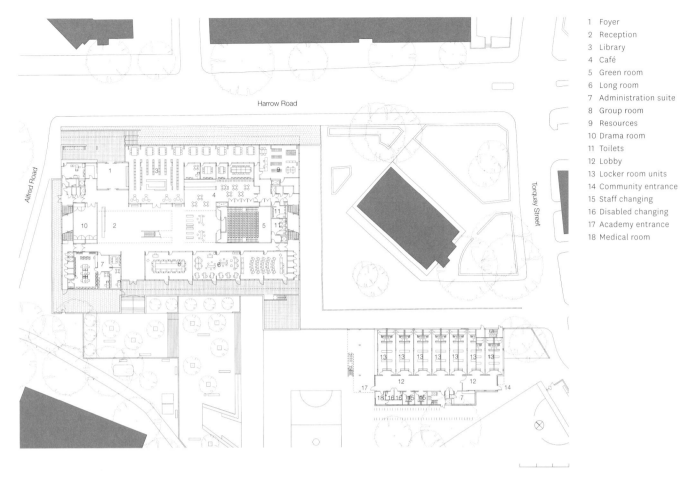

1 Foyer
2 Reception
3 Library
4 Café
5 Green room
6 Long room
7 Administration suite
8 Group room
9 Resources
10 Drama room
11 Toilets
12 Lobby
13 Locker room units
14 Community entrance
15 Staff changing
16 Disabled changing
17 Academy entrance
18 Medical room

WESTMINSTER ACADEMY / Ground floor plan. This large school in central London accommodates 1175 pupils from diverse ethnic backgrounds.

At Westminster Academy, the toilets were designed specifically to deal with the threat of violence and bullying. A door on either side of the toilets provides an escape for students.

The cubicles are assembled next to each other in a long room. Internally each cubicle contains a sink and a dryer. The toilets are tiled and clad with stainless steel creating the appearance of a cared-for space.

MUNKEGÅRDSSKOLEN IN GENTOFTE, DENMARK [Dorte Mandrup Arkitekter, 2009]

Despite the toilets being internal the spaces feel light and vibrant. The architects designed a bright green plastic laminate with a bold botanical graphic that is used for the cubicle walls, doors and the floor.

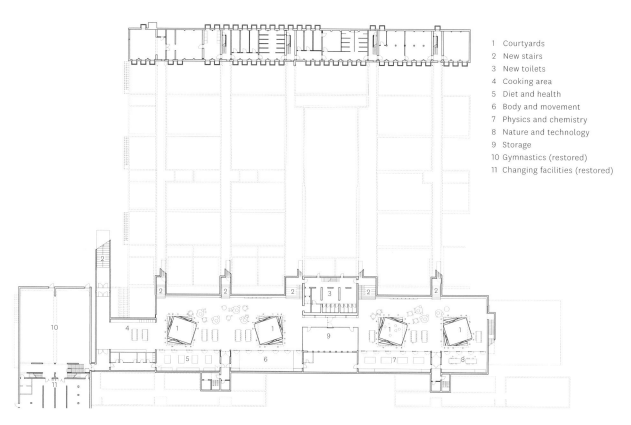

1 Courtyards
2 New stairs
3 New toilets
4 Cooking area
5 Diet and health
6 Body and movement
7 Physics and chemistry
8 Nature and technology
9 Storage
10 Gymnastics (restored)
11 Changing facilities (restored)

Ground floor plan. The school, originally designed by Arne Jacobsen, received an underground extension designed around four 'crystal-like' courtyards that flood the spaces internally with light.

sists of a repeated structure of buildings and courtyards. The new, beautiful, underground extension used this theme, establishing daylight in the parterre plan via four large courtyards, designed as 'crystal-like openings.'

The toilets, however, are internal, without external light to aid the comfort and atmosphere of the space. In order to give them coherence and drama, the cubicle walls, doors and the floor are all made of the same bold, contemporary, rambling botanical design in a bright green plastic laminate. This combined with the well-designed lighting installation makes the toilets feel luxurious and special, one large sculptural form.

Finally the toilets in a school can be a learning space. An internal refurbishment of **Earlham Primary School**

EARLHAM PRIMARY SCHOOL IN FOREST GATE, LONDON, UK [Prue Chiles Architects, 2009]
Two large diagrams on the wall inform students about how water was saved and how energy technologies like photovoltaic panels were used to make the toilets sustainable. The diagrams become three-dimensional with the integration of energy and water meters. Internally the cubicles feature photographs of Epping Forest as well as famous monuments in central London – here Trafalgar Square – which many students in this multi-cultural neighbourhood have never visited.

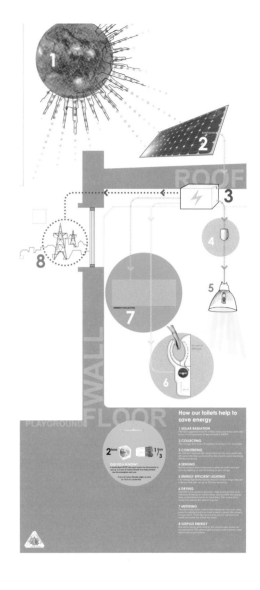

in Forest Gate, London, UK [Prue Chiles Architects, 2009] had sustainability and working with the children as key objectives. Located in a similar gritty, urban and multicultural area as Westminster Academy, Earlham Primary School had some problems of violence and police was often in attendance at the main entrance. The head governor and headteacher were very keen to do something

unique and special for the children and to reorganise the space to make the school feel different with a modest investment.

The toilets were old and inconvenient, and took up a lot of space that could better used. The solution was to open the toilets to the circulation space, make them half the size but with a more rationalised layout. This

EARLHAM PRIMARY SCHOOL / In a series of workshops with the students the design of the toilets was determined. Children wanted the spaces to feel like a part of the nearby forest which inspired the wall panels and the foliage-like roof for the cubicles.

opened up a large space to transform into a much-needed music room. The key aim was to make the new toilets 'sustainable', raising the profile of sustainability and encouraging the children to realise the importance of saving water and using the power of the sun.

The school wanted the children to be involved in the design of the toilets. A model-making exercise to create interesting and imaginative cubicles highlighted how even the inside of a toilet cubicle can be informative and fun. Early discussions with the children established how few had been to central London and the Tower of London, only 12km away. Neither had they been to Epping Forest, the hunting forests of King Henry VIII in the 16th Century, of which Forest Gate is the southern tip.

Thinking about the toilets as a landscape, similar to the toilets at Munkegårdsskolen, the children were keen to make the toilets feel like a forest with a canopy. They were also eager to bring central London into the school,

so photographs of some of the main monuments were commissioned and the favourites chosen for the cubicle doors. Two large graphic wall diagrams explaining how water was being saved and how the photovoltaic panels, visible in the playground, were collecting the energy from the sun, were placed each side of the entrance – water on one side and energy on the other. The graphics become three-dimensional as the energy and water meters become part of the diagram. Understanding the processes still might be difficult for the younger ones without the teachers present but they are a permanent reminder that something is going on. The trough wash-hand basins with energy saving sensors and the eco-hand dryers are fun to use. The toilets are incredibly popular and full of laughing children; they are a colourful and playful way of learning about energy, passing on the lesson in a visible way.

REFERENCES

1 This is well discussed in Prakash Nair and Annalise Gehling, 'Life Between Classrooms: Applying Public Space Theory to Learning Environments', in: *Building Schools for the Future (BSF)*, London: British Council for School Environments, 2010, pp. 26–33.

2 DEGW (for the British Department for Children, Schools and Families), 'Space for Personalised Learning', 2010. Cf. http://www.bdonline.co.uk/degw%E2%80%99s-personalised-learning-research-project/5000988.article. Accessed 26 August 2014.

3 The SKUB programme is explained in Introduction: Perspectives on New School Building, pp. 16–17.

4 The Parque Escolar programme is discussed in Introduction: Perspectives on New School Building, p. 16.

5 This school is also discussed in chapter 1, From Ideas for Learning to Architectural Form, pp. 32–33 and in chapter 10, Furniture and Equipment in Learning Spaces, pp. 221–224.

6 From McGarry Ni Eanaigh Architects' website. http://www.mcgnie.ie. Accessed 15 March 2014.

7 Based on authors' visit to school in 2009 and discussions with teachers and pupils.

8 http://www.docstoc.com/docs/50544949/Raholt-Secondary-School-Eidsvoll-Norway

9 S. Rose, 'Big Green Teaching Machine', *The Guardian*, 7 January 2008.

10 This school is also discussed in chapter 9, Refurbishment and Extension of Existing Schools, pp. 198–201.

11 From Dorte Mandrup Arkitekter's website. http://www.dortemandrup.dk. Accessed 15 March 2014.

Summary

6 LEARNING OUTSIDE THE CLASSROOM

1. A school with pupils everywhere, with movement and activity and a sense of openness is becoming more desirable. **Central atria, wide staircases with places to linger** as well as more intimate spaces are integral parts of today's learning environments.

2. **Incidental spaces in schools** often go unnoticed or are forgotten about; they are under-utilised or simply not prioritised in the design and use of the school. Used well, they can transform a school and provide places for learning and socialising.

3. New and existing schools can develop a physical environment which supports a more **student-led, personalised approach to learning**. It is often the informal, incidental spaces that provide the best learning places.

4. **Entrance spaces** are the first thing the visitor and the pupils see as they enter a school and are vital to the image of a school and the possibility of exhibiting what the school has to offer; they need to be welcoming, spacious and inspiring.

5. **Corridors and other circulation spaces** are an opportunity to create small intimate spaces to meet and work in small groups. Colour used deliberately adds contrast and stimulation and can help the children orientate themselves and identify parts of the school.

6. **Toilets** are often a good indicator of the design quality and innovation in a school building and can inspire children to learn. They can provide a moment of glamour as well as safety.

7. **Materials** are often under-valued in new school design; but materiality is vital to create interest and provide a quality environment. Utilitarian materials used cleverly can create a better quality of space and keep the building within the required costs limits.

7 Learning in the Landscape / HOWARD EVANS

This chapter focuses on how we can use our school grounds to enhance both a school's place within its community and a child's learning experience. For many of us, our experience of a school playground is limited to a sea of flat, cracked, grey tarmac surrounding the main school building; the tarmac was in turn bounded by a wide plain of flat mown grass. These unappealing expanses were animated seasonally by goal posts or athletics equipment and a seemingly random array of white painted lines. For a lucky few these barren wildernesses were punctuated by lone trees or raised brick planters filled with compacted soil and unidentifiable shrubs. It is these sights that are often the first experience a visitor has of a school. And yet there are examples around the world that illustrate a wide array of landscape interventions that set the identity of the school within its community, create spaces that support teaching activities and encourage uses that sometimes even define the form of the buildings. Good exterior spaces and playgrounds, however, are still rarer than good new school buildings.

JARDIN EL PORVENIR KINDERGARTEN IN BOGOTÁ, COLOMBIA [Giancarlo Mazzanti Arquitectos, 2009]
The school provides a place of stability within the densely populated shanty town.

HALLFIELD PRIMARY SCHOOL IN LONDON, UK [Denys Lasdun, 1952]
This modernist icon and listed building embraced the idea of an 'external classroom'.

Learning outside: using the school landscape

In the early 20th century the Open Air School movement in Europe developed a series of schools, such as the Open Air School in Suresnes, France [Eugène Beaudouin, 1931], that embraced the idea of schools connecting as closely as possible with the external environment to immerse the children in the health giving properties of clean air. The main buildings and classroom pavilions maximise the relationship between the inside and the outside, be that visual or physical. The walls of the classroom were highly glazed and able to slide away, creating a seamless link between classroom and the outdoor environment. Weather permitting, daily rest periods took place on sun decks on top of the classrooms which were accessed via the covered walkways. In between and around the buildings the premises are like a park with varied mature trees and areas of soft landscape and grass. In this school the built fabric becomes part of the external landscape by using the roofs, the walls, the windows and the covered areas all as part of the education experience. Although such total immersion in the outdoors was relatively short lived as an educational pedagogy, the idea of learning in outdoor environments has continued to be revisited over the decades. Hans Scharoun's famous unrealised Darmstadt School plan of 1951 proposed that each classroom had its own dedicated sheltered external courtyards. These courtyard gardens provided small-scale protected areas for the younger children and larger interconnected learning spaces for older children and separated sports provision as part of the wider campus. This enabled the landscape to respond and reinforce the scale and identity of the various parts of the school. This idea was explored in **Hallfield Primary School** in London, UK [Denys Lasdun, 1952] Is playful, intimate and sophisticated. A long and curved building has single-storey pavilions and outside classroom spaces. the infant classrooms were to feel like a 'home from home'.[1] The intimate courtyard spaces

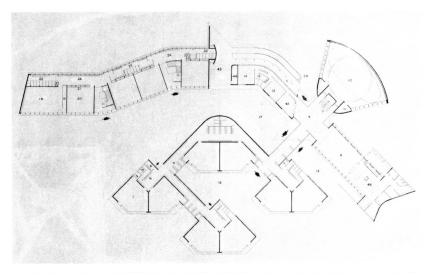

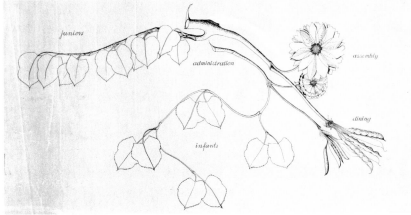

HALLFIELD PRIMARY SCHOOL / Lasdun's concept took its cue from the structure of a plant: the classrooms are arranged like leaves on a branch, the central hall is the flower and the dining hall is located where the seed pods are.

provide a secure play-space more akin to a domestic garden than school grounds. The concept of an 'external classroom' that enables a class to relocate to learn in a less formal environment or the ability to open the classroom out to embrace the external environment has become increasingly popular.

Recent examples of successful external school environments in the UK do exist but these are typically small-scale projects rather than larger and more holistic schemes like Hallfield Primary School. Whilst a whole campus design was often considered as part of the UK Building Schools for the Future programme, these schemes are rarely realised to their fullest potential. Examples with a successful holistic concept are, however, beginning to emerge: they immerse the school into its site and offer a wealth of experience to both the school and the wider community.

It is not by accident that in the UK, private sector schools often make the most of the Georgian or Victorian landscape legacy surrounding their buildings where the maturity of the planting and grand approaches down tree-lined avenues offer an image of solidity, experience and excellence. Indeed at Stowe School in Stowe, Buckinghamshire, UK, a leading public school that utilises a former country house and its wider landscape, there is a sense of pride in the architectural and landscape legacy that includes work by some of the greatest historical figures in the history of British architecture and landscape design: Sir John Vanbrugh, William Kent, James Gibbs, Robert Adam, Thomas Pitt and Sir John Soane. Stowe was the former seat of the Dukes of Buckingham, and the current house dates back to 1711. The landscape was Capability Brown's first major commission, dating to the 1740s. This is an extreme case but the significance of a school landscape is becoming increasingly important in the education of our children in the 21st century.

'School grounds are an invaluable resource and should be inspirational environments for playing and learning, not neglected after-thoughts,' said Catherine Andrews, chief executive of Learning Through Landscape, a UK

KANTONSSCHULE ENGE UND FREUDENBERG IN ZURICH, SWITZERLAND [Jacques Schader, 1959]
A series of terraces is set in an extensive mature landscape. The site plan shows how footpaths connect the school grounds with the urban surroundings.

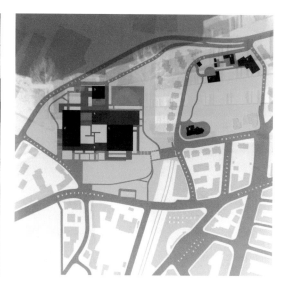

charity dedicated to enhancing outdoor learning and play for children. 'Yet most new secondary schools are failing to transform their outdoor space.'[2]

As land values and financial pressures faced by schools to maintain and improve their facilities increase, the school estate can be seen as a potentially valuable asset. The transformation of school grounds is often seen as a lower priority than that of its building stock but surely this should not be the case.

'As a society, we recognise that our young people are being offered ever fewer opportunities for safe, challenging and collaborative play. Lack of these opportunities can lead to health issues, apathy, social and behavioural issues. School grounds can help raise achievement and self-esteem, improve behaviour and health, and help children and young people develop a wide range of skills.'[3]

A community playground

Schools often occupy one of the largest areas of open green space within a community. They have the potential to form a crucial environmental resource, both ecologically and socially. Keeping school grounds open can be a difficult line for a school to tread, often the wider campus is surrounded by a high security fence, hindering movement through a neighbourhood and preventing the school from becoming the heart of a community.[4]

There are countries like Switzerland where the school grounds are open outside school hours to the wider public as a shared amenity space. **Kantonsschule Enge und Freudenberg in Zurich**, Switzerland [Jacques Schader, 1959] is an example of the success of this policy.

The buildings of both schools, set in a now mature landscape, emerge from an urban parkland setting. The extensive school grounds shared by the schools are connected via footpaths to the surrounding city fabric and to adjacent transport links. The building consists of a series of terraces located on the slope of a hill. Light wells punctuate the upper terrace allowing for light penetration deep into the semi-subterranean spaces such as the sports halls. Wide stairs effortlessly link the different levels. Narrow ramps and stairs wrap themselves around trees, further embedding the school into the landscape. The ensemble is capped by two modernist pavilions whose mass is separated from the upper terrace level by a glazed podium, ensuring that the landscape is visible from within the building.

Many schools across the world now have shared community facilities, forming a greater pivotal role within the neighbourhood. A more holistic approach considers the size and position of the school grounds within a community, potentially forming a more rewarding relationship between both parties. The benefits extend beyond merely improving the physical context to potentially bettering social and health aspects of a community as well.

'Improving physical environments can greatly increase young people's opportunities for health, particularly by removing the barriers to participation in physical activity and by reducing the risks of injury. Multi-sectoral attention to this issue is particularly important in low-income communities, as children and adolescents from such communities may face greater environmental risks and have fewer opportunities for physical activity. Schools

JARDIN EL PORVENIR KINDERGARTEN IN BOGOTÁ, COLOMBIA [Giancarlo Mazzanti Arquitectos, 2009]

The geometric building form creates landscapes for play on both sides of its boundaries.

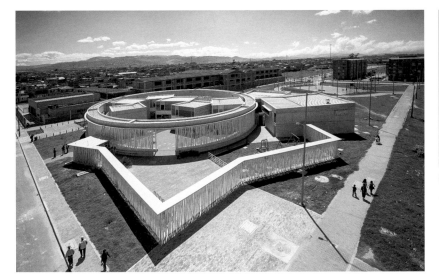

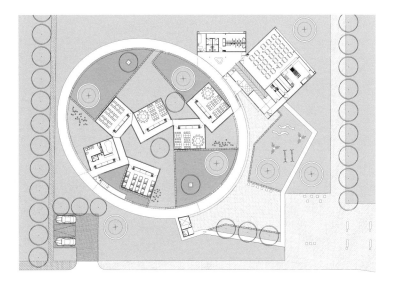

The site plan shows that the building and landscape are conceived as one.

Landscape creeps between the building forms.

The layered perimeter wall acts as security, defines spaces and also provides shaded area for play.

ROMMEN SKOLE & KULTURSENTER IN OSLO, NORWAY [L2 Arkitektur with Østengen og Bergo, 2010]
The building and the contoured roofs are considered as part of the landscape and the sedum roofs merge into the wooded surroundings. Play equipment for different ages is integrated between the building and green landscape.

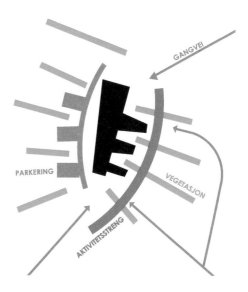

Conceptual plan showing the relationship between soft landscape, hard landscape and building.

and communities have an important role to play in boosting the protective factors associated with positive environments and physical activity.'[5]

Located in one of the city's shanty town suburbs, **Jardin El Porvenir Kindergarten** in Bogotá, Colombia [Giancarlo Mazzanti Arquitectos, 2009] seeks at once to raise community aspirations, provide sports facilities within the neighbourhood whilst also creating a refuge for the children, directly addressing the issues raised by the

World Health Organisation. In this project, Mazzanti Arquitectos have created a building as a symbol for urban regeneration and a boost for social change. The significance of the boundary treatment is a key driver to the project. Much of the plot of land in which the school is built remains open to the community, creating a much-needed green lung to the dense urban grain of the shanty town. The school buildings are wrapped in a ring of tall white angled columns that form a sheltered colonnade, giving the school its striking identity. The treatment of the wrap as a sculptural element erodes the negative connotations of typical boundary conditions. The angled columns afford views into and out of the play spaces reinforcing the link between community and school. Although the school is secure, a continuous bench around the exterior of the colonnade allows the whole neighbourhood to come right up to the building perimeter and use the benches, making the most of all the open space surrounding the school.

A single larger element housing the school hall breaks this ringed colonnade and is in turn wrapped in a more angular screen that forms both a secure entrance courtyard and gives access to the school hall. This outer courtyard means that the local community can use the school hall without entering the main educational spaces out of school hours. Within the ring, the classrooms are created by a series of angled cubes. The interstitial space then creates a sequence of play spaces, streets and sheltered wooded courtyards. The play spaces adjacent to each class space are simple flat areas that are linked to the architecture by the use of bold graphics and animated by light and shadows cast by angled columns of the wrap.

Topography and existing soft landscape

A good school should develop its grounds to provide learning opportunities that support core curriculum aims. The grounds should be ecologically diverse and stimulating environments, closely related to the topography and the natural surroundings. Scandinavian schools are particularly adept at realising strong links to the external environment. This is partly a cultural phenomenon in countries where citizens have close relationships with nature and the outdoors. The work of landscape architects such as Østengen og Bergo in Norway illustrates a sensitivity towards integrating building and landscape as well as acknowledging the potential to create environments that both stimulate creative play and physical ac-

tivity. The close collaboration between architect and landscape architect at **Rommen Skole & Kultursenter** in Oslo, Norway [L2 Arkitektur with Østengen og Bergo, 2010] has resulted in a new school and community facility that responds to the surrounding landscape whilst creating school grounds that are as much part of the educational environment as the classrooms.

The building sits on a north-south axis allowing the landscape to flow from the wooded hills and ravines to the west of the site to the community to the east. Many of the mature trees on site were preserved and have been augmented by new planting that extend right into the alternating fingers of landscape and building. The landscape fingers reach deep into the building plan and have been furnished with a variety of informal seating, play equipment and timber decks that respond to the age groups taught within the adjacent building finger. The timber decks form outdoor classrooms and are equipped with outdoor digital equipment. Access to the school makes the most of the surrounding topography to create a variety of experiences as well as to respond to the needs of differing age groups attending the school. A more direct path leads up the hill towards the end of the school housing the older students and the community library. Contrasting with this, a low-gradient wheelchair-accessible path winds its way up towards the end of the school housing the kindergarten.

The greening of the school campus also extends to how site drainage is controlled. The roof of the school is highly visible from the surrounding housing and roads and its tilting forms have been planted with sedum mats that help to reduce the run-off from the school's large roof area and that accentuate the relationship between building and landscape. The water from the large parking areas is collected in planted swales that feed into a large overflow pond. The holistic approach to the building, site design and the landscape has provided both the school and the local community with a considered and well-resolved learning resource.

EVELYN GRACE ACADEMY IN BRIXTON, LONDON, UK [Zaha Hadid Architects with Gross Max Landscape Architects, 2010] With limits on space the running track shoots through the school buildings. Buildings and walkways are orientated to overlook the school's sports fields.

Recreation and sport

Large areas of grass dedicated to sports provision are not always available to schools. Even when they are, as seen previously at Rommen Skole, they should be integrated carefully with a wider landscape strategy. New thinking on how sports and recreational activities are undertaken have led to some interesting recent explorations. Hampden Gurney Primary School sold its playground to partially fund the construction of a new school. Its recreational and educational facilities have been consolidated

onto a tight urban site where vertically stacked play decks face onto the street. The Thomas Deacon Academy added a further dimension in the debate over the importance of recreational space. The headteacher of the academy saw the academy as providing a 'maximum learning' environment whilst reflecting that the public 'recognises that youngsters can play in their own time'[6]. In structuring the lessons into longer, more consolidated blocks 'break time' is removed. The school is not without grounds and boasts a comprehensive array of sporting

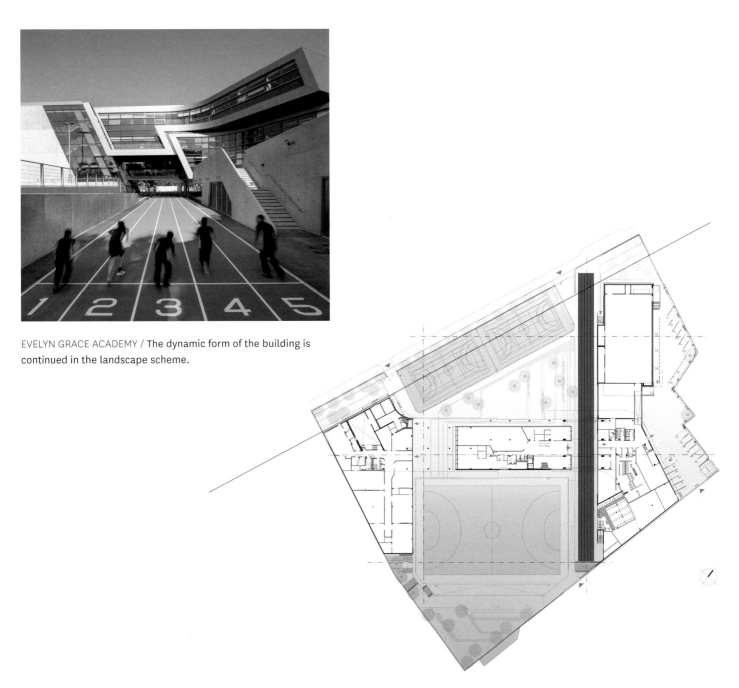

EVELYN GRACE ACADEMY / The dynamic form of the building is continued in the landscape scheme.

Ground floor plan. The school's outdoor sporting facilities are cleverly knitted into this inner city school campus.

facilities and extra-curricular activities. The more business-like structuring of the school day does raise questions over the importance of recreation time and space. Tim Gill, former director of 'The Children's Play Council' (now 'Play England') sees the over-structuring of the school day as problematic: 'That seems to me to be extremely damaging in the long term because children need to have some time where they take responsibility and they make everyday decisions about what they're doing.'[7]

Although the two above examples are perhaps at the extreme end of the scale, both acknowledge the importance of learning environments that are not classroom-based. At the **Evelyn Grace Academy** in Brixton, London, UK [Zaha Hadid Architects with Gross Max Landscape Architects, 2010] we see perhaps the best compromise to the above issues. The school sits on a tight urban site, pinned between two roads. The building itself bears many of the Zaha Hadid Architects hallmarks in its striking isometric architecture; in line with its academy status, the school's outward appearance seeks to set aspirations high. One of its most striking features is the running track that bisects the site and carves its way through the building. The building brings together four smaller schools on to one site. The facilities needed as

GAMMEL HELLERUP SECONDARY SCHOOL IN GENTOFTE, DENMARK [Bjarke Ingels Group – BIG, 2013]
Responding to the brief for a new indoor sports hall, BIG set the hall at the heart of the school, at 5m underground. All surrounding buildings have subterranean access to the hall.

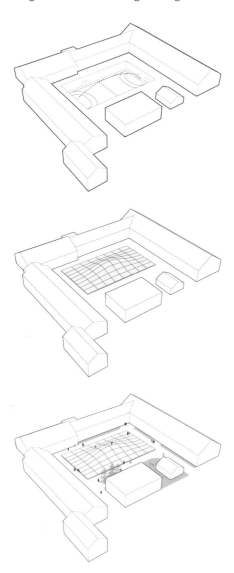

An internal view of the sports hall in use. The hall is lit naturally, as the roof has glazing along its perimeter and its surface is also perforated with glazing, connecting the inside spaces to the outside spaces.

Clad in timber, the roof creates a strong visual identity for the school, whilst combining sporting, learning and social interaction in a single element.

such for the enlarged school are increased, putting more pressure on how the site is used. The solution is elegant and well resolved. The building cuts across the site as a shallow Z-shape with single-storey elements running perpendicular to this, forming bookends at either end of the site. Enclosed within these arms, facing onto the street fronts are sports and multi-use pitches. The aforementioned running track cuts from one side of the site to the other. The track doubles as the main entrance path,

providing a sense of direction and perhaps urgency to those arriving at the school. The external space is not wholly dedicated to sports provision. Steps flow up the sloping geometry of the school, forming terraces and play spaces at roof level whilst a small horticulture garden occupies the southern corner of the site. Through careful planning, the site's potential has been maximised.

At **Gammel Hellerup Secondary School** in Gentofte, Denmark [Bjarke Ingels Group – BIG, 2013] the ar-

GAMMEL HELLERUP SECONDARY SCHOOL / Placed at the centre of the school, the curved roof of the hall turned into a social gathering space. It provides seating for social interaction and small group learning.

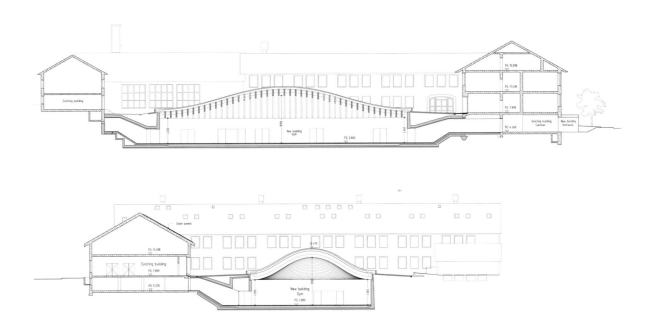

Longitudinal and cross section. The sports hall was placed below grade to avoid overshadowing the surrounding buildings, as well as to create a strong core for the school.

chitects have responded to the brief to provide a new indoor sports area by placing the hall in the centre of the school courtyard.[8] BIG's rationale for this move of putting the sports hall at the heart of the school was to avoid dispersing the campus further. Rather than losing the courtyard as a recreational and social space, the hall is set 5m down into the ground and accessed via subterranean connections from the existing school buildings. The roof to the hall is then used to create a gathering space that supports social and outdoor learning opportunities. A sliver of glazing runs around the perimeter of the roof, connecting inside and outside spaces as well as providing natural light to the underground space. The edge of the roof doubles as a seat around the perimeter of the hall before bulging out of the ground to form an altered topography in the middle of the school campus. The dome of the roof responds to the parabola of an item thrown inside the hall. Externally the roof is clad in timber

UTTERSLEV SCHOOL IN COPENHAGEN, DENMARK [KHR Arkitekter, 2006]
The school buildings are organised around a canal which runs through the site and is used as a learning and teaching tool.
On the canal, timber jetties provide the opportunity for the children to interact with the water and wildlife. Bottom: A pergola
running between the classrooms and the landscape mediates between the inside and outside.

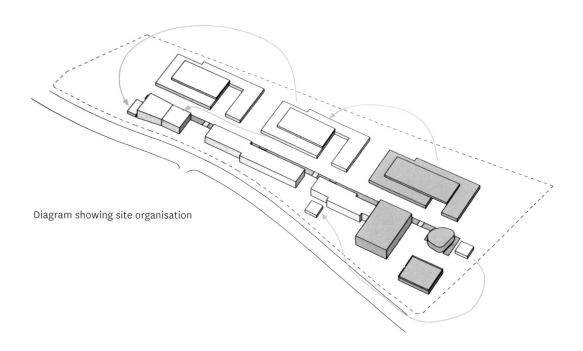

Diagram showing site organisation

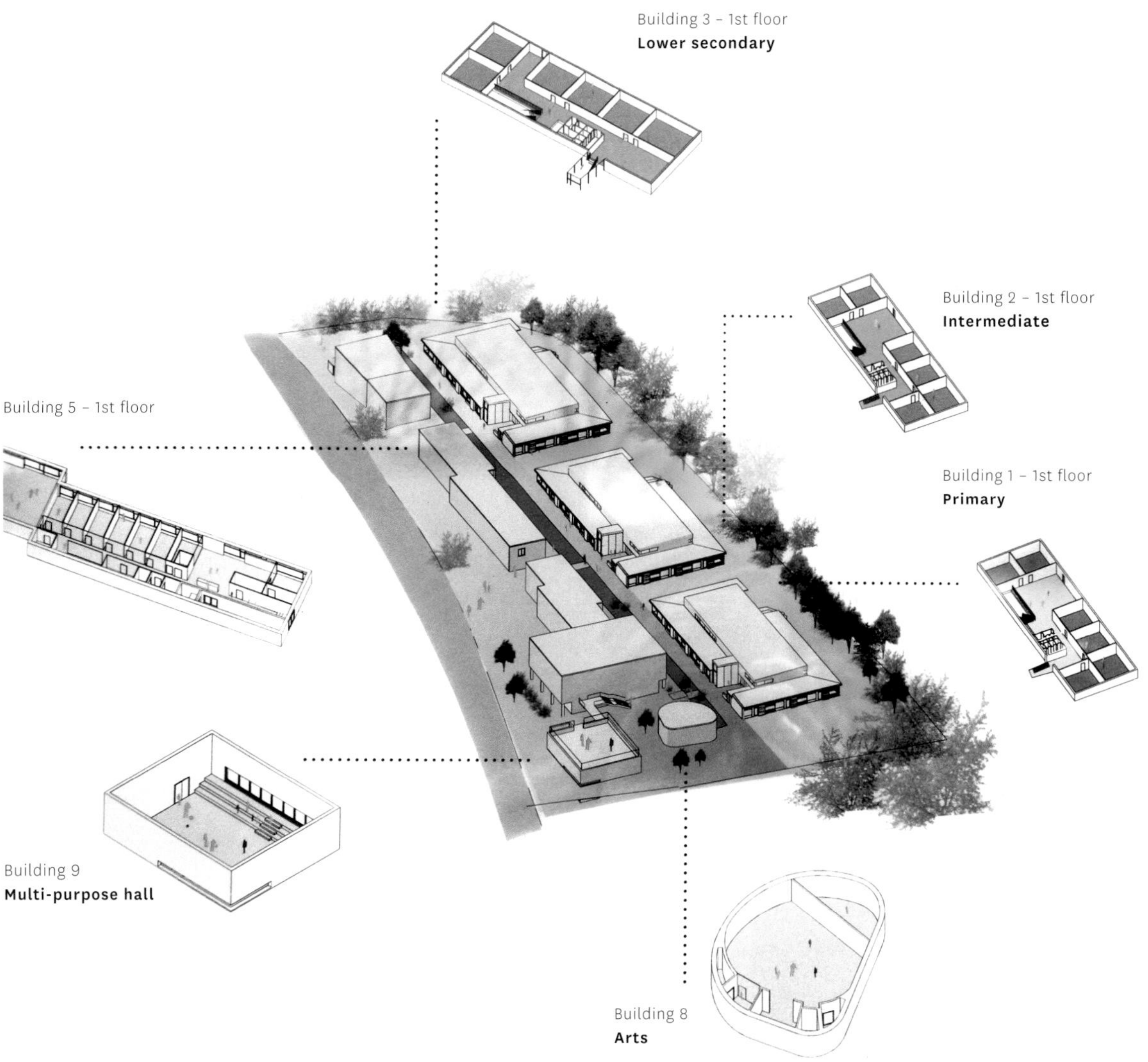

Building 3 – 1st floor
Lower secondary

Building 2 – 1st floor
Intermediate

Building 5 – 1st floor

Building 1 – 1st floor
Primary

Building 9
Multi-purpose hall

Building 8
Arts

UTTERSLEV SCHOOL / Diagram showing the make-up and spatial organisation of the school. The main circulation route follows the canal.

and a series of seats and benches form spaces for social interaction or small group learning. The scheme shows how a creative response to the requirement for more space can integrate sporting, learning and social needs as well as resulting in a strong visual identity for the school.

Teaching in the landscape

Outdoor classrooms are often seen as a beneficial addition to the school environment but it is important to understand how and why they might be used. In the UK, in 2006, the Department for Education and Skills published a manifesto for 'Learning Outside the Classroom' that aimed to deal with agendas such as remote learning and outdoor classrooms. In research undertaken for the Royal Horticultural Society teachers noted 'working in the garden gave them an arena in which they could encourage pupils to become active and independent learners'.[9] Certainly, it has been noted that use of external space and gardening 'can expand pupils' awareness of the natural world and promote their cognitive, social and personal development'.[10] With the right support a wide spectrum of the curriculum can be taught in outdoor classrooms. In the same research, it has been stated: 'The evidence from the ten case-study schools suggests that a significant amount of learning can take place in the garden, encompassing all curriculum areas (such as maths, science, languages, the humanities, personal, social, health and economic education and the arts) and a range of verbal, oral and personal and social skills'.[11]

School gardens are often seen as a feature oriented towards primary education but their significance at secondary level should not be overlooked. 'While younger children also have a variety of other play spaces, the importance of school grounds to teenagers is heightened by the fact that the 12–19 age group are one of the sectors of the population who are least likely to use public green spaces such as parks'.[12] Concerns over maintenance, budgetary constraints and health and safety issues are often cited as reasons that more creative provision is not made at secondary school level. The World Health Organisation has identified however that secondary schools are often better at providing structured physical activity. In a study of Norwegian schools, the following was noted: 'Secondary schools seemed more successful when physical activity was integrated into the teaching schedule and was used as a pedagogical method for learning.'[13]

Schools such as Kingoskolen in Slangerup, Denmark[14] prove that creative approaches to the design of school grounds can be informed by a strong pedagogical imperative and used to enhance both the school's identity and learning environment.

Utterslev School in Copenhagen, Denmark [KHR Arkitekter, 2006] was the first new school to be built in Copenhagen in 25 years. The linear nature of the site has been accentuated by a canal that cuts through the heart of the school, linking two major green spaces, Utterslev Square and Bispebjerg Cemetery. The building form lines either side of the canal forming a school that is both protective and yet an openly accessible cultural institution within the community. The landscape and school buildings make constant reference to the school's pedagogical interests in science and natural sciences. The canal collects rainwater from the roofs and provides a hands-on teaching aid: the plants attract wildlife and small locks in the canal create pools with fish in them, thus functioning as a science discovery centre. The school's main circulation route is intertwined with the canal and gives access to the lower school class blocks on one side and administration and shared spaces on the other. The circulation route is partially shaded by a planted pergola that links the three main blocks, creating a solid sense of proportion and unity to the site. Each classroom opens out into the school grounds forging a strong link between indoor and outdoor teaching. As a recreation space, the canal is used to reinforce ideas of learning through play. Utterslev School shows how landscape can be used creatively to benefit both school and the wider community.

REFERENCES

1   William Curtis, *Denys Lasdun: Architecture, City, Landscape*, London: Phaidon, 1994, p. 44.

2   'BSF grounds lag behind buildings', *Building Design*, 12 October 2007.

3   Play England, Play Sector Briefing, August 2007, (Department for Education and Skills, 2006:7).

4   This issue is explored in chapter 4, Schools and the Community.

5   'Socio-environmentally Determined Health Inequities Among Children and Adolescents', World Health Organisation, 2010, p. 4.

6   'No Playground for Super School', BBC News, 6 May 2007, http://news.bbc.co.uk/1/hi/england/cambridgeshire/6629655.stm. Accessed 5 November 2013.

7   Ibid.

8   'Gammel Hellerup Sports Hall by BIG', *Dezeen*, 28 June 2013. http://www.dezeen.com/2013/06/28/gammel-hellerup-gymnasium-sports-hall-by-big/. Accessed 5 November 2013.

9   R. Passy, M. Morris, F. Reed, 'Impact of Gardening on Learning', Final Report Submitted to the Royal Horticultural Society. National Foundation for Educational Research, 2010, p. 19.

10 Ibid, p. 4.

11 Ibid, p. 46.

12 B. Chillman, 'Do School Grounds have a Value as an Educational Resource in the Secondary Sector?' Sussex University – Learning through Landscapes, p. 3.

13 'Socio-environmentally Determined Health Inequities Among Children and Adolescents', World Health Organisation, 2010, p. 132.

14 The school is described in chapter 2, Nature, Ecology and Environmental Design, pp. 51–53.

Summary

7 LEARNING IN THE LANDSCAPE

1. **Establishing an identity**; many school buildings are set within a wider site. The interstitial band of landscape between the site and building entrances can be used to set the tone of the school's aspirations.
2. Many school buildings share resources with the local community. The World Health Organisation recognises that the **importance of sharing facilities** should extend to the grounds as well.
3. **Topography is important**. Careful consideration of the integration between building and its topography can define the physical built environment as well as impact on teaching pedagogies.
4. Working with the physical environment, **a holistic approach to the building of a school** and its surroundings can bring significant ecological benefits.
5. **Careful integration of sport and recreation facilities** can provide pupils with important access to external space even on the tightest of urban sites.
6. By improving teaching links with the school grounds, **learning in the landscape can cover all curriculum bases**. In this way, grounds can be designed to support creative learning throughout the school experience, whether this is cerebral or physical.
7. **Not all learning experiences need to be formal**. A school landscape is the perfect environment in which to support informal learning and those students who respond positively to being outside the classroom. By providing stimulating environments, creative play in recreation periods is facilitated, enhancing the student learning experience.

8 Special Schools should be Special / LEO CARE

This chapter addresses how school design for children with special educational needs is approached, either through specialist facilities for children with a specific disability or looking at how a mainstream school can be designed to be equitable for a diverse range of student needs.

Children with Special Educational Needs (SEN), whether mentally or physically disabled, are one of the most marginalised groups in the world. According to UNESCO: 'Of the 75 million children of primary school age who are out of school, one third are children with disabilities.'[1] This means that in the 21st century children with disabilities make up the world's largest and most disadvantaged minority. In developing countries, providing decent schools and education for able students is a challenge; young people with disabilities often struggle to even get to school, let alone have access to facilities that are designed to help them with their personal learning requirements. Within this 'at risk' group, girls with disabilities are perhaps the most neglected of all, with few educational opportunities. In 1994, a World Conference on Special Needs Education in Spain, developed the Salamanca Statement. Article 55 highlighted the plight of young women: 'Girls with disabilities are doubly disadvantaged. A special effort is required to provide training and education for girls with special educational needs.'[2]

Recently some exceptional schools have been built that have developed thoughtful and inspiring facilities for children with special needs – the group that clearly deserves our most special architecture.

STEPHEN GAYNOR SCHOOL IN NEW YORK, USA [Rogers Partners (previously Rogers Marvel Architects), 2008]
The school shares spaces and facilities with Ballet Hispanico, so children can interact with the dancers and other visitors on a daily basis, which the teaching staff regard as a crucial element to the children's personal development.

Mainstream or special schools?

In 2006, the United Nations prepared a convention on the rights of persons with disabilities, that member states were invited to sign up to. The convention came into force in 2008 and by 2013, 138[3] nation states had ratified the convention. Article 24 asserts that 'persons with disabilities can access an inclusive, quality and free primary education and secondary education on an equal basis with others in the communities in which they live; reasonable accommodation of the individual's requirements is provided; persons with disabilities receive the support required, within the general education system, to facilitate their effective education.'[4]

However, the convention also recognises that for children with certain disabilities, mainstream education may be inappropriate: 'Ensuring that the education of persons, and in particular children, who are blind, deaf or deaf-blind, is delivered ... in environments which maximise academic and social development.'[5] The convention suggests that the preference of individual families [of children with disabilities] should be taken into consideration. This poses a number of challenges to teachers, schools and authorities in terms of the support that they can offer on a one-off or ongoing basis. The effect of Article 24 has been felt around the world, with a range of national approaches to its implementation.

Countries vary substantially in the extent to which they include students with disabilities in mainstream schools or in special schools, and whether they mainly use special classes within mainstream schools or students are integrated into regular classes. 'This is a difficult area in which values as well as empirical evidence are strongly contested.'[6]

The in-between option is to have a special school co-located with a mainstream school. Co-located schools are often considered to offer the best of both worlds, but they are by no means without their own complications in design and delivery: 'Half our children go to some lessons in the mainstream school, and loads of their young-sters come over to us every day to help with classes. They look at what our children achieve, and learn to have respect for them. This is quite a deprived part of Eastbourne, but we've never had one incident of bullying. We share the same uniform and we join in on school trips.'[7]

The school design zeitgeist has moved away from a 'one-size-fits-all' approach for SEN pupils to a student-led design and pedagogy. This is clearly a big step forward as the umbrella term of special educational needs hides a vast array of disabilities. 'Special needs is just an administrative category ... The only thing these kids have in common is that they've been labelled "special needs".'[8] In design terms a stand-alone special needs school often caters for children with a specific problem and requires a well-informed response. A school for visually impaired children may be characterised by an interior that has high-contrast coloured surfaces and a range of textured, interactive elements, designed to aid way finding and to provide a sensory environment. Such an approach would be inappropriate for a school that supports students on the autistic spectrum, who may find the colours and textures distracting. In an inclusive school, SEN facilities are required to offer broader support and have built-in flexibility. This often leads to a less distinctive architecture and design.

One of the key aims for children with severe learning difficulties is to help them get to a point where they can play a meaningful and fulfilling role in society. Failing this, students are taught to become as self-reliant as they can. Life skills are a key component in all schools, but an added emphasis on day-to-day abilities means that special schools have a more homely design rather than the institutional or office-like design that mainstream schools possess. The scale of the architecture is often reduced, as part of the aim to make a school feel close to home, but also because of the reduced number of students. Providing design standards and guidance for SEN schools is particularly difficult because of specialist requirements. A good brief for the building is critical, the client and potential users of the building need to be fully in-

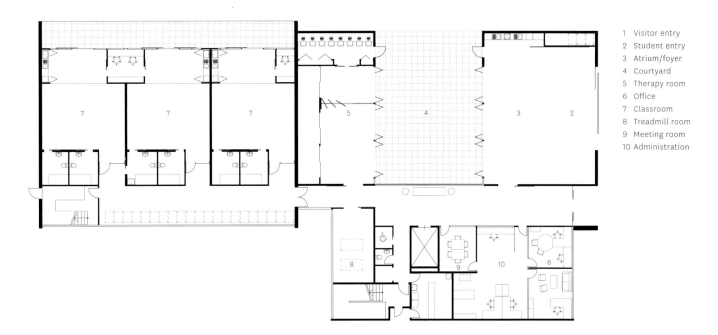

1   Visitor entry
2   Student entry
3   Atrium/foyer
4   Courtyard
5   Therapy room
6   Office
7   Classroom
8   Treadmill room
9   Meeting room
10 Administration

volved at every stage to lead the process so that the needs of each specific group are fully understood.

Legibility

Whilst some countries have had special schools since the 18th century[9], in many developed countries, providing specific facilities for children with special educational needs is relatively new. In New Zealand the first purpose-built special school was constructed in 2008, although special educational needs have been catered for in mainstream schools for some time. **Wilson School** in Takapuna, Auckland, New Zealand [Opus Architecture, 2008] acts as the 'base school' with other 'satellite classes' functioning in mainstream schools in the region. Within New Zealand, Wilson School is not only a model SEN facility but also sets new standards in the quality of mainstream school buildings. The building is characterised by its simplicity and transparency, two qualities that are also reflected in its teaching philosophy: 'A building which seeks to meet the needs of our most vulnerable children deserves the best possible architecture. ... The Wilson School [is] New Zealand's first purpose-built special needs school. ... Children arrive by car and enter a world which is theirs by right, not by compromise. An unwavering focus on the well-being of the pupils and staff and a genuine spirit of collaboration have allowed architect and client to create an extraordinary building, full of hope. It makes for architecture at its finest'.[10]

The building is a sophisticated collection of timber-clad boxes set among the mature trees of its well-established site. Easily legible, it is divided into three blocks dedicated to teaching, administration and social/communal activities. Classrooms have a fully glazed external wall looking out onto the countryside, providing a beautiful backdrop to learning and cleverly integrated break-out spaces for one-to-one teaching. A neutral materials palette consisting of timber flooring and off-white paint tones provide a robust frame for the colourful activities occurring in the school. The administrative areas are treated with as much care as the spaces for children, the staff 'lounge', positioned at the heart of the school, enables teachers to keep a watchful eye on the central courtyard and playground space whilst having a break from the demands of classroom activities.

Dealing with children that have severe physical and mental learning difficulties provides the school with a broad duty of care, which requires individual learning plans, but also very flexible spaces and places. This is manifest in the architectural design through the central courtyard, which acts as a security buffer zone, but more importantly provides a spatial focal point like an urban square. This simple architectural concept creates a social hub at the heart of the school, reflecting the nature of the place as a meeting point for children from across the region and those who only visit to touch base. A series of screens can be opened and closed to enable children and parents to filter from their drop-off point into

WILSON SCHOOL / Glazed classroom walls provide natural lighting, ventilation and views.

The double-height outdoor courtyard allows views between different parts of the school.

The outdoor courtyard opens onto a secure landscaped play area.

At the first floor, balcony classrooms provide a space for outdoor rest, recreation and learning.

the atrium and through into the courtyard. The suite of rooms enables students to easily congregate at the beginning of the day, which is no mean feat considering the range of support that each attending child needs.

The courtyard opens on to an external sensory play area that extends school activities into the landscape, connects the children to their surroundings and provides an attractive space for new arrivals. The landscape is another example of how Wilson School casts aside the notion that special schools have to function in isolation, out of sight and out of mind, and instead forms a hub for SEN provision in the region: accessible and open to all.

China has recently been challenged by the Human Rights Watch (HRW) organisation over its policy and practice of enabling children with disabilities to access education. HRW asserts that while all Chinese children are entitled to nine years of state-funded education the reality is somewhat different: 'Among the officially estimated 83 million people with disabilities in China, more than 40% are illiterate and at least 15 million live on less than 1 US$ a day, underscoring the lifelong consequences of a lack of access to education.' Many of the problems focus on the ability of local or mainstream schools to accommodate children with special needs. HRW reports that children with disabilities are being refused places at school because they may 'affect other children.'[11] The problem of integration is particularly challenging in an education system that is built on academic achievement. If a child is unable to deal with drills, rote teaching and extensive examinations,[12] then their ability to fit into the education system available to them is severely limited. With such barriers to accessing mainstream schooling there are seemingly few special schools available to these children, particularly in rural areas, where travelling long distances to get to school is often impractical.

Deyang is a prefecture-level city in Sichuan Province, comprising a series of conurbations, that are interspersed with large rural areas and a mountain range to the east. The area was ravaged by an earthquake in 2008,

leaving 90,000 people dead and 400,000 injured. Millions of people were affected as their homes and schools were destroyed. A huge rebuilding project has been undertaken since. The **Deyang School for Deaf & Intellectually Disabled Children** in Deyang, China [China Southwest Architectural Design and Research Institute, 2012], is a result of the rebuilding programme and an opportunity taken to transform the lives of disabled children in the region.

The design concept for the school is simple: to make it feel like home. Indeed the school is home to around 30 residential students with 60 others attending daily, offering comprehensive education to young people for the nine years of their compulsory education.[13] The scale of such a campus must be quite daunting for younger children. This issue has been addressed by the architects, who have divided the school into smaller house units, each with a pitched roof, giving it the appearance of an archetypal house that a child may draw. The pitched roof motif reappears throughout the school complex: in the sports pavilion and as a frame structure for an outdoor performance stage. Each element of the school is therefore recognisable as part of a unified whole. Large courtyards have been created by cutting voids out of the building. The walls overlooking the courtyards are covered in a patchwork of window openings, which help to break down the scale of the blocks and provide views out at different heights for children of all ages to appreciate. The many and varied roof lights create a sunlit and open interior.

Each house building has a defined use, yet is part of a wider architectural composition. The children with learning difficulties have their own building, as do the deaf children. Yet in between is the integrated learning building, which houses science labs, workshops as well as counselling rooms. This provides an opportunity for children of differing abilities to meet and socialise.

The organisation of the campus is conceived to give children a sense of security, with the buildings arranged

DEYANG SCHOOL FOR DEAF & INTELLECTUALLY DISABLED CHILDREN IN DEYANG, CHINA [China Southwest Architectural Design and Research Institute, 2012] The concept for the school is to make it feel like home for its 30 residential students and 60 students attending school daily. Internally the walls are rendered white to reflect the sunlight. The roof lights allow daylight to come through and open up the interior spaces visually.

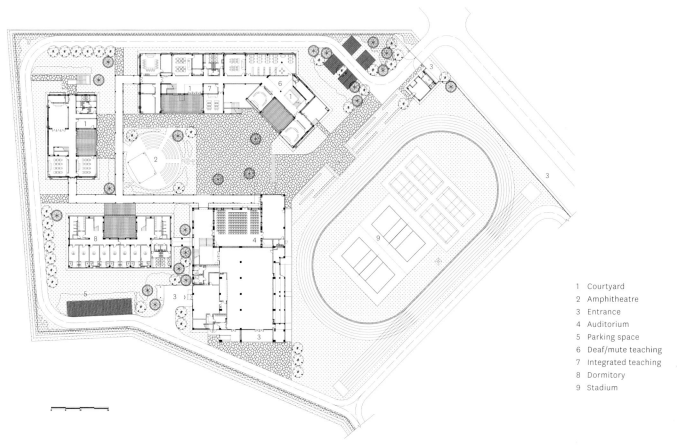

1 Courtyard
2 Amphitheatre
3 Entrance
4 Auditorium
5 Parking space
6 Deaf/mute teaching
7 Integrated teaching
8 Dormitory
9 Stadium

Site plan. Designed to give a sense of security to the children, the campus is arranged like arms that enfold the courtyard.

DEYANG SCHOOL FOR DEAF & INTELLECTUALLY DISABLED CHILDREN /
Windows open up to the courtyard and the atrium, in an effort to make the children more connected to outside world.

Children may find the scale of the school intimidating; to overcome the problem the architects divided the school into smaller house units, each with a pitched roof and many windows.

like arms enfolding the outdoor space. The white rendered walls reflect the sunlight and provide a clean and fresh appearance. Colour is used to animate the courtyard walls. The prominent location of an outdoor performance stage and amphitheatre highlight the value placed on arts and culture. This is reinforced by a suite of doors that open out from the music room into the atrium. It is easy to imagine music spilling out and flooding the other areas of the school. The array of sports facilities on offer at Deyang point towards a school where physical development is taken as seriously as academic learning. This is an institution where children are encouraged to express themselves in the outside world, rather than being confined to the classroom.

Deyang school has become well-known in China, as it provides an example of how young people with special educational needs can be valued, nurtured and supported in a high-quality facility. It does not answer questions about how children with learning difficulties in mainstream schools are supported, but it would be hard to argue that children in Deyang school are missing out or are being disadvantaged by the facilities on offer. Indeed mainstream students may be asking why their local schools are not up to this standard.

Inclusion and equality

There is ongoing debate about whether integrating students with special educational needs or separating them from mainstream schooling is more beneficial. On an international level, countries often have opposing views on this issue. The Organisation for Economic Co-operation and Development (OECD) report into special needs policy analysis across its 34 member countries highlights that there is no one solution to the levels of integration for SEN pupils: '... the same type of child could be in a special school in country X and fully included in a regular school in country Y. It is inevitable that the educational and social experiences of special schools and regular schools will be different, and this could well be inequitable in terms of students' access to post-compulsory education, the labour market and the wider society.'[14] As highlighted earlier, Wilson School offers an interesting approach to inclusion by acting as the hub for young people with special educational needs, but with links to surrounding schools, which perhaps suits the socio-demographics of the country. Yet, this model may be inappropriate elsewhere, in a different geo-social context.

Perhaps the most pressing issues to special school managers are ones of personal and social development which may appear to have little to do with architectural design. However, there are also significant design implications when considering inclusive schools or specialist facilities. Architects talk about the 'lines' or 'grades' of integration within combined schools, thresholds that separate mainstream students from those with learning difficulties, or points where all students can interact. Within combined or inclusive schools, these thresholds are explored in different ways. At one end of the spectrum is an adjoining doorway between the special needs

GOLDEN LANE CAMPUS IN LONDON, UK [Nicholas Hare Architects, 2008]

The campus is embedded intelligently in its urban context. It is integrated with its surroundings, whilst offering green views, calmness and a sense of safety to its students and staff. All outside play and learning spaces are shared, offering a high degree of accessibility, allowing all students to fully engage in mainstream class life.

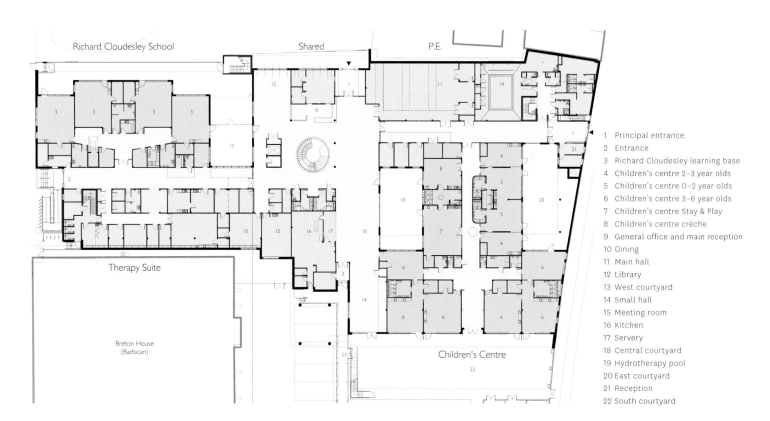

1 Principal entrance
2 Entrance
3 Richard Cloudesley learning base
4 Children's centre 2–3 year olds
5 Children's centre 0–2 year olds
6 Children's centre 3–6 year olds
7 Children's centre Stay & Play
8 Children's centre crèche
9 General office and main reception
10 Dining
11 Main hall
12 Library
13 West courtyard
14 Small hall
15 Meeting room
16 Kitchen
17 Servery
18 Central courtyard
19 Hydrotherapy pool
20 East courtyard
21 Reception
22 South courtyard

Ground floor plan. On the ground floor, Richard Cloudesley School for children with physical disabilities shares the core of services (library, dining hall, reception) with Fortune Park Nursery and Early Years Centre. Prior Weston Primary School is located on the first floor and is connected via a central spiral staircase.

GOLDEN LANE CAMPUS / Spaces are organised to offer opportunities for social interaction and integration between staff and students. Two separate schools and a nursery meet at a central spiral staircase and share entrances, a reception, a dining hall and library facilities.

Despite the tight, busy urban building site, all learning spaces have direct access to the outside, and they are day-lit.

wing and mainstream school, a boundary that is rarely breached. In some institutions dining areas are shared, which is as much a facilities management and financial issue as it is a gesture to enable social interaction. External spaces for SEN and mainstream pupils are often separated, to avoid the possibility of interpersonal issues developing through unmanaged play. Although understandable, this approach seems to negate the importance of children of all abilities interacting and learning through play. However, issues of personal security tend to prevail in such situations. Schools specifically designed for full integration are rarely seen, where children with special needs are fully integrated with mainstream students in everyday classroom situations. This is not to say that many schools cannot function as inclusive facilities, just that they have not been created to facilitate such use.

Whilst not providing a fully integrated SEN/mainstream learning environment **Golden Lane Campus** in London, UK [Nicholas Hare Architects, 2008] cleverly intertwines three schools with the urban surroundings to create a super school in both size and complexity. There are numerous points for impromptu student meetings, offering opportunities for interaction that are carefully afforded by the organisation of space – reducing barriers to integration. Richard Cloudesley School for children with physical disabilities is located on the ground floor with Fortune Park Nursery and Early Years Centre, whilst Prior Weston Primary School sits above on the first floor. The confluence of the three institutions occurs at a central

spiral staircase, off which flow the reception, dining area, hall and library facilities. In a sense the schools are rather like neighbourhoods around a civic centre. On plan there are clear lines of division between each neighbourhood, yet there are places for young people to meet informally without situations being contrived by staff or designers. The shared facilities sit at the heart of the plan and are accessed via generously proportioned circulation spaces to enable wheelchairs and walking frames to be used safely at peak traffic times.

The interaction of the schools transcends the physical: Richard Cloudesley pupils are able to join Prior Weston classes when appropriate, providing the opportunity for pupils with special needs to ease their way into mainstream school without the uncertainty of having to travel elsewhere or the need for additional support. The shared school ethos permeates to the staff as well, with a shared room on the second floor of the school, where staff are able to discuss how they can foster student interaction.

The high levels of natural light within the school benefit everyone and despite the tight urban location all classroom spaces have doors to external gardens and the views from the building are surprisingly green, given the schools' urban location. All outside play and learning spaces offer excellent security as well as accessibility, enabling pupils with special needs to take full part in mainstream class life where needed. The drop-off zone for pupils arriving by accessible transport has its own entrance with high-level pavements providing an easy route into school. Other entrances can be used by students as

POND MEADOW SPECIAL SCHOOL AND CHRIST'S COLLEGE IN GUILDFORD, UK [DSDHA, 2009]
The single-storey building of Pond Meadow Special School allows ease of access for all; the undulating roofscape nevertheless creates a visually interesting design.

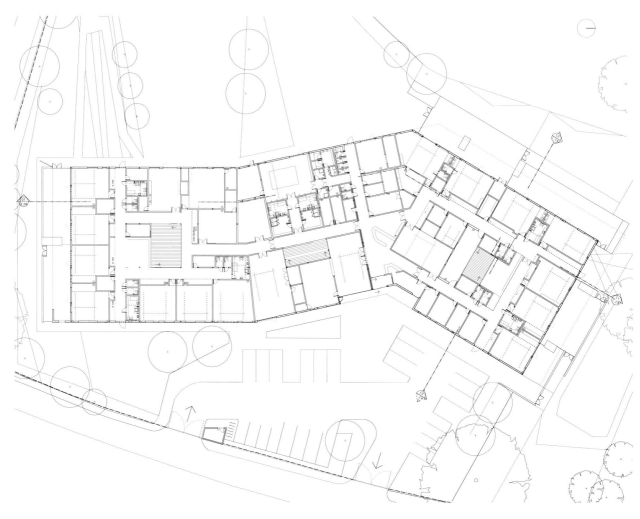

Site plan of Pond Meadow Special School

POND MEADOW SPECIAL SCHOOL AND CHRIST'S COLLEGE / Clearstories provide daylighting for the learning spaces. Inside, some facilities can be used by the wider community.

appropriate. Such a range of access points to accommodate all abilities helps to keep a sense of dignity for all students.

The benefits of co-location in this instance are three-fold; firstly, there is a high level of naturally occurring social interaction during break times; secondly, pupils with disabilities have the opportunity to push their own personal learning boundaries through carefully staged integration into mainstream lessons where appropriate. Finally, there is also the knock-on effect of shared facilities and reduced running costs, which has meant that a building of greater quality has been created than may have otherwise been possible for three separate schools.

At their 2003 summit the OECD committed to 'ensuring their education systems are equitable for all students, which requires them to provide for groups with diverse needs. An important part of this task is to structure programmes for students with disabilities, difficulties, and disadvantages in a way that respects and protects these groups' rights.'[15] The design of Golden Lane Campus has managed to meet these criteria; the careful consideration of pupil and institutional integration has created a school where all students, regardless of ability or disability are respected by staff and each other.

Co-location

One of the key beliefs agreed upon at the aforementioned World Conference on Special Needs Education in 1994 included the following: 'Regular schools with this inclusive orientation are the most effective means of combating discriminatory attitudes, creating welcoming communities, building an inclusive society and achieving education for all; moreover, they provide an effective education to the majority of children and improve the efficiency and ultimately the cost-effectiveness of the entire education system.'[16]

The **Pond Meadow Special School** and **Christ's College**, in Guildford, UK [DSDHA, 2009] offers an alternative approach to the co-location of SEN and mainstream schools. Designed by the same architect they sit as a pair of buildings in the landscape. There are no shared or combined facilities as such, but instead the two schools form a community of learning, aiming to be the catalyst for the kind of wider inclusive community that delegates at the world conference on Special Needs Education had envisaged.

On first inspection the road that separates the schools appears as a physical barrier to the interaction between the two institutions. In fact, it was implemented as a way of connecting the communities at either end and aids direct access for families to the schools which had been lacking in the past. The landscape around the buildings is still in its infancy and as this matures the recently planted trees will help to create a unified landscape around the two object buildings. In time Pond Meadow and Christ's College could be established as pavilions of learning or as Ellis Woodman describes it, Christ's college could appear as the 'country house' to Pond Meadows 'stable block'.[17]

Both buildings share common design aspects including the use of centralised courtyards to bring light into the schools. Both pieces of architecture make clever use of the same purple brick, sourced from Germany, although the bond is subtly adapted on Pond Meadow, using the stretchers to emphasise the sinuous form of the building. The openings on both buildings are playfully developed. Pond Meadow's seemingly random windows and doors are surface mounted whilst Christ's College windows are recessed into the wall. The roof-wall junction is also detailed in the same way. This material dialogue between the two buildings implies a connection, but leaves the viewer in some doubt as to how the material connection transfers to the use of the buildings.

The Pond Meadow student cohort has a range of physical and cognitive special needs. Some are so severe that life is a struggle for survival, let alone to achieve academically. This can make interaction with the mainstream school challenging, but older pupils from Pond Meadow do cross over the road to take part in Christ's College classes, a sign that integration is happening and that there is potential for wider-ranging inclusivity.

When thinking about the connectivity between the two schools, in terms of design and learning, it is also worth reflecting on the other two buildings that form part of the community of buildings. Firstly, an existing children's centre building forms an integral part of the educational continuity in the area, and secondly there is Christ's College's group learning and SEN building. Set to

one side of the college, but located on their side of the road this modest structure could play a vital role in linking activities between the two centres, bridging the physical divide and connecting to the wider community. With a simple single floor arrangement the space has the potential to act as a mixed-use community centre and like the rest of the school, without really shouting about it, make a real difference to the neighbourhood.

Community interaction

Despite the efforts made at Pond Meadow and Christ's College, connecting with the wider community effectively is a real challenge for contemporary special schools. One obstacle to overcome is often location – SEN schools are frequently situated in leafy suburban areas. Whilst this allows for quiet isolation, a safe buffer zone for the children and no closely positioned neighbours, schools can then be physically dislocated from their surrounding community. Because children that have particular learning needs may have few options in selecting a school, travelling long distances to go to school is common. This means that the communities surrounding special schools often have few children attending them, reducing the feeling of ownership and reinforcing disconnectedness.

With this in mind it comes as a bit of a surprise to find a special school in high-rise Manhattan occupying a multi-storey building in close collaboration with a dance company. The **Stephen Gaynor School** in New York, USA [Rogers Partners (previously Rogers Marvel Architects), 2008] makes a virtue of its urban surroundings, being at the heart of the city and wider community. Unlike other buildings in the area that offer street frontages of flat glazed façades, Stephen Gaynor school stands out, quite literally. The library is pushed out, forming a cantilevered reading bench with views down the street. There is also a recessed play balcony, animating the building and suggesting a break from the norm.

Children attending Stephen Gaynor School are of mixed ability, with what the headteacher describes as

STEPHEN GAYNOR SCHOOL IN NEW YORK, USA [Rogers Partners (previously Rogers Marvel Architects), 2008]
The school, set in an urban context, deliberately announces its presence. The generous staircase that winds up through the building provides interaction with Ballet Hispanico, housed in the same building. Bottom: School dining room

'learning differences'.[18] The school creates programmes that challenge and stimulate pupils with learning difficulties to achieve their full potential. In practice this is done through small class sizes and a dedicated team of staff.

Joined for social and financial sustainability, Stephen Gaynor and Ballet Hispanico have overlapping spaces and facilities, but separate access. This means that each organisation has its own identity, whilst also being interwoven – a clever move architecturally and organisationally. Both organisations share a staircase and lift, creating instances of interaction between dancers and children. People also using the building could be considered dis-

tracting, but at Stephen Gaynor, members of staff see the interaction with their neighbours as crucially important to the children's personal development.

Vertical circulation is challenging in special schools on open sites, particularly where children with physical disabilities are studying. Stairwells can be difficult to manage for staff and can make way finding challenging for students. This is overcome at Stephen Gaynor by using the stair as an orientation tool, a visual aid, but also a focal point for the school. The red ribbon stair meanders through the school and creates many instances of interaction between students in transit and those in class,

STEPHEN GAYNOR SCHOOL / The special school shares a high-rise building with Ballet Hispanico.

The high-rise location affords views across the city.

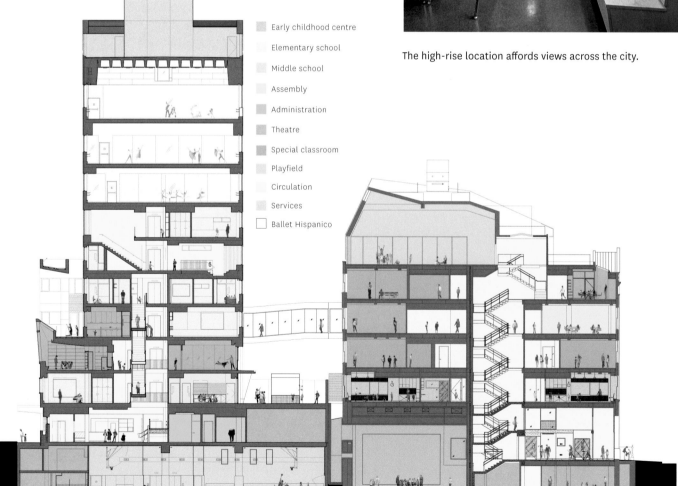

	Early childhood centre
	Elementary school
	Middle school
	Assembly
	Administration
	Theatre
	Special classroom
	Playfield
	Circulation
	Services
	Ballet Hispanico

The section shows how the space is used by the two schools. Although there are no shared facilities the schools' co-location provides a sense of inclusion.

SØGAARD SCHOOL IN GENTOFTE, DENMARK [CEBRA Architects, 2007]
The school is designed with domestic forms and proportions: a home away from home for the students. Carefully articulated windows, however, suggest a non-residential use despite the building form. Right: The perspective shows the relationship between the building and the landscape with small garden areas.

through cleverly positioned windows. The space on the stairs is generous, allowing children to dwell there without preventing others from passing by, making an informal meeting place.

External space is limited, but still provided through a rooftop playground at first floor level. However, the school usually undertakes physical education in neighbouring Central Park, proving that special school activities can be integrated into the locale without concerns of security, enabling students to feel part of the city's everyday life.

At **Søgaard School** in Gentofte, Denmark [CEBRA Architects, 2007] an alternative approach was taken to knit a special needs school into its physical and social context. Positioned in a suburb of Gentofte and surrounded by bungalows, the school is part refurbishment and part new construction. Rather than shoe-horn a larger institution into the neighbourhood, the architects have broken the building down into domestic-sized volumes and in doing so have made the learning environ-

ment appear like a collection of houses that have been knocked together. The beauty of such an idea, particularly appropriate for a special school, is that it becomes a home from home for students. It also enables a series of level changes, range of openings and thresholds between the adjoining houses in a multitude of informal learning spaces that offer plenty of niches for children to fit into. Around every corner is a new opportunity for learning, an example of which is a soft-play forest area, alongside student's lockers.

The outside of the building works in a similar way and must feel like playing in the back yard. The landscape is characterised by natural play equipment, and variations in ground textures define different zones within the space. The boundary of the school is carefully created by a hedgerow, which again fits into the context of carefully maintained gardens, and which is a good alternative to the high metal fences often in use, further reinforcing the school's open outlook. Like Pond Meadow School, Søgaard School uses a collage of windows to animate the

SØGAARD SCHOOL / Inside, classrooms are supported by a series of break-out spaces such as this play area.

High-level windows provide natural daylight in the sports hall, whilst retaining privacy at low level.

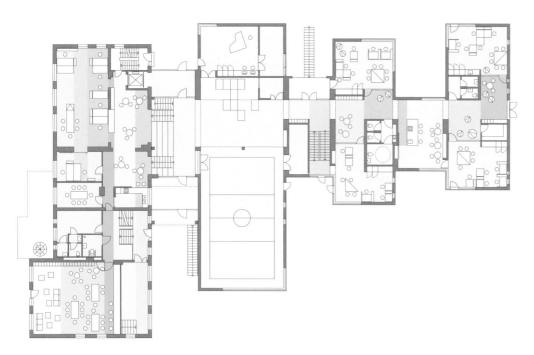

Ground floor plan

building. Looking from the outside it is not easy to identify a classroom or where the sports hall is hidden. Balconies sometimes project from the building and others are carved out of the gables. The white render reflects daylight and is complemented with a green shade used as an accent. The simple colour palette offsets the spatial complexity of the building and stops the building from becoming visually overwhelming. Indeed, the building is difficult to pick out as a school from the surroundings. Søgaard School proves that a special school can integrate seamlessly into a suburban context without the need for a sea of grass and perimeter fencing between it and the surrounding neighbourhood.

Preparing for adult life

Where countries do provide learning opportunities for all children with special educational needs, one of the key aims of the education is to teach young people to be self-reliant and to live independently. This is not always possible to achieve, but can make a huge difference to children and their families. Curricula focus on day-to-day practical considerations that many people take for granted, including personal hygiene and basic cooking skills. With support, it is hoped that young people with special educational needs may be able to play an active part in society: 'Young people with special educational needs

HAZELWOOD SCHOOL FOR THE BLIND IN GLASGOW, UK [Gordon Murray and Alan Dunlop Architects, 2007]
The school is located in a leafy suburb of Glasgow and the building winds its way between mature trees. Undulating façades create protected spaces for outdoor play and learning. Sensory surfaces on the floors and walls in the generous circulation spaces allow students to navigate the building independently.

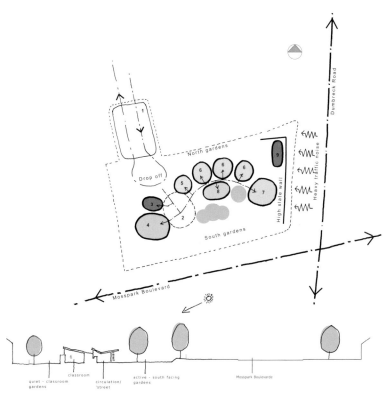

Conceptual site plan showing the main school building and the 'life skills house'

should be helped to make an effective transition from school to adult working life. Schools should assist them to become economically active and provide them with the skills needed in everyday life.'[19]

Hazelwood School for the Blind in Glasgow, UK [Gordon Murray and Alan Dunlop Architects, 2007] addressed the issue of personal development by designing a building that is conceived to support students' transition to adulthood and independence. The central spine corridor provides an indication of this, with tactile surfaces that guide pupils through the space, helping young people to explore their surroundings, whether inside the school or outside. The whole school is designed as a sensory landscape for visually impaired students. The majority of students can perceive changes in light level and therefore it is doubly important that the diurnal rhythms of day and night, dark and light can be understood by students within the classroom.

Adjacent to the main school building, a discreet distance away, is the 'life skills house'. Designed as self-contained apartments, older pupils can stay overnight and for longer periods where appropriate, to test out their domestic skills and prepare themselves for moving away from home. The house offers three bedrooms with adjacent (but not en-suite) bathrooms, shared kitchen and living space. The house has its own outdoor space and is very much a stand-alone unit, offering the bare essentials in a simple plan arrangement that is easy for students to navigate and settle in to. The house is almost a clone of the main building: its elegant simplicity, textural qualities and strong links to the school grounds distilled down into a smaller building.

The life skills house acts as a kind of destination point for pupils progressing from junior classes near the entrance of the school, along the sinuous circulation route to the class spaces of the senior and leavers' school. A visual connection is maintained between the senior classrooms and the house, providing reassurance for staff that unsupervised students are getting on with their own lives. A slate-clad wall acts as a comforting arm projecting from the main school building around the annexed unit, sheltering the school from the busy road beyond. Every aspect of the house has been considered to bridge the gap between school and life beyond. The next step for pupils is out into the real world, but perhaps the only downside with Hazelwood School is that it is so carefully designed, the pupils may never want to leave!

REFERENCES

1 'The Salamanca and Framework for Action on Special Needs Education. World Conference on Special Needs Education Access and Quality, Salamanca, Spain, 7–10 June 1994', http://www.unesco.de/fileadmin/medien/Dokumente/Bildung/Salamanca_Declaration.pdf. Accessed 9 May 2014.

2 Ibid.

3 http://www.un.org/disabilities/. Accessed 25 November 2013.

4 http://www.csie.org.uk/inclusion/rights-persons-disabilities.shtml. Accessed 22 November 2013.

5 Ibid.

6 'Diversity, Inclusion and Equity: Insights from Special Needs Provision', Education Policy Analysis, OECD 2003, p. 29. http://www.oecd.org/education/educationeconomyandsociety/ 26527517.pdf. Accessed on 20 December 2012.

7 Peter Gordon quoted in: Hilary Wilce, 'Special Needs Education: Does Mainstream Inclusion Work?', London: *Independent Newspaper*, 23 March 2006. http://www.independent.co.uk/news/education/education-news/specialneeds-education-does-mainstream-inclusion-work-470960.html. Accessed 20 December 2012.

8 Alan Dyson quoted in: Hilary Wilce, 'Special Needs Education: Does Mainstream Inclusion Work?', London: *Independent Newspaper*, 23 March 2006. http://www.independent.co.uk/news/education/education-news/specialneeds-education-does-mainstream-inclusion-work-470960.html. Accessed 20 December 2012.

9 Abbé de L'Épée (1712–1789) opened a school for deaf children in France. In Edinburgh, UK, Thomas Braidwood (1715–1806) developed a similar organisation. http://www.bris.ac.uk/Depts/DeafStudiesTeaching/deafed/Session%202A.htm. Accessed 29 November 2013.

10 From the citation for Wilson School, in 'New Zealand Architecture Awards 2009', http://www.eqoleung.com/awards_092.php. Cf. also Opus Architecture's website, http://www.opusarch.co.nz/. Accessed 12 May 2014.

11 Maya Wang, 'Chinese Children with Disabilities Denied Access to Education', originally published in the *South China Morning Post* and republished on the Human Rights Watch website, 17 September 2013. http://www.hrw.org/news/2013/09/17/chinese-children-disabilities-denied-access-education. Accessed 22 November 2013.

12 Daniel Bardsley, 'Educators Criticise China's Way of Teaching', *The National*, 5 March 2011. http://www.thenational.ae/news/world/asia-pacific/educators-criticise-china-s-way-of-teaching. Accessed 12 May 2014.

13 http://e.weibo.com/deyangtexiao. Accessed 29 November 2013.

14 'Diversity, Inclusion and Equity: Insights from Special Needs Provision', Education Policy Analysis, OECD 2003, p. 29. http://www.oecd.org/education/educationeconomyandsociety/26527517.pdf. Accessed 20 December 2012.

15 Ibid, p. 10.

16 'The Salamanca and Framework for Action on Special Needs Education. World Conference on Special Needs Education Access and Quality, Salamanca, Spain, 7–10 June 1994', p. IX. http://www.unesco.de/fileadmin/medien/Dokumente/Bildung/Salamanca_Declaration.pdf. Accessed 9 May 2014.

17 Ellis Woodman, 'Double Chemistry', London: *Building Design*, 22 January 2010, pp. 10–14. Christ's College is described in chapter 3, Flexible Space for Learning, pp. 76–77.

18 'From Self-Esteem to Self-Advocacy', http://www.stephengaynor.org/academic_excellence. Accessed 12 May 2014.

19 'The Salamanca and Framework for Action on Special Needs Education. World Conference on Special Needs Education Access and Quality, Salamanca, Spain, 7–10 June 1994', p. 34. http://www.unesco.de/fileadmin/medien/Dokumente/Bildung/Salamanca_Declaration.pdf. Accessed 12 May 2014.

Summary

8 SPECIAL SCHOOLS SHOULD BE SPECIAL

1. Special schools are leading the way in design quality for mainstream schools to follow. The **complex and individual requirements** of special schools have often been the catalyst for creative architectural responses and richly textured sensory environments, rather than hampering the design process.

2. **Legibility, simplicity and transparency** are three qualities that are reflected in the best special schools.

3. Architecture and design can contribute to achieving **integration between SEN and mainstream students** at an institutional level. Good integrated schools show how choice and equality can be delivered through thoughtful design and close collaboration with multiple schools.

4. Special schools can be **central to their communities**, whether in a high-density urban context or a suburb. A successful special school will usually be characterised by a conscious response to the physical and social context within which they are based.

5. There are many approaches to achieving education and social equality for young people of all abilities through the design of schools. However, there is **no one-size-fits-all solution**. The best results come from an in-depth knowledge of the culture, people and place.

9 Refurbishment and Extension of Existing Schools / HOWARD EVANS

Schools often see refurbishment as an opportunity to reinvent their teaching practice or their image to the outside world. A creative refurbishment project can produce innovative and inspiring solutions to help realise this ambition.

It is clear that the reconditioning of school building stock will become an increasingly important part of school modernisation and procurement. At least equal or even more resources are used for refurbishment and renovation of existing school premises as are invested in the construction of new schools. This chapter looks at the complexity associated with existing buildings and at the innovative ways this has been tackled by architects and the schools.

Much has been made of the profligacy of school construction programmes, such as the UK's Building Schools for the Future (BSF). The necessity of demolishing schools rather than emphasising repair and refurbishment has been questioned by commentators and critics of such programmes; new construction usually makes the procurement easier as the school can continue in its existing premises while a new school is built. The UK's BSF programme was originally designed to be 50% new construction and 50% refurbishment; however, the earlier BSF schemes focused on the complete redevelopment of the schools most seriously in need of replacement. Following the decision to stop the BSF programme in June 2010, of the 180 schools that had been completed as part of the programme, 47% were refurbished or had undergone renewal of ICT facilities.

BRENTWOOD SCHOOL IN BRENTWOOD, ESSEX, UK [Cottrell & Vermeulen, 2011]
The addition to this 450-year old institution is an example of how a school reinvented its educational practice and image to the outside world.

FRIEDRICH FRÖBEL SCHOOL IN OLBERSDORF, SAXONY, GERMANY [AIZ Bauplanungsgesellschaft, 2011]
The 1928 building, classified as a cultural monument, previously housed a secondary school and was converted to accommodate a special school. It was sensitively upgraded and given better lighting, acoustics and energy performance.

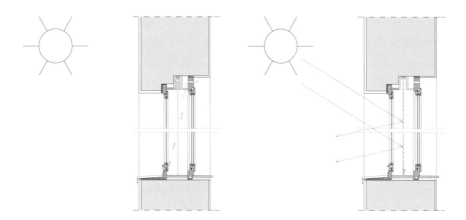

The section through the box window shows the improved daylighting concept.

Transforming school buildings

Following the global economic downturn different countries have seen wildly differing economic policies imposed on them from central government. In the UK it was the complete cessation of the BSF programme and the cancellation of the Primary Capital Programme[2]. These major programmes have been replaced by initiatives such as 'Free Schools'[3], set up by parents or individuals with government funding following particular faiths or agendas. They aim to use and refurbish the existing building stock to provide the new schools. The 'Priority School Building Programme'[4] is another UK coalition government initiative to refurbish rather than replace very

run-down schools. The funding for refurbishment of these state-funded schools is through private sector sponsors with some subsidy from the government. If schools do not already have premises they are able to request the use of empty properties previously owned by the state such as Magistrate Courts or even Department of Education Buildings.[5]

Australia by contrast set up the 'Building Education Revolution' programme (BER) which sought to provide public sector funding as a way through recession. The BER programme specifically targeted the spending of 16.2 billion Au$ (11 billion euros) in four years from 2009 on the refurbishment of schools across Australia. The programme was broken into three distinct packages, all focusing on refurbishment and extension rather than new buildings. These sectors were: the National School Pride Project, Primary Schools for the 21st Century, and Science and Language Centres for 21st Century Secondary Schools.[6]

Global economic circumstances have seen significant reductions to capital budgets available for school building. It is clear that this situation will last into the foreseeable future, requiring educational bodies and school builders to focus on the management of their existing school stock. Existing school buildings often offer better space standards than are achieved in newly built schools, although can be limited in their scope to integrate ICT and modern inclusive circulation.

In Germany, whilst no central programme dominates, the emergence of initiatives such as the Federal Ministry of Economics and Technology's Research for Energy Optimised Building (EnOB) looks at the retrofit of existing building types to meet modern energy performance standards.

Friedrich Fröbel School, a pilot project developed in close consultation with Hochschule Zittau/Görlitz and the University of Technology Dresden in Olbersdorf, Saxony, Germany [AIZ Bauplanungsgesellschaft, 2011] is an important example of a regional school, from the Weimar period and built in 1928. Classified as a cultural monument, it has housed a secondary school in recent years and was converted to accommodate a special school. The refurbishment, although fairly simple, improved the quality of light and resulted in a substantial upgrading of energy performance. In order to encourage a 'learning atmosphere', the refurbishment also intends to improve the acoustics and air quality, while lowering the indoor temperatures in summer. Digital displays illustrate the energy efficiency of the school building to the school pupils, teachers and parents.

In the UK, the post-war system schools developed in Hertfordshire[7], enabled schools to be built cheaply and quickly by means of a prefabricated system. Between 1948 and 1973, 350 schools were built, some of which are now listed structures. In 2006, the non-listed schools were analysed with a view to potential demolition.[8] However, Hertfordshire County Council decided that the inherent flexibility of the frame structure would enable the remodelling of the schools with minimal disruption. The steel frame structures were in sound condition, providing a highly adaptable and low-carbon alternative to the rebuilding of the whole county's school estate.

In refurbishment projects it is vital that the building is fully understood, in order to maximise the success of the project. An investment of time at the early stages of the project on surveying and understanding the existing building fabric and space will uncover issues and raise opportunities to work with the building. The following case studies look at successful alterations and additions to three buildings of differing scale and age.

Elm Court School in Lambeth, London, UK [JM Architects, 2009] was originally built in 1912 in the heart of what has now been designated a conservation area. The building was originally designed as a school but had fallen into disuse. It was in a poor state of repair by 2007 when Lambeth Council started its Building Schools for the Future Programme. A special needs school chose the building in part because of the existing architectural language that exuded 'school'. It also sits at the heart of the community where bringing a cherished building back to life is seen as a positive move.

The refurbishment sought to rationalise the internal layout of the school building, raising floor levels to minimise the various steps in the existing floor plan whilst giving an improved relationship to window sill heights which are now lower by comparison. Large classrooms with generous areas of glazing were seen as beneficial to supporting the learning and teaching goals of children with a variety of special educational needs. The school hall is stripped back to reveal the original architectural qualities of the space. An atrium is created at the heart of the building, resulting in a space that helps with orientation

ELM COURT SCHOOL IN LAMBETH, LONDON, UK [JM Architects, 2009]

Two new additions at the back of the school contrast in style with the existing building and are linked by a careful landscape strategy.

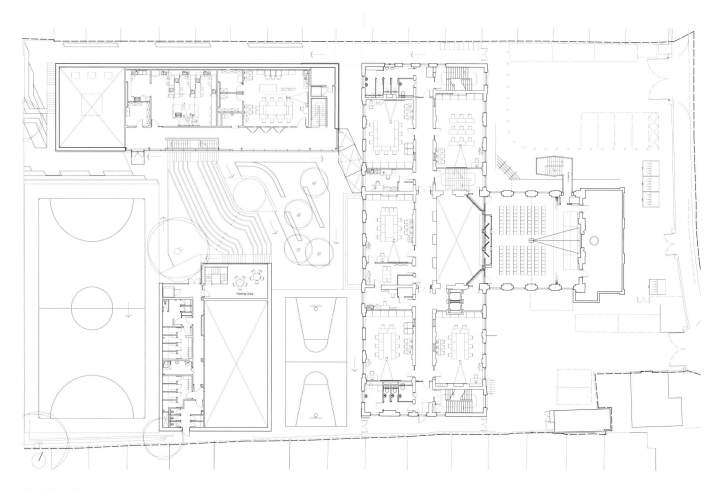

First floor plan

ELM COURT SCHOOL / A new and highly glazed external stair at the front of the building offers an indication that the school has been transformed.

An existing courtyard that has been glazed over helps to rationalise circulation in the old school building.

around the school whilst flooding the space deep within the plan with natural light. Levels of thermal insulation throughout the building have been significantly improved and, together with the holistic strategy for natural ventilation, these measures have resulted in a BREEAM 'very good' rating for energy efficiency performance.[9]

The additions are not stylistically contiguous with the existing building, the old and new elements are clearly legible and contrasting. From the front of the school a new planar glazed stair presents a visual cue of the changes that the building has undergone. To the rear, a pair of blocks containing the sports hall, design and

technology and music classrooms are realised in an overtly contemporary language, creating a school that offers a variety of spaces of different scales. The landscape adapts to the level changes across the site and ties the various building elements together. The result is a school that sensitively celebrates the best aspects of the original whilst creating a collection of spaces with different moods and atmospheres.

Dealing with a historically significant building requires a deep understanding of the merits of the original architecture to determine how to make alterations and additions that do not compromise the design intent or func-

MUNKEGÅRDSSKOLEN IN GENTOFTE, COPENHAGEN, DENMARK [Dorte Mandrup Arkitekter, 2009]
The new structure inserted into an existing double-height hall space keeps its distance from the original building. The 'underground' additions to this 1956 Arne Jacobsen building are lit by a series of light wells.

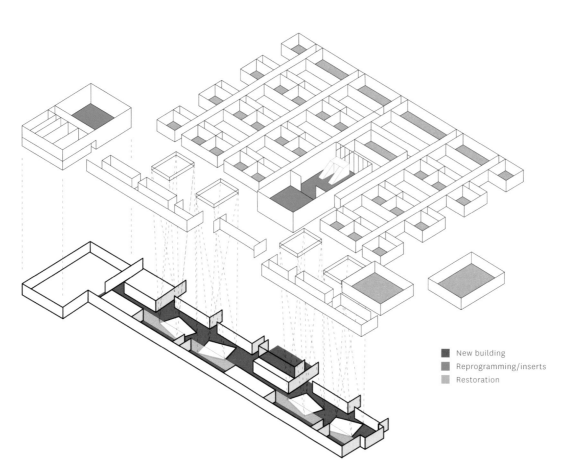

- New building
- Reprogramming/inserts
- Restoration

A diagram shows the three types of intervention in the school; new building, reprogramming/inserts and restoration.

MUNKEGÅRDSSKOLEN / The underground additions such as the experimental classroom are truly contemporary in their design and stand apart from Jacobsen's architecturally significant design above.

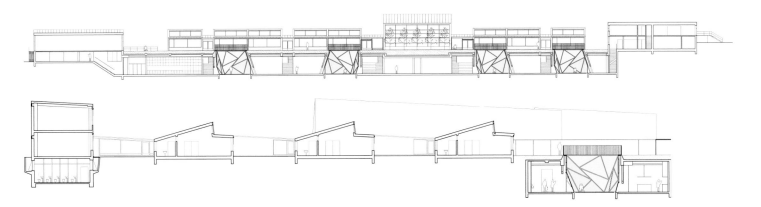

The sections shows how the crystalline underground light wells and underground additions minimise the impact of the refurbishment on this historic school.

tionality of the space. **Munkegårdsskolen** in Gentofte, Copenhagen, Denmark [Dorte Mandrup Arkitekter, 2009] was initially designed and built in 1956 by Arne Jacobsen and is considered one of his finest projects.[10] The school was registered as a protected building in 1995 in recognition of its architectural significance. The school was one of the first Danish single-storey schools. After some 50 years, the school was in need of significant overhaul and

modernisation to meet modern educational standards and provide contemporary facilities. Dorte Mandrup Arkitekter worked with the Gentofte Architecture Advisory Panel to modernise and restore the school.

The original building comprised a series of pavilions arranged in a grid system, enclosing a series of courtyard gardens. Jacobsen designed everything from the building plan to the door handles and even the furniture at

SCHULZENDORF PRIMARY SCHOOL IN SCHULZENDORF, BERLIN, GERMANY [Zander Roth Architekten, 2007]
Views of the building in its original state. Inside the new atrium spaces, the building has been stripped back to the original structure and reinvigorated with bold colours.

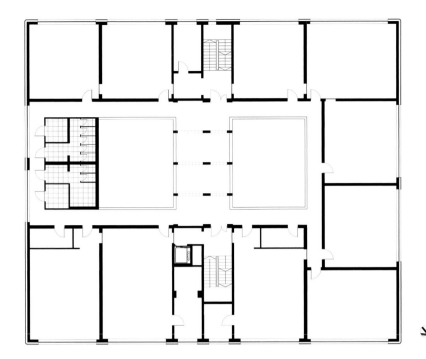

SCHULZENDORF PRIMARY SCHOOL / The plan form is a simple arrangement around the new atrium spaces. The new footprint allows for additional teaching space and services.

Model views. The original H-shaped plan has been squared to provide additional teaching space and enclose two atrium spaces.

which the children were to sit. The new work sought to restore the original building whilst enabling the school to respond to modern teaching pedagogies. The new additions allow for more open-plan teaching spaces, improved circulation and common facilities such as eating areas and toilets. The new areas are located under the original school yard and follow the strict grid set out by the Jacobsen building. The architects worked closely with the Daylight Laboratory at the Royal Academy of Fine Arts in Copenhagen to maximise daylight conditions deep within the space. Four crystalline light wells puncture the surface of the school yard dropping daylight into the new underground spaces. This move ensures the legibility of Jacobsen's original plan is retained whilst creating new and dynamic space at the heart of the school, making it relevant and useable for the 21st century.

Not all schools are of significant architectural merit or need to be. At the **Schulzendorf Primary School** in Schulzendorf, Berlin, Germany [Zander Roth Architekten, 2007] the school has been transformed from a tired 1960s school building into a refreshing and inspirational learning environment. The structure of the original H-shaped building was a simple concrete frame clad in rendered brick and single-glazed metal windows. The architects proposed two simple moves: the first was to retain

the existing structural elements and the second was to envelop the building in a new highly insulated skin.

The structure is stripped back to the essential frame and floor slabs. Two new linear elements are added to either end of the H-plan, creating two light wells in the middle of the building plan. These atria help to open up the centre of the building and define the building's horizontal and vertical circulation. The building is then encased in generous layers of insulation before the last skin of woven willow. This willow skin refers to the traditional industry in the area of willow harvesting, making a building that is at once overtly modern and yet highly contextual.

These three case studies highlight a number of common themes when working with existing buildings. Firstly, the importance of understanding and working with an existing structure, regardless of historical significance or architectural merit. Secondly, the importance of good light levels in creating spaces that are animated and enjoyable to use and learn in. Thirdly, the creative refurbishment of buildings can enable significant improvements in the energy efficiency performance of a building. Fourthly, careful reworking of buildings can make significant contributions to the local streetscape and the wider community.

MELBOURNE GRAMMAR SCHOOL IN MELBOURNE, AUSTRALIA [John Wardle Architects, 2005]

The new Nigel Peck Centre for Learning and Leadership incorporates a library, ICT provision, a large lecture theatre and an administration centre. The façade of this addition to the school creates a dynamic street presence. Study areas in the library look out towards the city, rather than into the campus.

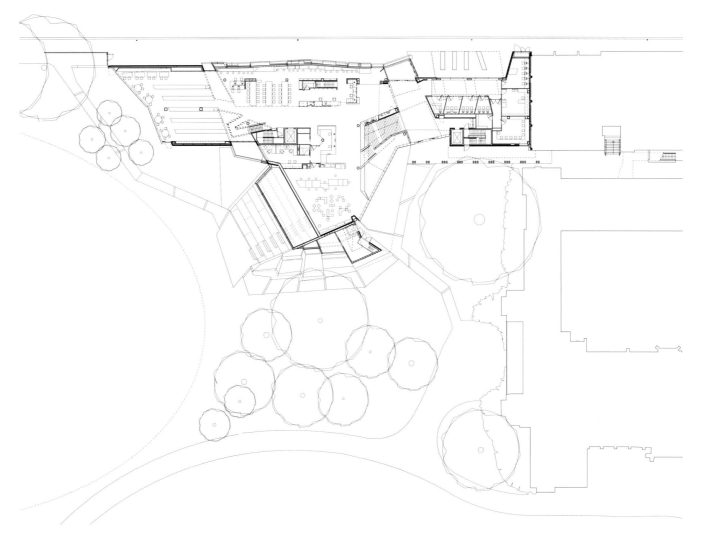

MELBOURNE GRAMMAR SCHOOL / Ground floor plan

Creating new or reinforcing existing identities

The idea that a refurbishment or extension of a school can impact on the community is an important consideration in any project. Many older school buildings have been at the heart of their neighbourhoods and make a contribution to their local streetscape. A refurbishment or extension project may be a chance for a school to consolidate an existing identity or for some to create a new face. In a world where clear presentation and marketing are increasingly important, the public façade of a school is a key way to communicate its identity and values.

Melbourne Grammar School in Melbourne, Australia [John Wardle Architects, 2005] is a well-renowned school in the heart of Melbourne. Established in 1858, the original building sits in the middle of a large campus, surrounded by sports fields. Later additions to the school

reinforced the focus towards the pitches, turning the school's back on the street. In 2004, the school commissioned the architects to design the new Nigel Peck Centre for Leadership and Learning. The building incorporates a new library, ICT provision, a large lecture theatre and an administration centre.

The project was seen as a valuable way for the school to create a very public street presence with a large shop window into the learning centre. The new building uses a dark brick that references the stone hues of the original building, whilst the angular geometric forms suggest forward-thinking modernity. A diagonal glazed cut through the building reveals the façade of the 1858 west quadrangle.

The street front window gives views into a learning space that supports both traditional and modern forms of learning, presenting a school with a long history yet capable of delivering cutting-edge teaching. The large

BRENTWOOD SCHOOL IN BRENTWOOD, ESSEX, UK [Cottrell & Vermeulen, 2011]

The addition of the new assembly hall significantly impacts the street elevation, creating a bookend to the long string of Edwardian buildings.

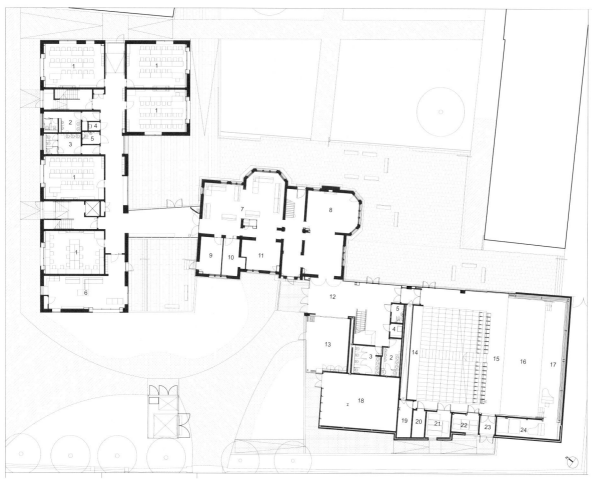

1   Classroom
2   Male WC
3   Female WC
4   Cleaners' cupboard
5   Disabled WC
6   Praepostors
7   Common room
8   Social/study room
9   Head of sixth form
10 Deputy head
11 Tea point
12 Foyer
13 Green room
14 Bleacher storage
15 Assembly hall
16 Loose stage
17 Fixed stage
18 Plant room
19 Switchroom
20 Exam store
21 Exam tables and chairs store
22 Chair store
23 Escape lobby
24 Drama store/side stage

Ground floor plan

BRENTWOOD SCHOOL / The new assembly hall echoes the existing buildings with strong gables and red brickwork.

An existing Victorian building sits between the two new additions.

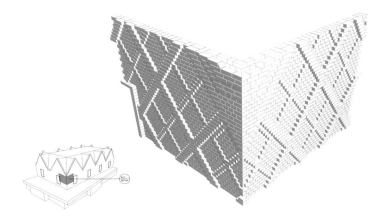

The detail of the brickwork pattern on the new assembly hall building makes reference to the older school buildings.

areas of glazing use a mixture of form and technology to control solar gain.

The architecturally diverse campus at **Brentwood School** in Brentwood, Essex, UK [Cottrell & Vermeulen, 2011] reflects its 450-year history. The latest addition is overtly contemporary whilst playfully referencing the materiality and forms of the older campus. The project was conceived to support the school's pedagogical shift to prepare pupils both toward UK A-Levels and the International Baccalaureate in their sixth form programmes. The evolution of the project involved complex negotiations with planning and conservation officers that resulted in the retention of a Victorian vicarage in the middle of the proposed site. The resulting tripartite composition is the better for the long gestation, reflecting the internal programme of learning, social areas and assembly spac-

es. The composition significantly impacts on the public street elevation, creating a bookend to the long string of buildings that start with the school chapel to the north. The main Edwardian school building is sat back from the road, creating a long open forecourt that is now contained by the addition of the new assembly hall.

The use of brickwork ensures a strong material continuity with the original buildings. The diaper pattern references the older buildings whilst giving a strong visual identity to the new buildings. On the classroom block the simple surface pattern wraps up the walls and continues onto the roof. The auditorium sees the diaper pattern used as a large bold relief, recessing three and half bricks deep. The multiple gables give the large block a scale that externally resembles the scale of the existing building. Internally this is used to animate the ceiling of the audi-

OSLO INTERNATIONAL SCHOOL IN BEKKESTUA, NORWAY [Jarmund/Vigsnaes Architects, 2008]
An extension clad in coloured panels created a new identity for the school: timber-clad pavilions provide learning spaces within the courtyard.

torium. The restored vicarage building's external appearance gives little clue to the nature of the internal spaces where the strategic removal of walls has created a flowing open-plan space.

The project has not only given the school a series of modern learning and teaching spaces addressing the older students but has resulted in a positive streetscape that benefits the wider urban landscape. The architecture projects the school as a place of solid educational values whilst being forward-thinking and embracing change.

The **Oslo International School** in Bekkestua, Norway [Jarmund/Vigsnaes Architects, 2008] aims to encapsulate the practice's ethos that 'the preservation and

renovation of existing buildings is essential for a greater sense of cultural continuity.'[11] The refurbishment of a 1960s school building that had previously served families on the local NATO military base has brought a freshness and new identity to the school. The existing school was already successful in providing a well-rounded education but the tired building was in need of repair and lacked spaces to allow for expansion.

Jarmund/Vigsnaes' analysis of the school recognised the good parts of the school, from the simple modular structure to the good circulation afforded by the single-storey plan. The school also benefited from a strong relationship with its site which provided good daylight levels,

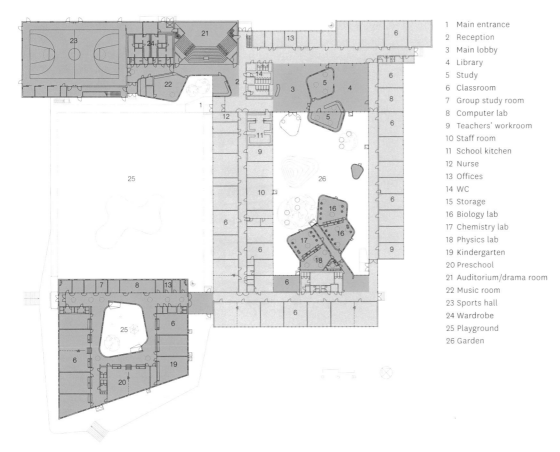

OSLO INTERNATIONAL SCHOOL / The additions (yellow) are placed around the existing courtyard building.

1 Main entrance
2 Reception
3 Main lobby
4 Library
5 Study
6 Classroom
7 Group study room
8 Computer lab
9 Teachers' workroom
10 Staff room
11 School kitchen
12 Nurse
13 Offices
14 WC
15 Storage
16 Biology lab
17 Chemistry lab
18 Physics lab
19 Kindergarten
20 Preschool
21 Auditorium/drama room
22 Music room
23 Sports hall
24 Wardrobe
25 Playground
26 Garden

access to the outside and surrounding woodland. The decision to refurbish the school meant that the school could remain open throughout the construction work.

The resulting scheme made a phased proposal. The first phase of the work reconditioned the original building, creating a new entrance, extending into the courtyard to build new learning pavilions containing science laboratories, a library and assembly space. New insulation and mechanical services greatly improved the energy performance of the school buildings. The new pavilions forge a stronger relationship between the school and the internal courtyard whilst creating a new architectural language of softly rounded timber structures. The second phase encompasses a new kindergarten and administration offices to the front of the school. The building is clad in vertical strips of bright colour that envelop and protect the younger pupils. The final phase will house gymnasium and performance spaces.

The new building creates a new identity for the school that suggests fun and sophistication. The harmony between old and new is achieved through a good understanding of the merits of the original structure and the appropriateness of scale of the additions.

Unifying the campus

Many school campuses develop over time as a collection of buildings of mixed merit. It is not always possible to 'wrap' a school campus in a new skin or to consolidate a collection of buildings with a single addition that reinforces a clear existing identity. More often, an addition to the school campus will seek to make accommodation that supports new teaching pedagogies or meets new standards of access. Successful additions can have no less effect on the school than a new building and can even establish a new identity for the school.

The Gentofte Kommune's school building programme (SKUB) has witnessed the overhaul of its school estate with a mixture of new buildings, refurbishment and extension projects. The project at **Bakkegårdsskolen** in Gentofte, Denmark [CEBRA Architects and Søren Robert Lund, 2003] involved an addition that went well beyond just creating a new gymnasium.

The school sits at the heart of a low-lying residential area. The original four-storey brick block is resonant of the early 1950s Scandinavian modernism with its simple brick treatment, windows contained within framed hori-

BAKKEGÅRDSSKOLEN IN GENTOFTE, DENMARK [CEBRA Architects and Søren Robert Lund, 2003]
View of existing building. A gymnasium was added that provided a roof garden and connected previously disparate school buildings. The changes in grade have been used to create exciting spaces for play and transition. The architects' sketch demonstrates the interesting juxtaposition.

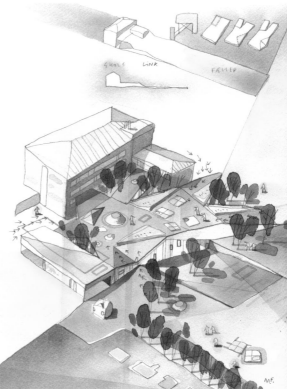

BAKKEGÅRDSSKOLEN / **Interior of the new gymnasium**

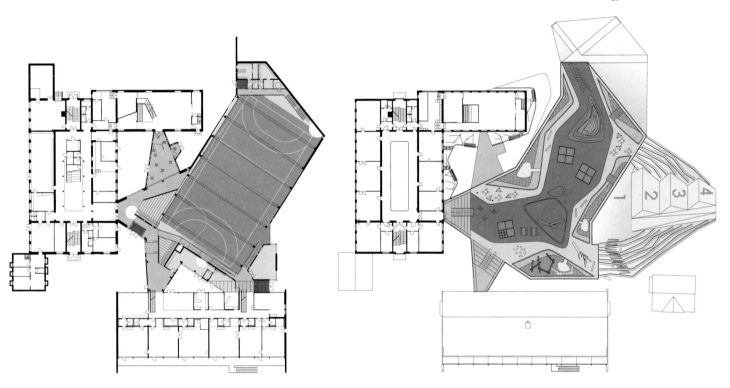

The ground floor plan (left) shows the internal connections created between the existing buildings, whilst the roof plan (right) shows how a new external landscape has been created.

zontal bands and a low-pitched copper roof. Internally the classrooms are based around a light-filled atrium with elegant handrails framing views throughout the building. A lower building added later contains the home bases for the kindergarten years.

The project started with the school, pupils and parents establishing core values which should be used to guide future developments. These were laid down in a document that informed the collaborative design process with the architects and other stakeholders. The resulting building sits at the heart of the campus, providing physical links between the existing buildings and extending out into the landscape. An angular volume clad in bold colours creates a strikingly contrasting addition. The connection with the existing buildings is where the scheme really excels. Internally, the division between old and new is blurred through narrow connections that lightly touch the existing whilst creating a series of light wells that are resonant of the original building.

The playground has been displaced by the new gymnasium building with its sinews that connect to the older structures, and it has been cleverly relocated to the new roof level. Kragh & Berglund's landscape works harmoniously with the building, and the angles found in the plan

ESCOLA SECUNDÁRIA D. DINIS IN LISBON, PORTUGAL [Bak Gordon Arquitectos, 2008]
The addition to the school weaves in between four existing pavilions. As well as accommodating a new auditorium this building
provides internal circulation between the previously separate pavilions.

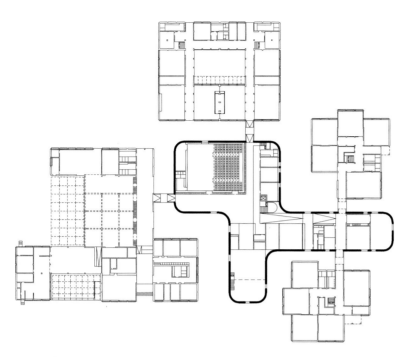

ESCOLA SECUNDARIA D. DINIS / The space between the new and old buildings allows natural light to enter the existing pavilions.

Ground floor plan. The added pavilion pushes in between the older buildings.

inform the section of the building which flows down to meet the wider school grounds. This single move does more to unify the campus than perhaps anything else. The children are able to access the school grounds from the principal classroom level on the first floor. At this raised level, the imposing four storey edifice of the original building appears reduced in scale to better fit that of the surrounding predominantly two-storey domestic context. The elevation of the playground also connects the children to the wider cityscape by affording them views over the suburban roofs and flat topography of Copenhagen.

The scheme is both bold and sensitive. The central move of inventing a topography that flows from inside to outside makes for an immensely inspiring and playful environment in which to learn, and yet this is countered by the understanding and lightness of touch in the renovation of the existing buildings, helping to tie the campus together.

The Portuguese Government's Secondary School Modernisation Programme[11] (SMP) run by Parque Escolar EPE, an autonomous government agency, sought to refurbish and modernise over 300 schools by 2015. Portugal as most of Europe has faced increased financial pressures since the global financial crash of 2007. In spite of this many of the first three phases of the programme were realised between 2007 and 2010. Although the programme was suspended in 2011 it has produced some remarkable results. **Escola Secundária D. Dinis** in Lisbon, Portugal [Bak Gordon Arquitectos, 2008] is one of four schools completed in the first phase.

The original building is typical of nearly 70% of modern Portuguese secondary schools. Constructed in the 1970s, it was based on a series of simple metal-framed pavilions. These buildings were often poorly insulated, both thermally and acoustically. The pavilions were separated from each other, linked by external canopies, causing functional and programmatic issues. Bak Gordon's proposals sought to develop a response that could be repeated with ease at other schools of a similar nature.

The resulting building weaves its way between the older pavilions, connecting in turn to each. The new central building houses communal functions that were either separated from the pavilions or absent all together. The new block steps down the site from single storey to the north to a double-height structure at the south accommodating a new large auditorium. Other facilities housed within it include a library, study areas and departmental support rooms. The building becomes the physical and metaphorical heart of the school, giving the previously disparate campus much greater focus.

CLAPHAM MANOR PRIMARY SCHOOL IN LONDON, ((UK)) [DeRijke Marsh Morgan Architects – DRMM, 2009]
The extension bridges between the old buildings.

The building is materially very simple. A steel frame structure was chosen for the necessity of fast construction time as much as for economic reasons. This was then covered in a robust insulated steel cladding. The white of the cladding externally marries the school to the surrounding pavilions, which in turn have been insulated and painted white. Internally a new red floor flows through old and new, again helping to unify the campus. The existing pavilions have also been reglazed to ensure further continuity in both visual quality and energy performance between old and new.

In a 2012 review by the Organisation for Economic Cooperation and Development (OECD), the Portuguese SMP was commended for its approach to the renovation of its existing school stock and the quality of the results from those projects completed so far. The report highlights 'that good architectural design improves the quality of education', stating that the SMP has responded to this with constantly achieving good quality spaces that support effective learning.[13]

Strategic alterations and phased development

The projects explored so far have been sizeable additions or alterations to schools. Smaller projects can have just as significant an impact on the performance of a school. The piecemeal approach to updating schools often results in the degradation of the building. A clear strategy can help to focus how and where development should occur to provide maximum benefit to the school. This may be the creation of a new entrance to improve accessibility to the school or the reorganisation of the internal layout to create new teaching spaces.

Clapham Manor Primary School in London, UK [DeRijke Marsh Morgan Architects – DRMM, 2009] sits on a tight urban site in central London. The Victorian board school had already been much expanded and needed to strike a careful balance between maintaining external play and sports facilities with the need for additional teaching space to support growing student numbers.

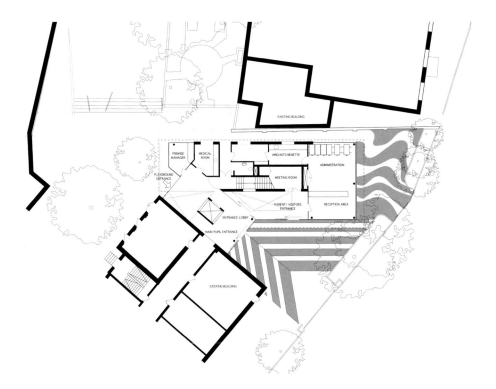

CLAPHAM MANOR PRIMARY SCHOOL / Ground floor plan. A new lift and stair well improve accessibility to the old buildings.

The colourful façade provides a new identity to the school at the front of the site.

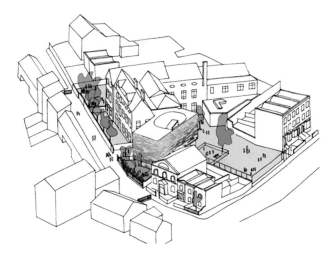

The school sits on a tight urban site in central London.

The architects' bold scheme utilises a tight corner of the site to create a new block that benefits the school and the wider urban realm.

The bold striped colours of the exterior are in stark contrast to the surrounding soft yellows of London stock bricks. The stripes carefully conceal the change of scale between old and new, fitting four new floors to the original building's three. This clever shift in scale creates an extra floor of accommodation which would have been difficult to achieve elegantly in a more traditional approach. The extension also enables new circulation: an attractive external glazed staircase bridges the different levels creatively and acts as a design highlight.

The openness of the glazed junction between old and new allows the ground floor space to visually flow from the front to the rear of the site. Bold colours accentuate the new façade. Internally, the space is equally playful with bold floor graphics of the local area street map, asymmetric and unconventional placing of the windows. The bold colours are more subdued in the interior but continue to enhance the playfulness of the new learning spaces.

PINE COMMUNITY SCHOOL IN BRISBANE, AUSTRALIA [Riddel Architecture, 2009]
Several small additions improved this primary school: The library space received an attractive glazed corner and a new canopy highlights the entrance.

Pine Community School in Brisbane, Australia [Riddel Architecture, 2009] is a small primary school in the Arana Hills suburb of Brisbane. The school had developed steadily and outgrown its existing facilities.[14] The school used the Australian Government BER funds[15] to expand the school, build a new library, office and store. Although modest in ambition, a series of small-scale additions have made a significant impact on the school and the community using it. A new glazed corner in the library space forms the most obvious architectural statement and surveys the approach to the school. A new canopy and roof structure clearly highlight the entrance to the building and bring unity to new and old elements. The existing walls are reclad and thermally insulated to improve the environmental performance of the building. The resulting project is a school that retains the small-scale domestic atmosphere of the original building whilst creating a new strong identity for the future.

Adaptation of other buildings and prefabrication

Previous examples in this chapter explored the benefits of intelligent refurbishment and extension of existing school buildings. Following the end of the UK's Building Schools for the Future programme in 2010, the new 'Free Schools' initiative[16] calls for the greater use of prefabrication and the reuse of existing buildings in the creation of new educational facilities.

Standardisation and prefabrication is not a new approach to making cost-effective and expedient school buildings. The CLASP[17] system was developed in the late 1950s to deliver cost-efficient prefabricated buildings quickly. The programme sought to address skill and materials shortages in post-war Britain. Although perceived to be hugely successful, many of the buildings are now reaching the end of their life span or suffer maintenance issues caused by the use of materials such as asbestos or poor construction quality. It is hoped, however, that new advances in prefabrication technologies and the industrial creation of building components can provide new high-quality results.

Duggan Morris Architects were commissioned by the London Borough of Croydon to develop a series of buildings for a number of schools under 'The Cooking Spaces Project'. The projects sought to answer the government's challenge to create 'off-the-shelf', modular design. Duggan Morris' approach shows how a basic palette of materials in flat pack and prefabricated elements can make buildings that respond both to site and programme. Two projects have been realised, the first at **Westwood Girls' College** in Croydon, London, UK [Duggan Morris

WESTWOOD GIRLS' COLLEGE IN CROYDON, LONDON, UK [Duggan Morris Architects, 2010]
The project shows the possibilities of an 'off-the-shelf', modular design. The simple and rectilinear form makes use of a repeated grid structure and allows for prefabricated elements that simultaneously create interesting, flexible spaces whilst responding to the site and the users.

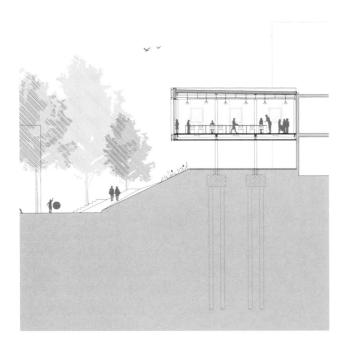

Section through dining hall

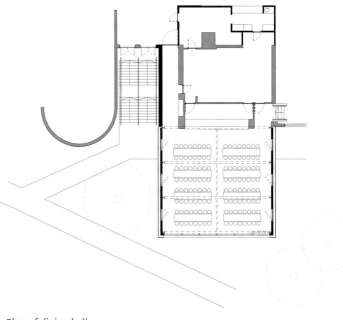

Plan of dining hall

WESTWOOD GIRLS' COLLEGE / Glazing becomes a continuous screen across one side of the building.

Architects, 2010] and the second at Virgo Fidelis Convent School in Croydon, London, UK [Duggan Morris Architects, 2011]. The two schemes use the same palette of materials in simple and legible layers. A rectilinear form is used to exploit a repeated grid structure. At Westwood Girls' College the structure abuts the front of the existing school building and is cantilevered above the ground. Whilst the form is simple, the set of components provides enough flexibility to make the schemes responsive to their sites. Glazing becomes a continuous screen across one end of the building at Westwood Girls' College, whilst smaller glazed panels frame views of the surrounding school grounds at Virgo Fidelis, creating a more intimate environment. The façade of insulated steel-clad panels is more reminiscent of an industrial shed than a school. A clever use of an expanded mesh for wrapping the box lifts the architectural language of the scheme. The mesh is also used to apply colour to the buildings, silver in the case of Westwood and gold in the case of Virgo Fidelis. Glazing further enhances the schools' appearances. The schemes aptly demonstrate the importance of good design to all buildings, especially when using standardised and prefabricated elements.

The other strand of current educational thinking in the UK is the reuse and inhabitation of buildings that are not necessarily educational buildings. Here, too, clever thinking and good design are at the heart of creative reuse of existing structures. The UK 'Free Schools' initiative has proposals for both the creation of new buildings and the refurbishment of older buildings. What is clear is that in any conversion, be it of an old school building, a steel-framed warehouse or a disused car showroom, strong consideration needs to be given to the core requirements of all educational buildings. Circulation, adaptability, pedagogical ethos, environmental factors and above all the classroom experience should be at the fore.

The **University Technical College** in Sheffield, UK [HLM Architects, 2013] is an entirely new school that aims to forge a link between the city's universities, leading industry partners and Sheffield College in order to provide vocational training in engineering and manufacturing, and creative and digital media industries for 14–19 year olds. The school aims to fill a perceived void in skills training for adolescents and to improve the employability of local young people. Deputy Prime Minister Nick Clegg said: 'Lots of local employers tell me even at a time now when people are looking for work and finding it difficult to find work, employers are finding it difficult to find people with the right skills. ... This is a tradition for the past it is also a tradition we can draw on for the future.'[18] The new school occupies a site at the centre of the Cultural Industries Quarter (CIQ)[19] and is a mixture of old and new buildings. As the location is a tight city centre site, every available space has been used, from the careful rehabilitation of the old industrial buildings on site to the roof top multi-games pitches, dramatic dining room and social suite providing views across the city. The building and site has been carefully planned and utilises the landscape courtyard to attenuate risk from its flood plain location next to a culverted river.

At the core of the design is the use of some of the oldest surviving buildings within the CIQ, instantly creating a

UNIVERSITY TECHNICAL COLLEGE IN SHEFFIELD, UK [HLM Architects, 2013]
View outside to Cultural Industries Quarter (CIQ) in which the school occupies some of the oldest surviving buildings. Located in a tight city centre site, every space was utilised. Timber beams, industrial fireplaces, the brickwork cleaned and chimneys were left exposed, recognising the inherent value in retaining the old industrial structures and the craft heritage of the city of Sheffield.

direct link to Sheffield's craft and industrial heritage; themes that pedagogically underpin the new school. The new elements create a street frontage along two edges of the site, forming a courtyard to the rear, echoing the traditional form of the old 'little mesters', i.e. master craftsmen's cutlery workshops. Internally, the material qualities of the old building are revealed with brickwork cleaned as well as industrial fireplaces and chimneys and timber beams left exposed. The school's internal circulation routes deliberately exploit the level differences between the old and new building elements. New elements result in an active street frontage with large areas of glazing revealing workshops, design and manufacturing studios. The servicing, neatly hung from the concrete soffits, is deliberately left exposed with the pipework labelled, creating a 1:1 scale service diagram, displaying how the building transports heat and water.

For a new school, it would have been cheaper and easier to knock down the old buildings and start again. In recognising the inherent value in retaining the old structures, the vocationally oriented teaching pedagogy of the new school instantly grafts on to the industrial and craft heritage of the city whilst making a bold statement of intent to the future that draws on the success of the industrial past in the city.

REFERENCES

1 'School Buildings Scheme Scrapped', BBC News Education and Family, 5 July 2010. www.bbc.co.uk/news/10514113. Accessed 2 August 2012.

2 The Primary Capital Programme ran in the UK from 2008–2009 and made additional funding available to authorities. It aimed to renew at least 50% of primary schools over 14 years, subject to future spending plans. It was cancelled in 2009.

3 Free schools were introduced in the UK by the Conservative-Liberal Democrat coalition following the 2010 general election making it possible for parents, teachers, charities and businesses to set up their own schools.

4 The Priority School Building programme (PSBP) is a centrally managed programme set up to address the schools most in need of urgent repair. Through the PSBP, 261 schools in the UK will be rebuilt or have their needs met. The first school will be completed in 2014.

5 'First Special and Alternative Provision Free Schools Given the Green Light', *Daily Telegraph*, 14 November 2011.

6 'Building the Education Revolution – Waste Blows out to $1.1bn', *The Australian*, 9 July 2011.

7 In the late 1940s, Hertfordshire County Council pioneered a system, specifically for schools, of standardised prefabricated parts, which could be constructed in factories and assembled on site.

8 There are a total of 38 post-war listed structures in the UK. 'Refurbishing Historic Buildings', *English Heritage*, January 2010, p. 6.

9 'Refurbishing Historic Buildings', *English Heritage*, January 2010, p. 5.

10 The school is also described in chapter 6, Learning Outside the Classroom, p. 152.

11 'Jarmund/Vigsnaes Architects Transforms a Worn 1960s-era School Building into a Vibrant Learning Environment', *Architectural Record*, July 2009. http://archrecord.construction.com/projects/bts/archives/k-12/09_Oslo/. Accessed 1 August 2012.

12 The Secondary School Modernisation Programme in Portugal, launched in 2007 and implemented by Parque Escolar EPE, has three fundamental objectives: 1. to renovate and modernise the school buildings, 2. opening the schools up to the community, 3. creating an efficient and effective school building management system

13 Modernising Secondary School Buildings in Portugal, OECD, 2012, p. 44.

14 'Pine Community School / Riddel Architecture', *ArchDaily*, 3 May 2010. www.archdaily.com/58425/ Accessed 2 August 2012.

15 'Building the Education Revolution' (BER) is an Australian government programme administered by the Department of Education, Employment and Workplace Relations (DEEWR) to provide new and refurbished infrastructure to all eligible Australian schools. The programme was part of the Australian Government's financial stimulus package following the global financial crisis of 2008.

16 The 'Free School' programme was introduced by the UK Conservative Government in 2010 following the cancellation of the Building Schools for the Future Programme. Free schools in England are funded by taxpayers, and are free to attend, and not controlled by a local authority.

17 CLASP is a system of steel frame elements on a planned structural grid which in turn is governed by a basic module dimension.

18 BBC News, 10 October 2011. www.bbc.co.uk/news/uk-england-south-yorkshire-15246900. Accessed 6 November 2013.

19 The Cultural Industries Quarter is a district in the city centre of Sheffield, England, and one of the 11 quarters designated in the 1994 City Centre Strategy.

Summary

9 REFURBISHMENT AND EXTENSION OF EXISTING SCHOOLS

1. It is important that refurbishment projects **work with the building** in order to maximise the success of the project. Investment in time at the early stages of the project and understanding the existing built fabric before developing the brief will uncover issues and raise opportunities to respond to the building.

2. **Smaller innovative projects can have a significant impact** on the performance of a school. A clear strategy can help to focus how and where development should occur to provide maximum benefit to the school. This may be the creation of a new entrance to improve accessibility to the school or the reorganisation of internal spaces to provide new teaching spaces.

3. The **conversion of other building types into school buildings** can, with clever thinking and good design, be an excellent strategy to reuse, creatively and economically, existing redundant buildings.

4. Refurbishment and extensions can be used to **consolidate the identity** of a school and its campus, regardless of scale.

5. Refurbishment and extensions can be a **celebration of the local community** and the school's place within it through the careful consideration of form, material and use of space.

6. **Prefabrication of new facilities** requires as much thought as in situ construction to ensure maximum benefit to the school and its wider community.

10 Furniture and Equipment in Learning Spaces / ANNA HOLDER

Furniture can be instrumental in the success of the school. It can also compromise an otherwise successful space. As the most direct interface between children and their environment, furniture can be used to organise space or provide vital storage to support the whole gamut of learning activities. In schools, furniture mediates between our environment and ourselves. Chairs, tables, lockers, benches, screens, cupboards: these are the elements we will lay our hands on every day. They shape our actual experience of a learning space.

This chapter explores the role of furniture, fixtures and equipment in supporting the pedagogical approach of a learning environment and providing the interface between users and building in a variety of different ways. It describes how innovative approaches to the design of furniture pioneered around the globe have addressed the needs of pupils, teachers and visitors in a range of different ways.

The chapter looks at how furniture can be used to organise the space for learning, access and storage of equipment, thus enhancing readiness for learning and creating spaces that welcome and aid way finding. The examples discussed also present a range of different methods of procurement, from architect-designed bespoke solutions through the selection of appropriate pieces by furniture consultants, to integrating furniture into strategies for art.

ROC AVENTUS IN APELDOORN, THE NETHERLANDS [Jurgen Bey, Tjep., Tejo Remy and René Veenhuizen with Kunst en Bedrijf and AGS Architekten & Planners, 2004] The design of furniture has progressed to respond to the wide range of learning types. In ROC Aventus, each learning space has bespoke furniture with strong graphic prints, created by young designers, to assist learning and encourage creativity.

Making and marking space

Chairs and desks

Complementing or contradicting the overall design of spaces, furniture can provide us with visual and haptic clues as to how we might use a space, both through the design of individual elements and the arrangement of elements in space.

Chairs that allow us to change both our position and the configuration of seat height, back of chair and relationship to a working surface make us sit comfortably and thus foster longer concentration.[1] Tables that let us converse with others, sitting face-to-face and proximate, suggest that we might work together and collaborate in learning; screens made of materials that soften the surrounding noise and can hide us from view will enable concentration and quiet reflection.

Precious fabrics and expensive or delicate materials make a space feel special and enjoyable to experience and might make us reticent to move furniture and make our own arrangements of space, or might make us think about using furniture with consideration. Conversely, solid chairs or tables in 'everyday' materials might be sat on, stood on, stacked, scratched and bashed without thought. The sort of furniture we have seen a hundred times before, in many different settings, will not necessarily fire the imagination, while one unfamiliar item could instigate a rethinking of the entire room. The ability to change and arrange spaces according to the requirements of different tasks also has the potential to give school users (pupils, teachers and support staff) a greater sense of agency over their learning and teaching, and a feeling of ownership and comfort in their environment.

Furniture types and arrangements in schools have changed over time to reflect trends in pedagogy and views of the role of the pupil in society.[2] For instance, 19th-century school rooms were furnished with rows of solid timber desk and bench units, heavy and virtually immovable, locking pupils into a fixed sitting position and a spatial configuration enforcing the dominance of the teacher as the controller of the learning space. Changes in pedagogy over the last century have seen desks give way to grouped tables and chairs, recognising the role of group and peer learning, and the benefits of flexibility in setting up different types of learning spaces.[3]

Creating a sense of entrance

Several examples of using furniture to form spaces or give identity and human scale to larger areas are demonstrated at **ROC Aventus** in Apeldoorn, the Netherlands [Jurgen Bey, Tjep., Tejo Remy and René Veenhuizen with Kunst en Bedrijf and AGS Architekten & Planners, 2004][4]. This technical college is the flagship of a Dutch national programme to integrate vocational and technical learning into mainstream education.[5] The college takes the form of an interior 'high street' with functioning businesses including a mechanic, travel agent and hairdresser. Here students can learn on the job, while in the upper floors of the building lecture theatres, classrooms and open-plan office spaces provide a setting for theoretical learning across a range of subjects.

A series of specially commissioned and adapted furniture was procured for the college from a selection of young but internationally renowned designers. The procurement of furniture for education spaces is often handled by large Furniture and Fittings (FF&E) consultants or taken on by the school themselves, but in this case the importance of a tailored approach led to the commission being facilitated by Kunst en Bedrijf, an agency which specialises in integrating artwork into buildings and public spaces, allowing innovative designers to create site-specific pieces which enliven the architecture and define spaces within the college.

Subject areas are grouped spatially, and each grouping is provided with its own reception area, comprising space for administration, group working and break-out or touchdown learning.[6] Entering the area for health studies and nursing, the visitor is immediately drawn to a large white reception desk, faced in moulded plastic but with a pattern reminiscent of upholstery – the effect is clean

ROC AVENTUS IN APELDOORN, THE NETHERLANDS [Jurgen Bey, Tjep., Tejo Remy and René Veenhuizen with Kunst en Bedrijf and AGS Architekten & Planners, 2004] The design and graphics study area feels like a modern studio. Suspended curtain tracks and lighting allow the space to be easily reconfigured. Reclaimed furniture was transformed with graphic prints co-ordinated with the floor finish to give identity to a specific subject area. Bottom: In the area for health studies, the visitor first encounters a large white reception desk while an arched tent structure suggests a canvas 'field hospital'.

and fresh but not quite clinical. Just beyond, an arched tent structure suggests a canvas 'field hospital', with desk and chairs within providing a semi-private meeting space. Students sit and chat before class on comfy furniture of various types.

In the subject grouping for design and graphics, existing furniture was reused, but updated and made unique. Standard metal-framed tables, chairs and waste-paper baskets were printed with a graphic of wireframe and component drawings combining in a monochrome landscape. Design magazine are scattered across the table and a curtain with the same graphic can be drawn to bi-

sect the space, creating a quiet place for product research or small group meetings. The area is defined by a vinyl floor, again with a complementing graphic, and surrounded by small glass-walled meeting rooms. This, along with the repurposed furniture, gives a 'design studio' atmosphere to what would otherwise be a standard office space.

These elements of furniture each have a distinct use, but also combine to make a welcoming space with a clear purpose and intent. Creating reception spaces for each subject grouping helps to define the experience of the overall building, as each area has its own sense of

NEW LINE LEARNING PLAZA, OLDBOROUGH MANOR COMMUNITY SCHOOL IN MAIDSTONE, KENT, UK
[Alsop Architects with FFE Consulting, 2006, and Gensler Architects, 2009]
Plaza 1 (left) by Alsop Architects addresses younger pupils with tiered and brightly coloured seating units. Plaza 2 (right), designed by Gensler Architects in 2009, has a demure colour scheme, that fits the needs of older pupils.

entrance and arrival. The design has humour, with its tongue-in-cheek references to each vocation, and the budget material palette is offset by an attention to detail in design and manufacturing.

Dividing space

As well as making spaces feel distinct, furniture can work to divide larger spaces and create a hierarchy of uses or experiences within an open plan. At the **New Line Learning Plaza**, Oldborough Manor Community School in Maidstone, Kent, UK [Alsop Architects with FFE Consulting, 2006, and Gensler Architects, 2009] for 566 pupils, this new type of learning place was piloted, and termed a 'learning plaza'. The concept was for a large-scale, flexible space for project-based learning which might involve large groups of pupils receiving information from a teacher, pupils working together in smaller groups to develop ideas and then working in pairs or individually on producing pieces of work, with information technology integrated throughout. Incorporating several different styles of

learning and the ability to move swiftly between styles requires a considered approach to the furniture, fixtures and equipment. The space itself was a converted sports hall so it had no internal partitions and allowed great flexibility of use. The architect worked with an experienced FF&E consultant to source the range of furniture and equipment to create the different working spaces.

The problem of seating the maximum capacity of 90 pupils, whilst still being able to quickly transform the space for smaller group work, required a bespoke solution. In Plaza 1, designed by Alsop Architects in 2006, tiered and brightly coloured seating units, addressing younger pupils, were constructed from MDF over a steel frame and faced with fabric and leather and mounted on wheels. Each unit seats 30 pupils and they can be grouped together or spread throughout the space. Off-the-shelf solutions were sourced for the furniture for group working, with propeller-shaped tables each seating 12 students, and further desk spaces provided by perimeter tables.

'SUPERCLASS' AT ACLAND BURGHLEY SCHOOL IN CAMDEN, LONDON, UK [SCABAL, 2012]

Using an existing assembly hall as a testing bed for project-based learning, the architect and the client worked together to design a flexible, open-plan space. Redundant furniture was used to create this 'Internet Bar', made from lift-top desks, which hold computer screens and support laptops.

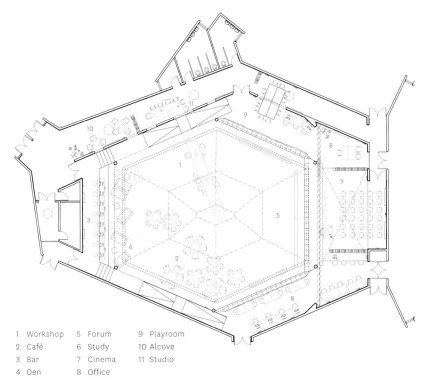

1 Workshop
2 Café
3 Bar
4 Den
5 Forum
6 Study
7 Cinema
8 Office
9 Playroom
10 Alcove
11 Studio

Ground floor plan

Bespoke furniture was made from recycling old and redundant furniture retrieved from the school's stores.

Section

In 2009, Plaza 2 was given a more demure colour scheme that fits the needs of older pupils. The furniture and its arrangement was refined, to allow for more flexibility and adaptability from the first iteration of the Learning Plaza.

Another example of a flexible space aimed at project-based learning is the **'Superclass' at Acland Burghley School** in Camden, London [SCABAL, 2012]. The project was initiated as part of an interim intervention in a school earmarked for further 'Building Schools for the Future' funding. Making use of the existing assembly hall, client and architect collaborated on an architectural and educational experiment to inform approaches to pedagogy and use of space in the school. The design and layout of this space was developed in dialogue with teachers and school governors. Pupil and staff perceptions and learning experiences were observed over the course of a year and eventually informed the brief for the new school building.

Furniture is integral to the design and construction of the Superclass, both for shaping and defining the different learning areas and opportunities offered and also for providing the project's building materials. Old, damaged and redundant furniture from the school's stores was given a new lease of life, with component parts being recycled into a range of bespoke furniture pieces. This furniture is used to create a variety of smaller areas, called settings, within the main space. These support different learning experiences and are also intended to be flexible, allowing different spatial configurations and approaches to be tested.

The different settings are created through the use of customised furniture pieces, all of which are reused from old school furniture. For example, 'floating' tables made from old-fashioned lift-top desks, with their lids raised to hold computer screens, support laptops and create an 'Internet Bar' area overlooking the main space. Long tables and benches of joined, reclaimed timber form the 'Workshop', describing both a setting and the activity intended for it. Tables painted to match brightly coloured new chairs offer break-out working space in the 'Alcove'.

The idea behind creating a range of spaces is to encourage pupils to be self-motivated in tailoring their learning experience, finding ways to work at their own pace, and moving between individual study and more sociable group and event-based learning. Some new furniture has been specified, such as beanbags for the more informal 'Den' space, but mostly the Superclass offers a creative mingling of the reused and remade. This frugal ingenuity, intended to be exemplary, means that the space was kitted out for only 105,000 £: a budget which includes new lighting and acoustic devices as well as the creation of structural openings, making connections between the hall and adjoining corridors, to show how old spaces can be used anew.

'Where are we going to put everything?': furniture for storage

From our research visits to many different schools of all types, storage stands out as a problem common to most new schools. It is one which is often difficult for designers and schools to address, as design guidance sets limits for space and the budget allocated to storage, but school storage needs are seemingly unlimited. A common sight in newly built schools is to have an overflow of equipment and resources across classrooms or housed in 'off-the-shelf' storage units jammed into corridors, as the built-in storage provided proves inadequate.

This section describes two approaches to designing a strategy for storage furniture: the first incorporating mobile storage into spaces designed to be used flexibly and the second demonstrating a successful incorporation of storage furniture into the building fabric and overall design of the school.

Heimdalsgades School in Copenhagen, Denmark [Kant Arkitekter, 2001]

The architects created a combination of fixed, built-in storage units as well as moveable storage containers. In the corridors storage walls are hidden behind polycarbonate screens. Bottom: Wheeled furniture means that whole spaces can be cleared and thus become more flexible.

Fixed and mobile storage solutions

The problem of providing sufficient storage had to be addressed also at **Heimdalsgades School** in Copenhagen, Denmark [Kant Arkitekter, 2001], a converted bakery on a tight urban site. With a focus on flexibility and adaptability, and keen to avoid the institutional feeling of the traditional school building, learning at Heimdalsgades School is organised across four themes, each with associated physical areas: a physical and musical area, called the 'Studio'; the practical and aesthetic area, termed the 'Workshop'; the international and cultural area, referred to as the 'Station'; and the scientific and experimenting area, the 'Laboratory'. Within each area, spaces are left largely free from permanent partitions and provided instead with moveable screens that allow them to be easily reconfigured into different spatial arrangements. This means there is less space for storage to be built into walls or arranged against partitions.

The school adopted a strategy for storage that combined instances of fixed, wall-mounted furniture where possible, with moveable units on castors. Storage for the pupils is provided in the more traditional form of built-in lockers in the entrance area, which doubles in purpose to give the children a sense of ownership of the reception space with their own piece of personal space in the school. Storage of equipment for science lessons is also

YPENBURG LYCEUM IN THE HAGUE, THE NETHERLANDS [DP6, 2006]
Bold graphics transform the white storage walls. Also the furniture is covered in graphics, thus adding vibrancy to the simple material palette of the building. Bottom: The wall is punctured with display units that provide interest along the circulation spaces.

wall-mounted, as is appropriate for one subject where tasks are 'fixed' and location-specific. In addition to this, the designers chose to provide storage boxes on wheels, which can be moved around the building adding to flexibility of use, and, when combined with the screens and tables which are also on wheels, give many possibilities of different spatial arrangements. The same type of storage boxes are used as 'teacher stations', meaning that instead of having distinct areas, teachers work with the school's shifting approach to territory, and move themselves and their equipment to spaces which they can then configure according to the learning approach they require.

Integrating storage into the building

At **Ypenburg Lyceum** in The Hague, the Netherlands [DP6, 2006], student and classroom storage has been fully incorporated into the design of the building fabric, and was also integrated into the school's art strategy. Positioned around a four-storey central atrium, classrooms are arranged in rings around the exterior of each floor plate, encircling the loops of circulation space and a large main stair. A deep wall between the classrooms and circulation space at each level is 'inhabited' with student lockers and school storage cupboards (facing into the atrium) and storage for classes (facing into the rooms). These inhabited walls are punctuated with glazed display niches, providing space for display in each classroom and enlivening the corridors. They also create visual connections between the classrooms and the rest of the school whilst avoiding the distracting and uncomfortable 'goldfish bowl' effect of glass partitions. Largely glazed exterior walls in every classroom allow for good natural lighting, and natural ventilation is achieved through opening lights. Daylight penetrates throughout the building by means of skylights and internal courtyards so the storage 'wall' also provides a visual effect of solidity and separation in an otherwise very transparent and visually connected building.

What makes the approach so successful, however, is the incorporation of a bold black and white abstract

YPENBURG LYCEUM / The central atrium is lined with deep walls housing storage and display units.

The walls also provide storage and display space within the classrooms.

graphic pattern, which runs across the surface of the locker doors throughout the school, at a scale that can be 'read' across floors when seen from the atrium. Small keypads at regular intervals provide access to the locked storage using individual numerical codes, thus removing the need for key locks on each unit and allowing the locker fronts to be read as an uninterrupted visual surface. The 1% art budget for the school was allocated to the decoration of the locker fronts and was designed by a graphic artist in collaboration with the architects. As well as creating a striking visual impact this approach to decoration visually connects every level of the school, contributing to orientation for users.

Furniture components: a variety of approaches

Convertible furniture

An alternative approach to furniture, fixtures and equipment is demonstrated at **Fuji Kindergarten** in Tokyo, Japan [Tezuka Architects, 2007]. This building has won awards for its innovation as a learning environment and the sensitivity of its architectural concept.[7] The kindergarten is designed to accommodate 500 children, making it the biggest preschool in Japan, and its ring-shaped floor area is left almost entirely open in plan. The kindergarten is operated along principles of Montessori, encouraging pupil-directed learning and exploration of the environment as a tool for developing skills. Choices of furniture, fixtures and equipment support this pedagogical approach in a number of ways. Firstly, to enable pupils to inhabit the largely open-plan interior and exterior spaces

of the building, chairs and tables are supplemented with a system of three sizes of stackable timber boxes, which are used for sitting, as a work surface, storage, display and dividing space through the construction of small walls. The boxes are constructed from Paulownia, a hardwood timber indigenous to China, that is both light and soft, meaning that children can move the boxes easily and are not hurt if they fall or knock into them.

Secondly, while the kindergarten's sliding exterior glazed walls make for good daylighting, the artificial lighting provided adds another layer of learning through experience for pupils, with a series of individual ceiling-mounted electric lightbulbs each being controlled by a pullchord and dimmer. Children are encouraged to experiment with making changes to their space by manipulating the lighting as well as thinking about where the electricity for lighting comes from and how it is made.

A similar approach has been developed for water provision. In the large oval courtyard at the centre of the kindergarten, metal water troughs, buckets and taps are surrounded by ground paved with timber rounds. These are used by the children for water play, but also by teachers to encourage children to question where water comes from, and where it goes to, as it soaks between the paving and into the ground.

Furniture integrated with fixtures and services

Another interesting example is **De Kikker School** in Amsterdam, the Netherlands [DOK Architecten (previously Van der Pol), 2006], part of an education complex including two primary schools, a daycare centre and

FUJI KINDERGARTEN IN TOKYO, JAPAN [Tezuka Architects, 2007]

Moveable timber boxes make up the furniture which can be used for sitting, as a hard working surface, storage, display and can be stacked to create partitions in the open space. Bottom: Fuji Kindergarten follows the pedagogical principles of Montessori, where children are encouraged to learn by engaging with their environment.

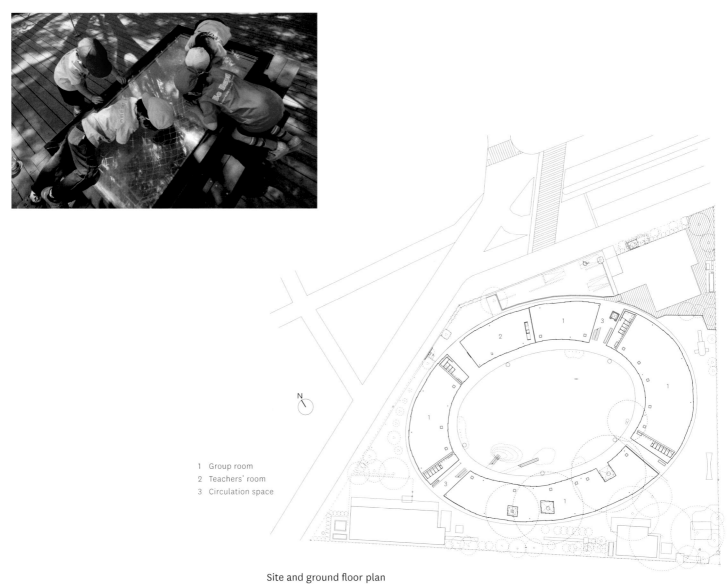

1 Group room
2 Teachers' room
3 Circulation space

Site and ground floor plan

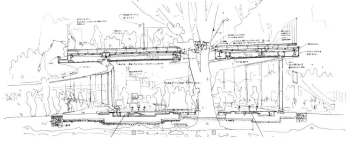

FUJI KINDERGARTEN / Design sketch. All the existing trees were kept and integrated into the design as well as the learning.

Designed as ring-shaped open floor, the exterior glazed walls slide to maximise natural daylight and allow children to explore outdoors.

The environment is important for developing social and learning skills. Here, the building becomes a prop that engages children with their environment. For instance, in the courtyard there are metal water troughs, buckets and taps to prompt the question: where does water come from?

DE KIKKER SCHOOL IN AMSTERDAM, THE NETHERLANDS [DOK Architecten (previously Van der Pol), 2006]
In each classroom, the service core is located under a small mezzanine space that allows the remaining classroom space to be used without any interruptions.

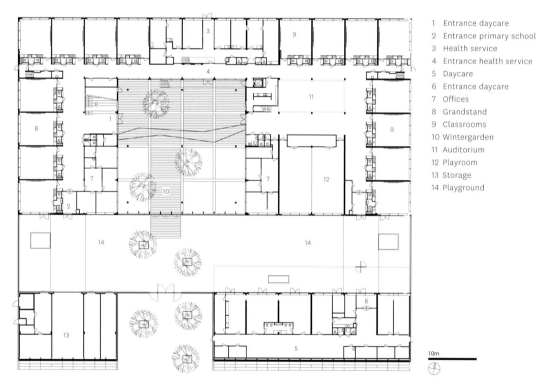

1   Entrance daycare
2   Entrance primary school
3   Health service
4   Entrance health service
5   Daycare
6   Entrance daycare
7   Offices
8   Grandstand
9   Classrooms
10 Wintergarden
11 Auditorium
12 Playroom
13 Storage
14 Playground

Ground floor plan. The entrance to each classroom is marked by a 'core' containing storage and services.

health facilities, known as a 'Broad School'. The idea behind the school is to try to integrate children's education with services that support parents' needs as well. This concept of integration and support is carried through in the spatial arrangement of the built fabric, with the different functions sharing communal spaces. Within classrooms, services are integrated into a 'core' of fixtures, which holds services such as toilets, kitchen equipment and information technology workstations slotted under a small mezzanine space which is used for break out and a reward space. This arrangement of varied fixtures and equipment, once designed, was easily replicated for each classroom and thus combines several fixed elements in the same area, allowing for more flexible use of the remaining classroom space.

FRAN KRSTO FRANKOPAN PRIMARY SCHOOL IN KRK, CROATIA [Randic and Turato, 2005]
The generous circulation spaces provide circulation between levels and also provide places to congregate. The school fits neatly into the urban fabric of its setting, a historic Croatian walled town.

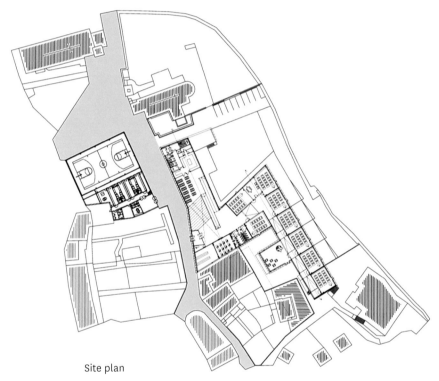

Site plan

Using the building fabric

A more conventional approach to built-in furniture, where the school fabric itself forms the sitting areas is relatively common. However, this is demonstrated elegantly in **Fran Krsto Frankopan Primary School** in Krk, Croatia [Randic and Turato, 2005], a school which fits neatly into the urban fabric of its setting, a historic Croatian walled town. Following the existing contours of the site, the school is arranged along two adjacent linear circulation spaces, and the slope of the wider of the two traverses the ground plane via a series of low wide steps. Surfaced in timber, and in a soft yellow painted space, bathed in natural light, these steps become a natural sitting and gathering space for pupils, wide and broad enough to accommodate a school assembly, but also tranquil enough for cosy playtime chats. This is one of the

KINDERGARTEN PUSTEBLUME IN BUCHEN, GERMANY [Ecker Architekten, 2006]
The cupboard doors are blue and white laminate, forming a checkerboard pattern visible from outside. Each classroom has a storage wall that is both functional and attractive.

simplest and most effective ways to make successful social space in a school.

Another way to use the fabric of the building to give a particular feel to the school is exemplified in the **Kindergarten Pusteblume** in Buchen, Germany [Ecker Architekten, 2006]. This small preschool for children with developmental or physical learning difficulties, has built-in furniture that takes on a more domestic aesthetic suited to the size and human scale of the building. A timber 'storage wall' in each of the six classrooms incorporates cupboards and a sink area. The cupboard doors are blue and white laminate, forming a subtle checkerboard pattern. Colour is important in the school, and the wall contrasts with deeper coloured flooring and bright interior walls in the central atrium space. More built-in storage is provided in the therapy rooms.

REFERENCES

1   D. Breithecker, *'Beware of the Sitting Trap in Learning and Schooling'*, Design Share: Designing for the Future of Learning, 2006. http://www.designshare.com/index.php/articles/sitting-trap/. Accessed 16 June 2014.

2   P. Cornell, 'The Impact of Changes in Teaching and Learning on Furniture and the Learning Environment', *New Directions for Teaching and Learning*, vol. 92, Winter 2002, pp. 33–42.

3   M. Kennedy, 'In Position to Learn', *American School & University*, February 2010. http://asumag.com/Furniture/versatile-education-furniture-201002/. Accessed 16 June 2014.

4   The school is also described in chapter 1, Ideas for Learning and Architectural Form, pp. 32–33, and in chapter 6, Learning Outside the Classroom, pp. 142–143.

5   The programme is called 'Voorbereidend middelbaar beroepsonderwijs' (VMBO) and is a four-year preparatory vocational education.

6   This concept of 'touchdown learning' calls for spaces where students might only stop for a short length of time to undertake specific tasks or activities.

7   Awards include the Association for Children's Environment, ACE Award, Design Category (2007), the Design for Asia Grand Award (2007) and the Japan Institute of Architects Prize (2009) among others.

Summary

10 FURNITURE AND EQUIPMENT
IN LEARNING SPACES

1. Furniture can be **instrumental in the success of the school** but it can also compromise an otherwise successful space.
2. Furniture can be used **to organise space or provide vital storage** to support the whole gamut of learning activities.
3. Furniture **mediates between our environment and ourselves** and can bring colour, form and visual interest into the spaces of a school.
4. Furniture can **create a sense of entrance** forming spaces or giving identity and human scale to larger and more anonymous areas.
5. Furniture can work to **divide larger spaces** and create a hierarchy of uses or experiences within an open plan.
6. Storage stands out as a problem common to most new school designs. Two key approaches exist: **mobile storage containers** which can be used flexibly or **storage furniture** which can be incorporated into the building fabric and overall design of the school.
7. Schools can encourage pupil-directed learning, and careful design or procurement of **furniture, fixtures and equipment can support particular pedagogical approaches**, for example the exploration of the environment used as a tool for developing skills.
8. Using the building fabric, for example **circulation spaces and steps, can create a natural sitting and gathering space** for pupils, wide and broad enough to accommodate a school assembly, but also tranquil enough for small groups. **Scale and colour** is also important to the feel and inviting quality of the gathering or sitting space for children.

Selected Bibliography and Further Reading

The design of schools

Adams, E., *Shaping Places: Built Environment Design Education*, Kent: The Kent Architecture Centre, 2006.

Beard, A., *Picturing School Design: A Visual Guide to Secondary School Buildings and Their Surroundings Using the Design Quality Indicator for Schools*, London: CABE, 2005.

Beard, A., 'Do PFI Schools Have to be so Boring?', autumn 2005, http://www.century21schools.com.

Bentley, T., Fairley, C., Wright, S., *Design for Learning – Joinedupdesignforschools*, London: DEMOS, 2001.

Buvic, Karin, *Primary and Secondary Schools, Options when Designing School Buildings*, Oslo: Norwegian Board of Education, 2001.

CABE, *Picturing School Design: A Visual Guide to Secondary School Buildings and Their Surroundings Using the DQI for Schools*, London: CABE, 2005.

CABE, '*Assessing Secondary School Design Quality – Research Report*', London: CABE, 2006.

CABE – Ultralab, *21st Century Schools: Learning Environments of the Future*, London: CABE and RIBA, 2004.

Care, L., Chiles, P., Primary Ideas: Projects to Enhance Primary School Environments, London: The Stationary Office, 2006.

Chiles, P., 'The Classroom as an Evolving Landscape', in M. Dudek (ed.), *Children's Spaces*, Oxford: Architectural Press, 2005, pp. 101–113.

Chiles, P., 'Classrooms for the Future: an Adventure in Design and Research', *Architectural Research Quarterly*, vol. 7, no. ¾, September 2003, pp. 244–261, doi:10.1017/S1359135503002215.

DfES, *Schools for the Future – Designs for Learning Communities, Building Bulletin 95*, London: The Stationary Office, 2002.

DfES, *Classrooms of the Future*, London: DfES, Department for Education and Schools, 2003.

Dudek, M., *Architecture of Schools – The New Learning Environments*, Oxford: Architectural Press, 2000.

Dudek, M. (ed.), *Children's Spaces*, Oxford: Architectural Press, 2005.

Dudek, M., *Schools and Kindergartens – A Design Manual*, Basel: Birkhäuser, 2007. Second and revised edition 2015.

Fisher, K., 'Revoicing Classrooms: A Spatial Manifesto', *FORUM: for promoting 3–19 comprehensive education*, 46 (1), 2004, pp. 36–38.

Ford, A., Hutton, P., *A Sense of Entry – Designing the Welcoming School*, Mulgrave, Victoria: Images Publishing Group, 2007.

Franklin, G., Harwood, E., Taylor, S., Whitfield, M., *England's Schools 1962–1988: A Thematic Study*, London: English Heritage, 2012.

Futagawa, Y., *School – GA Contemporary Architecture*, Edita GA, 2010.

Harwood, E., *England's Schools: History, Architecture and Adaption*, London: English Heritage, 2010.

Hille, R. T., *Modern Schools – A Century of Design for Education*, New York: Wiley, 2011.

Kramer, S., *Schools: Educational Spaces*, Salenstein: Braun, 2009.

Kroner, W., *Architecture for Children*, Stuttgart: Karl Krämer, 1994.

Qin, Li, *School Buildings*, Hong Kong: Design Media Publishing Ltd., 2012.

Seymour, J., et al., *School Works Toolkit*, London: School Works Ltd., 2001.

Sorrell, J., Sorrell, F., *Joinedupdesignforschools*, London: Merrell Publications, 2005.

Taylor, A., 'The Learning Environment as a Three-Dimensional Textbook', *Children's Environments*, 10 (2), 1993, pp. 170–179.

The Lighthouse, *Design Strategies – Design for Learning: 21st Century Schools*, Glasgow: The Lighthouse – Scotland's Centre for Architecture, Design and the City, 2004.

Verstegen, T. (ed.), *Contemporary Dutch School Architecture – A Tradition of Change*, Rotterdam: NAi Publishers, 2008.

Landscape, environment and schools

Brink, L., Yost, B., 'Transforming Inner-City School Grounds: Lessons from Learning Landscapes', *Children, Youth and Environments*, 14 (1), 2004, pp. 208–232.

Burke, C., *Play in Focus: Children Researching their Own Spaces and Places for Play*, *Children, Youth and Environments*, 15 (1), 2005, pp. 27–53.

David, T. G., 'Environmental Literacy', in T. G. David, B. D. Wright (eds.), *Learning Environments*, Chicago: The University of Chicago Press, 1975, pp. 161–179.

Day, C. Environment and Children: Passive Lessons from the Everyday Environment, Oxford: Architectural Press, 2007.

DfES, *Designing School Grounds – Schools for the Future*, London: The Stationary Office, 2006.

Dyment, J. E., 'At That Age, You Just Accept What You Have. You Never Question Things: Student Participation in School Ground Greening', *Children, Youth and Environments*, 14 (1), 2004.

Ford, A., *Designing the Sustainable School*, Mulgrave, Victoria: Images Publishing, 2007.

Ker, M., *Grounds for Design: The Improvement of School and College Grounds*, NSEAD National Society for Education in Art and Design, 1997, pp. 61–72.

Stine, S., *Landscapes for Learning: Creating Outdoor Environments for Children and Youth*, New York: Wiley, 1997.

Children, education and schools

Burke, C., Grosvenor, I., *School*, London: Reaktion Books, 2008.

Burke, C., 'About Looking: Vision, Transformation and the Education of the Eye in Discourses of School Renewal Past and Present', *British Education Research Journal*, vol. 36, no. 1, February 2010, pp. 65–82.

Chawla, L., 'Growing up in Cities: A Report on Research Underway', *Environment and Urbanisation*, 9 (2), 1997, pp. 247–251.

Chawla, L., 'Cities for Human Development', in L. Chawla (ed.), *Growing Up in an Urbanising World*, Paris: UNESCO and London: Earthscan Publications, 2002, pp. 15–34.

Chawla, L., 'Insight, Creativity and Thoughts on the Environment: Integrating Children and Youth into Human Settlement Development', *Environment and Urbanisation*, 14 (2), 2002.

Chawla, L., 'Toward Better Cities for Children and Youth', in L. Chawla (ed.), *Growing Up in an Urbanising World*, Paris: UNESCO and London: Earthscan Publications, 2002, pp. 219–242.

Clark, A., 'The Mosaic Approach and Research with Young Children', in V. Lewis, et al. (eds.), *The Reality of Research with Children and Young People*, London: Sage, 2004, pp. 142–156.

Council of Europe, 'Revised European Charter on the Participation of Young People in Local and Regional Life – Charter without the Status of a Convention' (10th session – 21 May 2003 – Appendix to the Recommendation 128), 2003.

Cutler, D., Taylor, A., *Expanding and Sustaining Involvement: A Snapshot of Participation Infrastructure for Young People Living in England*, London: Carnegie Young People Initiative & DfES, 2003.

Croll, P. (ed.), *Teachers, Pupils and Primary Schooling: Continuity and Change*, New York: Cassell, 1996.

DCSF, 'Aiming High for Young People: A Ten Year Strategy for Positive Activities', in Department for Children, Schools and Families (ed.), London: HM Treasury and DCSF, 2007.

DCSF Department for Children, Schools and Families, 'United Nations Convention on the Rights of the Child', *Every Child Matters*, 2003. http://www.everychildmatters.co.uk/uncrc.

Delpit, L. D., 'The Silenced Dialogue: Power and Pedagogy in Educating Other People's Children', *Harvard Educational Review*, 58 (3), 1988, pp. 280–298.

Design Council, 'Kit for Purpose: Design to Deliver Creative Learning', London: Design Council, 2002.

DfES, *Youth Matters*, London: DfES, 2005.

Higgins, S., et al., 'The Impact of School Environments: A Literature Review 2005', London: Design Council, 2005.

Hofmann, S., 'The Baupiloten: Building Bridges Between Education, Practice and Research', *Architectural Research Quarterly*, 8, 2004, pp. 114–127.

Holt, J., 'Involving the Users in School Planning', in T. G. David, B. D. Wright (eds.), *Learning Environments*, Chicago: The University of Chicago Press, 1975, pp. 181–203.

Hübner, P., *Kinder bauen ihre Schule – Children Make their Own School: Evangelische Gesamtschule Gelsenkirchen*, Stuttgart and London: Edition Axel Menges, 2005.

Hunjan, R., Lewis, M., Stenton, S., *Inspiring Schools: A Literature Review. Taking up the Challenge of Pupil Participation*, London: Esmée Fairbairn Foundation and Carnegie Young People Initiative, 2006.

Jans, M., 'Children as Citizens: Towards a Contemporary Notion of Child Participation', *Childhood*, 11 (27), 2004, pp. 27–44.

Kirby, P., Bryson, S., 'Measuring the Magic? Evaluating and Researching Young People's Participation in Public Decision Making', London: Carnegie Young People Initiative, 2002.

Kothari, U., 'Power, Knowledge and Social Control in Participatory Develoment', in B. Cooke, U. Kothari (eds.), *Participation: The New Tyranny?*, London and New York: Zed Books, 2001, pp. 139–152.

Linell, P., *Approaching Dialogue: Talk, Interaction and Contexts in Dialogical Perspectives* 3; Amsterdam and Philadelphia: John Benjamin's Publishing Company, 1998.

Magee, F., *The Floors Should Be Made of Chocolate – Unicorn Theatre and Tower Bridge Primary School Consultation Project, 2001–2004*, London: Unicorn, 2005.

Mayall, B., Hood, S., 'Breaking Barriers – Provision and Participation in an Out-of-School Centre', *Children and Society*, 15, 2001, pp. 70–81.

McGregor, J., 'Space, Power and the Classroom', *FORUM: for promoting 3–19 comprehensive education*, 46 (1), 2004.

Percy-Smith, B., 'Contested Worlds: Constraints and Opportunities in City and Suburban Environments in an English Midlands City', in L. Chawla (ed.), *Growing Up in an Urbanising World,* Paris: UNESCO and London: Earthscan Publications, 2002, pp. 57–80.

UNICEF, 'Convention on the Rights of a Child'. http://www.unicef.org/crc.

Participation and school design

Adams, E., Ingham, S., *Changing Places – Children's Participation in Environmental Planning*, London: The Children's Society, 1998.

Auriat, N., Milijeteig, P., Chawla, L., '*Overview – Identifying Best Practices in Children's Participation*', *PLA Notes (Participatory Learning and Action)*, 42, 2001, pp. 5–8.

Bartlett, S., 'Building Better Cities with Children and Youth', *Environment and Urbanisation*, 14 (2), 2002, pp. 3–10.

Blishen, E., *The School that I'd Like*, Harmondsworth: Penguin Books, 1967.

Blundell Jones, P., Petrescu, D., Till, J. (eds.), *Architecture and Participation*, London and New York: Spon Press, 2005.

Boyd, K., *A How-To Guide for Adults on Involving Youth in Community Planning: Youth Voices in Community Design,* Sacramento, CA: California Center for Civic Participation and Youth Development, 2004.

Checkoway, B., Richards-Schuster, K., 'Youth Participation in Evaluation and Research as a Way of Lifting New Voices', *Children, Youth and Environments*, 14 (2), 2004, pp. 134–139.

Clark, A., *Transforming Children's Spaces – Children's and Adults' Participation in Designing Learning Environments*, London and New York: Routledge, 2010.

Clark, A., Percy-Smith, B., 'Beyond Consultation: Participatory Practices in Everyday Spaces', *Children, Youth and Environments*, 12 (2), 2006.

Cooke, B., Kothari, U. (eds.), *Participation: The New Tyranny?*, London and New York: Zed Books, 2001.

Driskell, D., Bannerjee, K., Chawla, L., '*Rhetoric, Reality and Resilience: Overcoming Obstacles to Young People's Participation in Development*', *Environment and Urbanisation*, 13 (1), 2001, pp. 77–89.

Flutter, J., Ruddock, J., *Consulting Pupils: What's in it for Schools?*, London and New York: Routledge, 2004.

Flutter, J., 'This Place Could Help You Learn: Student Participation in Creating Better School Environments', *Educational Review*, 58 (2), May 2006, pp. 183–193.

Hansen, J. M., Childs, J., 'Creating a School Where People Like to Be', *Educational Leadership*, 5 (1), 1998, p. 14.

Hargie, O., Saunders, C., Dickson, D., *Social Skills in Interpersonal Communication*, London and New York: Routledge, second edition 1987.

Hart, R. A., *Children's Participation: The Theory and Practice of Involving Young Citizens in Community Development and Environmental Care*, London: Earthscan Publications, 1997.

Hickey, S., Mohan, G., *Participation: From Tyranny to Transformation? Exploring New Approaches to Participation in Development*, London and New York: Zed Books, 2004.

Hofmann, S., *Architecture is Participation – Die Baupiloten: Methods and Projects*, Berlin: Jovis, 2014.

Lawson, L., McNally, M., 'Putting Teens at the Centre: Maximising Public Utility of Urban Space through Youth Involvement in Planning and Employment', *Children's Environments*, 12 (2), 1995, pp. 45–65.

Neuburger, L., The Glass House (eds.), *Involving Young People in the Design and Care of Urban Spaces: What Would you Do with this Space?*, London: CABE Space and CABE Education, 2004.

Penrose, U., Thomas, G., Greed, G., 'Designing Inclusive Schools: How can Children be Involved?', *Support for Learning*, 16 (2), 2001, pp. 87–91.

Percy-Smith, B., Malone, K., 'Making Children's Participation in Neighbourhood Settings Relevant to the Everyday Lives of Young People', *PLA Notes (Participatory Learning and Action)*, 42, 2001, pp. 18–22.

West, A., 'Power Relationships and Adult Resistance to Children's Participation', *Children, Youth and Environments*, 17 (1), 2007, pp. 124–135.

Woolner, P. (ed.), *School Design Together*, London and New York: Routledge, 2015.

Wood, J. T., 'Celebrating Diversity in the Communication Field', *Communication Studies*, 49 (2), 1998, pp. 172–178.

Wright, S., 'User Involvement in School Building Design', *FORUM: for promoting 3–19 comprehensive education*, 46 (1), 2004.

Schools and the community

Haar, S., *Schools for Cities: Urban Strategies*, Washington D. C., National Endowment for the Arts, New York: Princeton Architectural Press, 2002.

US Department of Education, *Schools as Centers of Community: A Citizen's Guide for Planning and Design*, 1998. http://www.designshare.com/index.php/awards/principles.

Wright, S., 'Designing Schools for the Whole Community', *ExtraTime Special,* 107, 2003, pp. 1–4.

Index of Buildings, Architects and Locations

3XN Architects 25, 43, 45
A. P. Møller School, Schleswig, Germany 78–79
AA-Lab 121–122
Acland Burghley School, London, UK 225–226
Adam, Robert 159
Adelaide, Australia 42–43
AGS Architekten & Planners 32–33, 142, 221–223
AIZ Bauplanungsgesellschaft 194–195
Alan Dunlop Architects 189–190
All Saints School, Mansfield, UK 117–119
Allford Hall Monaghan Morris 149–150
Alsop Architects 224
Amsterdam, the Netherlands 80–82
Anna Heringer and Eike Roswag 56–57
Apeldoorn, the Netherlands 32–33, 142, 221–223
Archi5 33–34
Architerra Inc. 126–127
Arkitema 26, 79
Arkkitehtitoimisto Sari Nieminen Oy 99
ARX Portugal 131, 136
Auckland, New Zealand 175
Australian Science and Mathematics School – ASMS,
    Bedford Park, Adelaide, Australia 42–44
Bak Gordon Arquitectos 210–211
Bakkegårdsskolen, Gentofte, Denmark 207–209, 211
Baltimore, USA 100
Barnsley, UK 13, 114–115
Barreiro, Portugal 14
Baupiloten 115–117
BDP 13, 38–40, 103–104
Beaudouin, Eugène 158
Bedford Park, Australia 42–43
Bekkestua, Norway 206
Berlin, Germany 115–116, 200–201
Bexley Business Academy, London, UK 27–29
Bey, Jurgen 32–33, 142, 221–223
BIG 166–167
Birmingham, UK 13
Bjarke Ingels Group – BIG 166–167
Bogotá, Colombia 19–20, 157, 161–162
Bosch and Fjord 132–134
Bosuil, Overijse, Belgium 50
Brentwood School, Brentwood, Essex, UK 193,
    204–205
Brentwood, Essex, UK 193, 204–205
Bridge Academy, London, UK 103–105
Brisbane, Australia 214
Bristol Metropolitan College, Bristol, UK 71, 84,
    86–87
Bristol, UK 40–42, 71, 84, 86
Broekbakema Architects 134
Brown, Capability 159
Buchen, Germany 234
Building Design Partnership – BDP 13, 38–40,
    103–104
Building Trust International, UK 87–88
Bureau – design + research 114–115, 118

Buschow Henley 74–75
C. F. Møller 78
Caneças, Portugal 131, 136
Cape Town, South Africa 96, 98
Carl Bolle Elementary School, Berlin, Germany 115–
    117
Carlton Community College, Barnsley, UK 13
Cartagena, Colombia 21
CEBRA Architects 132–134, 187, 207–208
Central High School #9, Los Angeles, USA 20
Charlottenlund, Denmark 132–134
China Southwest Architectural Design and Research
    Institute 177–178
Christ's College, Guildford, UK 76–77, 182
City in the Sky, Wuhan, China 121–123
Clapham Manor Primary School, London, UK 9,
    212–213
Cole and McKillop 87–88
Coop Himmelb(l)au 20
Copenhagen, Denmark 25, 43, 45, 168, 170, 227
Corlaer College 2, Nijkerk, the Netherlands 134–136
Cottrell & Vermeulen 193, 204–205
County Meath, Ireland 145–146
Cowley St. Laurence Primary School and Children's
    Centre, Hillingdon, UK 109, 120–121
Darmstadt, Germany 158
Dartford, UK 38–39
Dartington C. of E. Primary School, Totnes, Devon,
    UK 54–55
De Kikker School, Amsterdam, the Netherlands 232
DeRijke Marsh Morgan Architects – DRMM 9, 212
Despang Architekten 60–61
Deyang School for Deaf & Intellectually Disabled
    Children, Deyang, China 177–179
Deyang, China 177–178
Die Baupiloten 115–117
Dinajpur, Bangladesh 57
DOK Architecten 232
Dorte Mandrup Arkitekter 17, 150, 152, 198–199
DP6 228
DRMM 9, 212
DSDHA 76, 182–183
Duggan Morris Architects 214–216
Ealing, UK 74–75
Earlham Primary School in Forest Gate, London, UK
    153–154
Ecker Architekten 234
Eidsvoll, Norway 148
Elm Court School, Lambeth, London, UK 195–197
Elmer A. Henderson: A Johns Hopkins Partnership
    School, Baltimore, USA 100–101, 103
Escola Secundária D. Dinis, Lisbon, Portugal 210–211
Escola Secundária de Santo André, Barreiro,
    Portugal 14
Espoo, Finland 18
Evelyn Grace Academy, Brixton, London, UK 164–166
Feilden Clegg Bradley Studios 138–139
FFE Consulting 224
Flexible Open Learning Space, P-12 School, Timboon,
    Australia 111–113
Flor del Campo School, Cartagena, Colombia 21
Foster + Partners 27–28, 35–37

Fourth Gymnasium, Amsterdam, the Netherlands
    80–82
Fran Krsto Frankopan Primary School, Krk, Croatia
    233
Fredrikstad, Norway 140
Friedrich Fröbel School, Olbersdorf, Saxony, Ger-
    many 194–195
Fuji Kindergarten, Tokyo, Japan 229–231
Gammel Hellerup Secondary School, Gentofte,
    Denmark 166–167, 169
Gando Primary School, Gando, Burkina Faso   56,
    124–127
Gando, Burkina Faso 124–126
Garthwaite Center for Science and Arts, Weston,
    Massachusetts, USA 126–128
Gensler Architects 224
Gentofte, Denmark 16–17, 21, 26, 150, 152, 166, 187,
    198–199, 207–208
Giancarlo Mazzanti Arquitectos 21, 157, 161–162
Gibbs, James 159
Glasgow, UK 189–190
GMB Architects 65
Golden Lane Campus, London, UK 180–181, 183
Gordon Murray 189–190
Greenhill Jenner Architects 94, 96
Gross Max Landscape Architects 164–165
Guildford, UK 76, 182–183
Hallfield Primary School, London, UK 158–159
Handmade School, Rudrapur, Bangladesh 56–57
Hanover, Germany 60–61
Harris Academy, London, UK 83–85
Hazelwood School for the Blind, Glasgow, UK 189–
    190
Heimdalsgades School, Copenhagen, Denmark
    227–228
Hellerup School, Gentofte, Denmark 26–27, 78–79
Henning Larsen Architects 29–30
Heringer, Anna 56–57
HHbR 74–75
High School, Caneças, Portugal 131, 136–137, 139
Hillingdon, UK 109, 120
HLM Architects 216–217
Hochschule Zittau/Görlitz 195
Huidobro, B. 33–34
HVDN Architecten 80–82
Ibaraki, Japan 72
Jacobsen, Arne 152, 199
Jardin el Porvenir Kindergarten, Bogotá, Colombia
    157, 161–163
Jarmund/Vigsnaes Architects 206
Jåttå School for Vocational Learning, Stavanger,
    Norway 29–31
JM Architects 195–196
Joensuu Lyceum, Joensuu, Finland 143–145
Joensuu, Finland 143–144
John McAslan + Partners 83–84
John Wardle Architects 202–203
Jurgen Bey, Tjep., Tejo Remy and René Veenhuizen
    32–33, 142, 221–223
Kant Arkitekter 227
Kantonsschule Enge und Freudenberg, Zurich,
    Switzerland 160

Kent, William 159

Kéré Architecture 124–126

Khayelitsha, South Africa 96, 98

KHR Arkitekter 168, 170

Kieran Timberlake Associates 63

Kindergarten Pusteblume, Buchen, Germany 234

Kingoskolen, Slangerup, Denmark 51–53

Kirkkojärvi Comprehensive School, Espoo, Finland 18

Kristin Jarmund Architects 148

Krk, Croatia 233

Kungälv, Sweden 91–92

Kunle Adeyemi – NLÉ 58

Kunst en Bedrijf 32–33, 142, 221–223

Kvernhuset Middle School, Fredrikstad, Norway 140–142

L'école buissonnière, Bosuil, Overijse, Belgium 50

L2 Arkitektur 162–163

Lagos, Nigeria 58–59

Lahdelma and Mahlamäki Architects 143–144

Lasdun, Denys 158–159

Leeuwarden, the Netherlands 33, 35

Leigh Academy, Dartford, Kent, UK 38–40

Lewis, Duncan 140

Lisbon, Portugal 210–211

London, UK 9, 12, 27–28, 83–84, 94, 96, 102–104, 138–139, 149–150, 153–154, 158, 164–165, 180–181, 195–196, 212, 214–216, 225–226

Los Angeles, USA 18–20, 83

Lund, Søren Robert 132–134, 207–208

Lycée Marcel Sembat, Sotteville-lès-Rouen, France 33–34

Mae Sot, Thailand 87–88

Maidstone, UK 224

Makoko Floating School, Lagos, Nigeria 58–59

Mansfield, UK 117–118

Mawson Lakes School, Mawson Lakes, Australia 65–66

Mawson Lakes, Australia 65

McGarry Ní Éanaigh Architects 145–146

Melbourne Grammar School, Melbourne, Australia 202–203

Melbourne, Australia 19, 202–203

Merchants' Academy, Bristol, UK 40–42

Mimers Hus, Kungälv, Sweden 91–93, 95

Mobile ECO LAB, Los Angeles, USA 83

Mossbourne Community Academy, Hackney, London, UK 102–103

MOVING School, Mae Sot, Thailand 87–88

Munkegårdsskolen, Gentofte, Denmark 17, 150, 152, 198–199, 201

New Line Learning Plaza, Oldborough Manor Community School, Maidstone, Kent, UK 224

New York, USA 173, 184–185

Nicholas Hare Architects 180–181

Nijkerk, the Netherlands 134

Noero Wolff Architects 96, 98

Ntakiyica, Aime 50

Office of Mobile Design 83

Olbersdorf, Saxony, Germany 194–195

Oldborough Manor Community School, Maidstone, Kent, UK 224

Open Air School, Suresnes, France 158

Opus Architecture 175

Ordrup School, Charlottenlund, Denmark 132–134

Ørestad College, Ørestad, Copenhagen, Denmark 25, 43–46

Ørestad, Denmark 25, 43, 45

Oslo International School, Bekkestua, Norway 206–207

Oslo, Norway 162–163, 206

Østengen og Bergo 162–163

Otonoha School, Ibaraki, Japan 72–73, 75

Outdoor Classroom in Ecclesall Woods, Sheffield 51

Pedro Matos Gameiro Arquitectos 14

Penoyre and Prasad 40–41

Peterborough, UK 35–36

Pine Community School, Brisbane, Australia 214

Pir II Architects 140

Piter Jelles Nijlân School, Leeuwarden, the Netherlands 33, 35

Pitt, Thomas 159

Pond Meadow Special School and Christ's College, Guildford, UK 182–184

Postfossil Ecowood Kindergarten, Hanover, Germany 60–62

Prue Chiles Architects 118, 153

Råholt Secondary School, Eidsvoll, Norway 148–149

Randic and Turato 233

Ratoath College, County Meath, Ireland 145–147

RAU – One Planet Architecture 33, 35

Reggio Emilia 26

'Remaking Learning', Barnsley, South Yorkshire, UK 114–115

Remy, Tejo 32–33, 142, 221–223

Richard Rogers Partnership 102

Riddel Architecture 214

ROC Aventus, Apeldoorn, the Netherlands 32–33, 142–143, 221–223

Rogers Marvel Architects 100, 173, 185–186

Rogers Partners 100, 173, 185–186

Rogers Stirk Harbour + Partners 102

Rommen Skole & Kultursenter, Oslo, Norway 162–163

Roswag, Eike 56–57

Rowan Opat Architects 111–112

Rubow Arkitekter 51–52

Rudrapur, Bangladesh 56–57

Russell & Yelland Architects 65

Sakarinmäki School, Sipoo, Finland 99

Sandal Magna Primary School, Wakefield, UK 49, 66–68

Sarah Wigglesworth Architects 49, 66

Sari Nieminen Oy 99

SCABAL 225–226

Schader, Jacques 160

Scharoun, Hans 158

Schulzendorf Primary School, Schulzendorf, Berlin, Germany 200–201

Schulzendorf, Germany 200–201

Sheffield School of Architecture 51

Sheffield, UK 51, 216–217

Sidwell Friends Middle School, Washington, USA 63–64

Sipoo, Finland 99

Slangerup, Denmark 51–52

Soane, John 159

Søgaard School, Gentofte, Denmark 187–188

Sotteville-lès-Rouen, France 33–34

Spowers 19

St. Benedict's School, Ealing, UK 74–75

St. Mary Magdalene Academy, Islington, London, UK 138–139

Stavanger, Norway 29–28

Stephen Gaynor School, New York, USA 173, 184–185

Stowe School, Stowe, Buckinghamshire, UK 159

Stowe, UK 159

'Superclass', Acland Burghley School, London, UK 225–226

Suresnes, France 158

Takapuna, Auckland, New Zealand 175

Tezuka Architects 229–230

The Hague, the Netherlands 228

Thomas Deacon Academy, Peterborough, UK 35–38

Timboon, Australia 111–112

Tjep. 32–33, 142, 221–223

Tokyo, Japan 229–230

Totnes, Devon, UK 54

Triangle Children, Young People and Community Intergenerational Centre, London, UK 94–97

University of Technology Dresden 195

University Technical College, Sheffield, UK 216–218

Usasazo Secondary School, Khayelitsha, Cape Town, South Africa 96–98

Utterslev School, Copenhagen, Denmark 168–170

UZU Architects 72

Van der Pol 232

Vanbrugh, John 159

Veenhuizen, René 32–33, 142, 221–223

Verstas Architects 18

Victoria, Australia 18, 21

Virgo Fidelis Convent School, Croydon, London, UK 216

Wakefield, UK 49, 66

Washington, USA 63

Westminster Academy, London, UK 149–151

Weston, Massachusetts, USA 126–127

Westwood Girls' College, Croydon, London, UK 214–216

What Architecture 109, 120

White Design 54

Wilkinson Eyre Architects 71, 84, 86

Williamstown High School, Melbourne, Australia 19

Williamstown, Victoria, Australia 19

Wilson School, Takapuna, Auckland, New Zealand 175–177

Wingårdh Architects 91–92

Wolff Architects 96, 98

Woods Bagot Architects 42–43

Wuhan, China 121–122

Ypenburg Lyceum, The Hague, the Netherlands 228–229

Zaha Hadid Architects 164–165

Zander Roth Architekten 200–201

Zurich, Switzerland 160

Illustration Credits

Cover photographs Adam Mørk

8 Clapham Manor Primary School: Jonas Lencer

13 Carlton Community College: David Barbour (left); BDP (right)

14 Escola Secundária de Santo André: Bernardo Ribeiro (left); Pedro Matos Gameiro Arquitectos (right)

17 Munkegårdsskolen: Adam Mørk

18 Kirkkojärvi Comprehensive School: Tuomas Uusheimo

19 Williamstown High School: Dianna Snape

20 Central High School #9: Duccio Malagamba

21 Flor del Campo School: Cristóbal Palma

24 Ørestad College: Adam Mørk

26-27 Hellerup School: Kontraframe (photographs); Arkitema (plans)

28-29 Bexley Business Academy: Nigel Young/Foster + Partners (photographs); Foster + Partners (plans)

30-31 Jåttå School for Vocational Learning: Monica Larsen (photographs); Henning Larsen Architects (plans)

32 ROC Aventus: Prue Chiles/BDR (top);Tjep. (bottom)

34 Lycée Marcel Sembat: Thomas Jorion (photographs); Archi5 (plans)

35 Piter Jelles Nijlan School: Christian Richters/RAU

36-37 Thomas Deacon Academy: Nigel Young/Foster + Partners (photographs); Foster + Partners (plans)

39 Leigh Academy: David Barbour/BDP (top left and right); BDP (plans); Leo Care/Bdr (bottom right)

41 Merchants' Academy: Rob Parrish Photography (top left and right); Penoyre and Prasad (section); Timothy Soar Photography (bottom left and right)

42 Merchants' Academy: Penoyre and Prasad (plan)

43-44 Australian Science and Mathematics School: Kevin O'Daly/Woods Bagot Architects (photographs); Woods Bagot Architects (plan)

45 Ørestad College: Adam Mørk (top left and right, bottom); Prue Chiles/Bdr (top centre); 3XN Architects (section)

46 Ørestad College: 3XN Architects (plan); Prue Chiles/Bdr (photograph)

48 Sandal Magna Primary School: Mark Hadden Photography

50 L'école buissonnière: Aimé Ntakiyica

51 Outdoor Classroom: Prue Chiles/Bdr

52-53 Kingoskolen: Nielson & Rubow/Rubow Arkitekter (photographs); Rubow Arkitekter (plans)

54 Dartington C. of E. Primary School: White Design

56-57 Handmade School: Kurt Hoerbst (photographs); Anna Heringer and Eike Roswag (plans)

58-59 Makoko Floating School: NLÉ works

61-62 Postfossil Ecowood Kindergarten: Despang Architekten

63 Sidwell Friends Middle School: Isaiah King

64 Sidwell Friends Middle School: Kieran Timberlake Associates (plan); Barry Halkin (bottom left), Isaiah King (bottom right)

65 Mawson Lakes School: Steve Rendoulis (top left); John Gollings/GMB Architects (bottom right); GMB Architects (photographs top right and centre, section)

66-67 Sandal Magna Primary School: Mark Hadden Photography (photographs); Sarah Wigglesworth Architects (plans, diagrams)

70 Bristol Metropolitan College: James Brittain

72-73 Otonoha School: Akiyoshi Fukuzawa (photographs); UZU Architects (plans)

74-75 St. Benedict's School: David Grandorge (photographs); HHbR (plan)

76 Christ's College: DSDHA

77 Christ's College: Hélène Binet (top left); Dennis Gilbert (top right); DSDHA (plan)

78-79 A. P. Møller School: Poul ib Henriksen (photographs); C. F. Møller (plans)

79 Hellerup School: Kontraframe

80-82 Fourth Gymnasium: John Lewis Marshall (photographs); Studioninedots (plans)

83 Mobile ECO LAB: Office of Mobile Design

84-85 Harris Academy: Richard Bryant/Arcaid (photographs); John McAslan + Partners (plan)

86-87 Bristol Metropolitan College: James Brittain (photographs); Wilkinson Eyre Architects (plans)

88 MOVING School: Building Trust International UK

90 Mimers Hus: Ulf Celander

92-93 Mimers Hus: Ulf Celander (photographs); Wingårdh Architects (plans)

94-95 Triangle Children, Young People and Community Intergenerational Centre: Charlotte Wood Photography (photographs); Greenhill Jenner Architects (plans)

96-97 Usasazo Secondary School: Heinrich Wolff (photographs); Wolff Architects (section)

99 Sakarinmäki School: Arno de la Chapelle (photographs); Arkkitehtitoimisto Sari Nieminen Oy (plan)

100-101 Elmer A. Henderson: A Johns Hopkins Partnership School: Albert Vecerka/ESTO (photographs); Rogers Partners (diagrams)

102 Mossbourne Academy: David Churchill (photographs); Rogers Stirk Harbour + Partners (sketch)

104 Bridge Academy: Martine Hamilton Knight (top, bottom left); Leo Care/Bdr (right)

105 Bridge Academy: Leo Care/Bdr (top left); Martine Hamilton Knight (top right); BDP (plan)

108 Cowley St. Laurence Primary School and Children's Centre: What Architecture

112-113 Flexible Open Learning Space, P-12 School: Rowan Opat Architects

115 'Remaking Learning': Leo Care/Bdr

116-117 Carl Bolle Elementary School: Jan Bitter Photography (photographs); Die Baupiloten (diagram, collage)

118 All Saints School: Leo Care and Howard Evans/Bdr

120-121 Cowley St. Laurence Primary School and Children's Centre: What Architecture

122-123 City in the Sky Li Xiao and Jiang Jiang/AA-Lab (photographs); AA-Lab (diagram)

124 Gando Primary School: Siméon Douchoud (top); Francis Kéré (bottom left and right)

125 Gando Primary School: Kéré Architecture

126-128 Garthwaite Center for Science and Arts: Chuck Choi/Architerra Inc. (photographs); Architerra Inc. (plan)

130 High School Caneças: FG + SG Fotografia de Arquitectura

132 Ordrup School: Adam Mørk (top left); Anders Sune Berg (top right, centre); CEBRA Architects, Bosch and Fjord (elevations)

133 Ordrup School: Anders Sune Berg (photographs); CEBRA Architects, Bosch and Fjord (plan)

134-135 Corlaer College 2: Rob 't Hart Fotografie (photographs); Broekbakema Architects (plans)

136-137 High School Caneças: FG + SG Fotografia de Arquitectura (photographs);ARX Portugal (plans)

138-139 St. Mary Magdalene Academy: Hufton & Crow (photographs); Feilden Clegg Bradley Studios (plans)

140-141 Kvernhuset Middle School: Pir II Architects

142 ROC Aventus: Tjep.

143 ROC Aventus: Prue Chiles/Bdr (photograph); Tjep. (diagram)

144-145 Joensuu Lyceum: Jussi Tiainen (photographs); Lahdelma and Mahlamäki Architects (plan)

146-147 Ratoath College: Richard Hatch Photography (photographs); McGarry Ní Éanaigh Architects (plan)

148-149 Råholt Secondary School: Stian Wiik (photographs); Kristin Jarmund Architects (plan)

150-151 Westminster Academy: Timothy Soar Photography (photographs); Allford Hall Monaghan Morris (plan)

152 Munkegårdsskolen: Adam Mørk (photographs); Dorte Mandrup Arkitekter (plan)

153-154 Earlham Primary School: Kevin Grieve (photographs); Prue Chiles Architects (diagrams)

156 Jardin el Porvenir Kindergarten: Rodrigo Davilla

158-159 Hallfield Primary School: Lasdun Archive/RIBA Library Photographs Collection (photograph); Lasdun Archive/RIBA Library Drawings Collection (drawings)

160 Kantonsschule Enge und Freudenberg: Howard Evans/Bdr (photographs); Jennifer Langfield/Bdr (plan)

161 Jardin El Porvenir Kindergarten: Rodrigo Davilla (photograph); Giancarlo Mazzanti Arquitectos (plan)

162 Rommen Skole & Kultursenter: Rolf Estensen (top left); Østengen og Bergo (top right); Espen Grønli (centre left); Østengen og Bergo (centre right)

164-165 Evelyn Grace Academy: Luke Hayes/VIEW (photographs); Zaha Hadid Architects (plan)

166-167 Gammel Hellerup Secondary School: Jens Lindhe/BIG (photographs); BIG (plans)

168 Utterslev School: Prue Chiles/Bdr (left and centre right); KHR Arkitekter (photograph top right, diagram)

169 Utterslev School: KHR Arkitekter

172 Stephen Gaynor School: David Sundberg/Esto

175-176 Wilson School: Patrick Reynolds/Opus Architecture (photographs); Opus Architecture (plan)

178-179 Deyang School for Deaf & Intellectually Disabled Children: Liu Yi (photographs); China Southwest Architectural Design and Research Institute (plan)

180-181 Golden Lane Campus: Peter Durant (photographs); Nicholas Hare Architects (plan)

182-183 Pond Meadow Special School and Christ's College: Timothy Soar Photography (photographs); DSDHA (plans)

185-186 Stephen Gaynor School: David Sundberg/Esto (photographs); Rogers Partners (section)

187-188 Søgaard School: Adam Mørk (photographs); CEBRA Architects (diagram, plan)

189 Hazelwood School for the Blind: Keith Hunter (top); Andrew Lee (photographs centre and bottom); Alan Dunlop Architects (plan)

192 Brentwood School: Paul Riddle

194 Friedrich Fröbel School: AIZ Bauplanungsgesellschaft

196-197 Elm Court School: JM Architects

198-199 Munkegårdsskolen: Adam Mørk (photographs); Dorte Mandrup Arkitekter (plans)

200 Schulzendorf Primary School: Andrea Kroth

201 Schulzendorf Primary School: Zander Roth Architekten

202 Melbourne Grammar School: Trevor Mein (top left), Dianna Snape (top right, bottom)

203 Melbourne Grammar School: John Wardle Architects

204 Brentwood School: Tom Cronin/Cottrell & Vermeulen (photograph); Cottrell & Vermeulen (plan)

205 Brentwood School: Tom Cronin/Cottrell & Vermeulen (top left); Paul Riddle (top right); Cottrell & Vermeulen (drawing)

206-207 Oslo International School: Ivan Brodey (photographs); Jarmund/Vigsnaes Architects (plan)

208-209 Bakkegårdsskolen: Adam Mørk (photographs); Mikkel Frost/CEBRA Architects (sketch); CEBRA Architects and Søren Robert Lund (plans)

210-211 Escola Secundária D. Dinis: Leonardo Finotti/Bak Gordon Arquitectos (photographs); Bak Gordon Arquitectos (plan)

212-213 Clapham Manor Primary School: Jonas Lencer (photographs); DRMM (plans)

214 Pine Community School: Christopher Fredrick Jones

215-216 Westwood Girls' College: Duggan Morris Architects

217 University Technical College: Prue Chiles/Bdr

220 ROC Aventus: Prue Chiles/Bdr

223 ROC Aventus: Anna Holder/Bdr (top left and right); Tjep. (bottom left and right)

224 New Line Learning Plaza: Maxine Pringle/Alsop Architects (left); Gensler Architects (right)

225 'Superclass' at Acland Burghley School: SCABAL

227 Heimdalsgades School: Kant Arkitekter (top left, bottom); Prue Chiles/Bdr (top right)

228-229 Ypenburg Lyceum: Prue Chiles/Bdr

230-231 Fuji Kindergarten: Tezuka Architects

232 De Kikker School: Arjen Schmitz (photograph); DOK Architecten (plan)

233 Fran Krsto Frankopan Primary School: Randic and Turato

234 Kindergarten Pusteblume: Constantin Meyer/Ecker Architekten